THE POLITICS OF AESTHETICS

Cultural Memory
in
the
Present

Mieke Bal and Hent de Vries, Editors

THE POLITICS OF AESTHETICS

Nationalism, Gender, Romanticism

Marc Redfield

STANFORD UNIVERSITY PRESS

STANFORD, CALIFORNIA

Stanford University Press
Stanford, California

Printed in the United States of America
on acid-free, archival-quality paper.

Library of Congress Cataloging-in-Publication Data

Redfield, Marc.
    The politics of aesthetics : nationalism, gender, romanticism / Marc
Redfield.
        p. cm.— (Cultural memory in the present)
Includes bibliographical references and index.
        ISBN 0-8047-4750-4 (paperback : alk. paper)
        1. Aesthetics—Political aspects.   2. Romanticism—Political aspects.
I. Title.   II. Series.
BH301.P64 R43 2003
111'.85—dc21   2002015100

Original Printing 2003

Last figure below indicates year of this printing:
12   11   10   09   08   07   06   05

Typeset by Alan Noyes in 11/13.5 Adobe Garamond.

For Molly

τᾶς κε βολλοίμαν ἔρατόν τε βᾶμα
κἀμάρυχμα λάμπρον ἴδην προσώπω
ἢ τὰ Λύδων ἄρματα κἀν ὄρλοιοι
πεσδομάχεντας

Contents

Acknowledgments

Earlier versions of Chapters 1, 3, 4, and 5 have appeared as essays in journals: *Diacritics* (Chapters 1 and 3); *Amsterdamer Beiträge zur neueren Germanistik* (Chapter 4); and *The Bucknell Review* (Chapter 5); two or three sentences in the Coda have been extracted and reproduced from a short text (a solicited response to an article by Tilottama Rajan) in *Literary Research/Recherche littéraire*. I thank these journals, the Johns Hopkins University Press, Bucknell University Press, and the International Comparative Literature Association for permission to republish these texts in revised form. Three of the essays were solicited by guest editors putting together special issues, and I'm grateful to Jonathan Culler and Pheng Cheah (editors of "Grounds of Comparison: Around the Work of Benedict Anderson," *Diacritics* 29, no. 4 [1999]), Martha Helfer (editor of *Rereading Romanticism, Amsterdamer Beiträge zur neueren Germanistik* 47 [2000]), and Ghislaine McDayter (editor of "Untrodden Regions of the Mind: Romanticism and Psychoanalysis," *Bucknell Review* 45, no. 2 [2001]) for their encouragement and critical comment. An invitation from William Flesch to contribute to a book on Paul de Man spurred into existence an early version of Chapter 3; the book fell victim to dire forces within the university press that had solicited it, but in the meantime I'd written the essay.

James Merrill's poem "b o d y" is quoted with the permission of Alfred A. Knopf, a division of Random House, Inc. (for full acknowledgment, see the copyright page). The illustrations in Chapters 1 and 3 appear courtesy of, respectively, AKG London and the Goethe Museum in Frankfurt. I'm particularly grateful to Jane Westbrook of AKG London for her help.

I thank those who have responded to drafts, orally delivered versions, or previously published versions of this book's arguments over the past few years. I owe particular thanks to Ian Balfour, Marshall Brown, David Clark, and Orrin Wang, who at various points provided erudite and very helpful critical commentary on part or all of the manuscript; to James Elkins, Molly Ierulli, David Mankin, Peter Redfield, and Liliane Weissberg, who at critical moments directed me to some appropriate texts; and to my research assistants Ellen Scheible and Mark Paloutzian, who helped me track down references and prepare the manuscript for publication. Cynthia Chase, Jonathan Culler, Neil Hertz, J. Hillis Miller, and Samuel Weber have offered me invaluable intellectual support over the years, as have my colleagues and students at Claremont and the many friends who have made the North American Society for the Study of Romanticism the best of annual conferences. Helen Tartar, who has become something of a Jérôme Lindon figure to scholars publishing in the field of critical theory in late twentieth-century America, is a peerless editor; it has been a privilege to work with her and with her assistants Amy Jamgochian and Kim Lewis Brown, and, subsequently, with my excellent production editor, Mariana Raykov, and copy editor, Karen Hellekson. Finally, thanks, as always, to Molly Ierulli and to Charles, Margaret, Tim, and Peter Redfield for their familial and intellectual friendship; and to Caroline, for being there.

Introduction: The Politics of Aesthetics

> In the sense that has been invented and legitimated for it in Germany, aesthetics is a word that notoriously reveals an equally perfect ignorance of the thing designated and of the designating language. Why is it still retained?
> —Friedrich Schlegel, *Lyceum Fragments*, no. 40

In the literary and cultural criticism of our era, few notions cause more trouble, and more misunderstanding, than that of the "politics of aesthetics." Explicitly or implicitly, this genitive construction often comes across as an insight—or an insult: across the spectrum of the culture wars, critics frequently write as though they imagined the terms *politics* and *aesthetics* to be antonyms yoked together, rightly or wrongly, by postmodern acts of synthetic judgment. The academic enterprise called "cultural studies" nourishes itself on the belief that it has demystified the aesthetic by politicizing it, a claim reinforced by the conservative voices in the academy and the highbrow to middlebrow wing of the culture industry that decry this putative act of politicization. On the left and on the right, aesthetics and politics appear as antithetical terms, with the dispute between the two camps taking the form of an argument about the legitimacy of submitting the former term to the latter. And yet from a certain perspective, *all* the combatants submit aesthetics to politics—or, more accurately, they go into battle armed with the common, if not necessarily conscious, presupposition that these two terms are inseparably entangled and with the notion that, sooner or later, aesthetic experience must resolve itself in the political realm. The politics of aesthetics: in a sense, no one really disagrees. From Friedrich Schiller to Matthew Arnold to T. S. Eliot, from the New Critics to the New Historicists and multiculturalists, aesthetic judgment has always in the end been understood to effect, somehow, a passage to cognition and humane action. Culture is acculturation—the forming of subjects, the reforming of the world.

To be sure, the priests of high culture and the postmodern cultural critics differ in their attitude toward the possibility of "disinterested" aesthetic judgments. But under inspection, this difference turns into a knot of interfiliations and ambiguities. Disinterestedness can never be absolute or pure in traditional aesthetic discourse. One must always be able to return—invigorated, educated—to the workaday world of intention, meaning, and action. Translated into the language of politics: disinterested criticism, according to Matthew Arnold, keeps its distance from "the political, social, humanitarian sphere" in the hope that it may "perhaps one day make its benefits felt even in this sphere, but in a natural and thence irresistible manner."[1] The humanities rely on this duplicitous itinerary for their institutional existence. Few defenses of poetry, and even fewer justifications of the teaching of poetry in schools and universities, can do without it. Even those relatively few critics who argue strongly for some version of *l'art pour l'art* find it difficult to avoid the sideways slide from aesthetics to politics. Harold Bloom does his best in his *How to Read and Why*: as a lifelong disciple of Pater and Wilde (as he reads these authors) and opponent of conventional Arnoldian humanism, Bloom is "wary of any arguments whatsoever that connect the pleasures of solitary reading to the public good."[2] Yet like a hidden gravitational field, the aesthetic's sociopolitical and therapeutic function exerts its force on his text. Good reading, Bloom tells us, "keep[s] alive civilized tradition" by warding off ideology and cant (143); it strengthens the self in ethical and occasionally even in frankly political ways ("Be open to a full reading of *King Lear*, and you will understand better the origins of what you judge to be patriarchy," he lectures an imaginary feminist reader [22]). Immersed as he is in the aesthetic tradition, Bloom cannot stop himself from drifting in these directions; the current is too strong.

Aesthetics, then, is always in principle and at the end of the day a political discourse. Yet its political dimension can, of course, be rendered thicker and more devious if, like the cultural critics on the other side of the aisle, one discovers political significance in the detour of disinterestedness itself. The aesthetic's (temporary) retreat from the heat and dust of "the political, social, humanitarian sphere" may be understood as itself a ruse, a pursuit of politics by other means. The universalizing force of disinterested aesthetic judgment, these critics point out, has historically served a specific political interest: that of an acculturated middle class entitling itself to speak for the national collective. In some respects, this critical insight is sound. We shall examine in detail later in this chapter—and in varying ways throughout this book—the political character of aesthetic disinterestedness. But here, too, things are not simple. Two broad preliminary observations bear consideration at this point. First, the critical reduction of aesthetic judgment to political calculation simply exacerbates the aesthetic tradition's essential pragmatism—the critique, that is, honors the telos of the discourse it claims to destroy. Second, and more tellingly, this critical reduction of aesthetics to politics does not in fact accomplish what it claims. Exiled to the false consciousness of "ideology," the aesthetic returns, dialectically inflated, to lift skyward the critique that negated it. It is here that we begin (though only begin) to confront the stubborn complexity of the relation between aesthetics and politics: because it sets the terms of its own critique, aesthetics is well prepared to survive an annihilation that it has in a sense predicted. Thus, in our era, the term *culture* unfurls to become a banner adjective for a *studies* as imperially broad as the aesthetic humanism it claims to replace.[3] Critics "expand" the canon to include authors and texts representative of certain ethnicities or genders rather than (or in addition to) nations or eras, and as *representative* figures, these authors and texts remain fully within the orbit of aesthetic discourse. Aesthetic–political synecdoches for particular social groups, they may always, in the next turn of the aesthetic spiral, become, like their canonical counterparts, synecdoches for humanity itself.[4] The physical symbol of this elasticized aesthetic frame is the literature anthology: endlessly reedited, but never fundamentally transformed; always somewhat unsatisfactory, but necessary to be had anyway, in most classrooms. Aesthetic humanism cannot simply be wished or theorized away, for it inheres in the structures, discourses, and practices of our pedagogical and cultural institutions. Those who write in opposition to this humanism, furthermore, repeatedly seek critical traction in the density or self-consciousness of aesthetic texts, and thereby reinstate versions of the aesthetic distance they deplore. The politics of aesthetics: ambiguously objective or subjective genitive. Though the aesthetic takes the political realm as its telos, no act of politicization seems able to make the aesthetic disappear.

To say, therefore, as we have, that aesthetics is irretrievably political and ineradicably part of modern cultural life, is only to lay out terms of approach toward a problem. The problem has a claim on us because the category of the aesthetic unquestionably names a site of complex, significant tension in our society. The culture wars play a loud version of a theme one encounters in numerous urgent critical conversations. Everywhere, aesthetics seems simultaneously to inflate and wither, most obviously, perhaps, in the various discussions of postmodernism and late capitalism that worry the turns of Fredric Jameson's influential claim that "aesthetic production today has become integrated into commodity production generally."[5] The Frankfurt School tradition that Jameson represents is only one of many attempts to characterize and come to terms with modernity as, among other things, an *aesthetic* disturbance. In the society of the spectacle and the age of the world picture, we suffer—we have been told this so often, in various idioms—a generalization of aesthetic experience that is also an evacuation of affect, a waning of aura, an experience of shock.[6] The aesthetic is everywhere and nowhere, triumphant and dead, or half-dead or undead; phantomlike, it returns to us—that is, to those of us who inhabit the wealthy pockets of the world—as the glossy sheen of high-tech commodities, images, weaponry, and Web pages. Literary high culture wanes, like the Shape in Shelley's *Triumph of Life*, in the light of a more terrible dawn. Cultural criticism and avant-garde art put their weight on differences that crumble away, as each act of transgression or demystification becomes another image to be marketed, another device of power. Yet the production of criticism and art continues unabated, as does the traditionalist backlash, and, in consequence, the so-called culture war. The wealth of argument about and in the humanities, furthermore, contrasts obviously with the ongoing defunding of the humanities, not just in the United States but in universities throughout much of the world. And though it may be tempting to conclude, as many have, that talk proliferates about the humanities because little is really at stake, it seems more accurate to say that ours is a culture at once obsessed with and contemptuous of the aesthetic—and also at times, as we shall see, deeply wary of it. And this ambivalence suggests that the notion of the aesthetic is a stranger phenomenon than we usually admit: the repository of half-repressed aversions and hopes; the locus of half-acknowledged complications. We assume far too quickly that we know what the aesthetic really is.

The Strange Case of Theory

Like its prequel, *Phantom Formations*,[7] this book sets out to explore the paradoxes of aesthetic discourse from a literary–critical vantage and takes as its point of entry the remarkable career of "theory" in late twentieth-century humanistic scholarship and cultural journalism. Many things turn peculiar within the orbit of the aesthetic, but the production and reception of "theory" surely ranks among the most intriguing high-cultural events of our era. I shall spare readers the quotation marks from here on, but the word belongs in them insofar as it functions less by referring to an identifiable object than by triggering figurative associations. One can, of course, sketch plausible pragmatic definitions of theory: in a lucid introductory survey, Jonathan Culler, for instance, proposes that the term nicknames a genre of writing that is reflexive, analytic, and speculative, "interdisciplinary in the sense of having effects outside an original discipline," and "a critique of common sense or of concepts taken as natural."[8] That definition nicely suggests the unmasterable expanse and heterogeneity of theory ("No matter how well versed you may think yourself, you can never be sure whether you 'have to read' Jean Baudrillard, Mikhail Bakhtin, Walter Benjamin, Hélène Cixous, C. L. R. James, Melanie Klein, or Julia Kristeva, or whether you can 'safely' forget them" [Culler, 16]), but it overlooks the odd fact that this seemingly capacious term has tended, over the past thirty years, to rollercoast around the same narrow loop of figurative associations. For when debates about theory grow heated, as sooner or later they generally do, theory sooner or later turns out to mean deconstruction. Deconstruction is "high theory," the theoretical essence of theory, and deconstruction in turn narrows, under polemical pressure, to mean "deconstruction in America," and above all Paul de Man's project of rhetorical reading. The fact that numerous texts and traditions rightly claim theoretical status in contemporary criticism—that dozens of proper names could be added to Culler's list, which is, of course, Culler's point—need not inhibit us from taking seriously theory's ideological gyrations. Though we shall be approaching these issues from a perspective that is considerably different from that advanced by John Guillory in *Cultural Capital*, his account of the figurative link between de Man and theory cannot be bettered:

The immense symptomatic significance of the *figure* of de Man has been indisputably confirmed by the paroxysm which passed through the entire critical profession in the wake of the revelations concerning de Man's wartime journalism. It would not have been necessary for so many theorists and antitheorists, de Manians and anti–de Manians, to "respond" to these revelations if *theory itself* were not perceived to be implicated in the figure of de Man. The easy condemnation in the media of theory along with de Man only confirmed a symbolic equation already present in the professional imaginary. (178)

At the end of the line, theory is deconstruction is de Man: the copulas are all the more persistent for being legibly fantastic. And the furor that theory has provoked is not simply a response to the sublimely extensible length of a theory reading list (all reading lists, after all, are sublimely extensible); it is keyed, in the final analysis, to theory's phantasmatic conflation with de Manian deconstruction, and has about it the obscurely motivated intensity of a genuine symptom. Obsession laces our response, positive or negative, to de Man precisely to the extent that de Man stands in for theory. This obsession still lingers, at the dawn of the twenty-first century, manifested in the stubbornly loving attentiveness of former students and the irritable rhetoric of antitheorists.[9] The hyperbole that deconstruction can inspire is remarkable. "Theory has not yet been blamed for the Gulf War or for the destruction of the ozone layer, but it may only be a matter of time," David Simpson joked in 1993; one could change the topical references and recycle the joke today, and probably for some time to come.[10] By the same token, de Man, repressed but never quite forgotten, remains a personification capable of bringing into focus the contradictory slurs that theory has always inspired: theory as foreign yet American, escapist yet totalitarian, trivial yet terrible—an ivory tower game and a threat to Western culture.[11] The ever-difficult problem of the politics of aesthetics turns particularly slippery here, as both on the left and the right, among the multiculturalists and the traditionalists, the politics of aesthetics-as-high-theory names the abjected politics of the other (the conservative aestheticism of traditionalism; the disease at the heart of multiculturalism). In engaging the specter of theory, we touch on a curiously sore spot in aesthetic discourse. No serious critique of aesthetics can avoid an engagement either with theory or with the literary critic who, however improbably from some points of view (for de Man certainly had none of the glamour of a conventional media figure), has for three decades provided this specter with a face and a name.

Indeed, a stronger claim is necessary. Not only must a critique of aesthetics account for theory's personification in and as "de Man" in late twentieth-century Anglo-American high culture; it must also engage this critic's actual work, which, as part of its own critique of aesthetics, offers us an argued version of the ideological sequence theory–deconstruction–de Man. "The advent of theory," de Man claims in his ironically program-matic essay, "The Resistance to Theory," "occurs with the introduction of linguistic terminology in the metalanguage about literature."[12] On the one hand, de Man is offering us here an explanatory history of the theory phe-nomenon—a narrative capable of getting us, say, from Wellek and War-ren's 1948 book *Theory of Literature* (where theory denotes an innocuously epistemological act of discursive self-reflection), to Wellek's 1983 position paper "Destroying Literary Studies" (where theory serves as the Godzilla-sized implied subject of the title's gerund).[13] Something happened in be-tween, something involving, as de Man says, such a variety of methods and names—structuralism, semiotics, psychoanalysis, certain elements of Marx-ism, "post-Husserlian phenomenology and post-Heideggerian hermeneu-tics"—that a forceful interpretive move becomes justifiable (7). On the other hand, as soon as de Man has defined literary theory as a certain kind of linguistic turn, he has aligned theory per se with his own work's central preoccupation—not linguistics in the ordinary or disciplinary sense of the word, but a "linguistics of literariness" (11), where literariness names the ir-ruption or revelation of an "autonomous potential of language" (10). The-ory *is* thus, in essence, rhetorical reading. Theory's embodiment in Paul de Man is certainly, from the point of view of (de Manian) theory, an egre-gious error, but nonetheless, it is a predictable one insofar as it recapitulates and literalizes the trope of personification that theory (as we shall see in somewhat greater detail later) identifies as a fundamental error of reading. Signing his name to this theory of theory, de Man ironically reconfirms and reperforms his own phantasmatic role in the academy as he reiterates, in the form of historical narrative and theoretical analysis, the gunpowder trail of associations that takes us from theory to the master teacher, the man who teaches theory.

Should we therefore take de Manian theory as a reiteration of a symp-tom? If so, how is that reiteration to be read: is it blind or knowing? ideo-logical or critical? John Guillory reads it as blind: his ambitious chapter on de Man returns the theory phenomenon to a cause external to theory's self-comprehension. In this account, theory responds to and reacts against the emergence of a professional–managerial class indifferent to the forms of cultural capital of an older bourgeois culture: "literary theory as a version of rhetoricism defends literature from its half-perceived and half-acknowledged social marginality" by redefining literature as literariness (180); theory's emphasis on "rigor," meanwhile, functions as an unconscious repetition of contemporary conditions of institutional life, by modeling "the intellectual work of the theorist on the new social form of intellectual work, the technobureaucratic labor of the new professional–managerial class" (181). Guillory's is a bold effort to confront and explain the event of theory, and I think he is right to seek links between theory as a social phenomenon and the professionalization of academic work over the last half century. Arguably, a figure like de Man could only become a locus of phantasmatic investment in a pedagogic–professional context in which critics produce and disseminate literary interpretations as a professional activity within an enabling bureaucratic apparatus. But it is nonetheless questionable whether Guillory's sociological interpretation adequately addresses the peculiarities of theory. He underplays the complications and the persistence of aesthetics as a discourse and web of institutions (if, for instance—to take only the example at hand—our culture were disinvesting in literature as a form of cultural capital without hedge positions, literary theory would probably have been received with somewhat more indifference, particularly in nonacademic venues).[14] And he seriously underestimates the degree to which de Manian theory, as a theory of its own reception, has a dense commentary to offer on these matters.[15] We shall have to come back to "The Resistance to Theory"—a considerably more difficult text than readers often acknowledge—just as we shall eventually need to engage at some length de Man's work as a whole. But for a guiding question at this point, it suffices to ask whether de Man's notion of "literariness" can be translated cleanly into a sociological idiom. De Man obviously intends the term to invoke the kinds of writing that literature departments have traditionally called "literature," but he also suggests its irreducibility to a sociological notion of literature as cultural capital. Before we exile de Man's claim to the looking-glass world of ideology—before we repeat, once again, the rapid trajectory of aesthetics to politics—we should first do our best to figure out what a phrase like "the autonomous potential of language" really means, and why a theory oriented toward the possibility of this autonomous potential has managed to function as such a visible irritant—and locus of excitement—within aesthetic culture. How does this literariness overlap with the aesthetic institution of literature? What makes that overlap a flash point in the wider context of aesthetic discourse?

"Nothing can overcome the resistance to theory, since theory *is* itself this resistance," de Man famously claims near the close of his essay (19). Theory theorizes itself as doubled or split, as blinded by and in flight from its own insight. I propose to dwell with that paradox here and to extend its implications through a set of overlapping terms: theory, aesthetics, technics, literature, romanticism. Theory as rhetorical reading enacts a self-difference, doubleness, or foreignness within aesthetics. The skewed interplay of aesthetics and theory, furthermore, helps illuminate the complex intimacy between aesthetics and technics, which in turn helps us understand the generalization of aesthetic effects consequent upon the unleashing of technical power in late-capitalist societies. "Literariness," I shall suggest, is best conceptualized in relation to figures of writing and inscription and thus names a kind of self-difference that cuts across our notions of high and mass culture and aesthetics and technics as separate fields. Rich expanses of the question of the politics of aesthetics, therefore, may be reached by voyaging through the narrow straits of literary and literary-theoretical debate. In this book's forerunner, *Phantom Formations*, I took as my starting point the semimythical genre of the *Bildungsroman* and its vexed relation to the aesthetic–pedagogical tradition of *Bildung*. Here, pursuing a related but different itinerary, we shall focus on the crisis-ridden period metaphor and academic field of romanticism. Both as a term and a field, romanticism has suffered instabilities to the degree that it has functioned as a trope for aesthetics—as, that is, the figurative locus of "aesthetic ideology" and "theory." The following pages will try to make good these claims, in preparation for a sequence of readings that explore saliencies of the romantic–aesthetic tradition in an effort to rethink the vexed interplay of aesthetics and politics.

Aesthetics

Though I review the political and epistemological ambitions of aesthetic discourse periodically in this book, it will be helpful, I think, to begin with a brief account of what aesthetics is and how I understand its complications. "No concept is more fundamental to modernity than the aesthetic," Geoffrey Galt Harpham rightly remarks; indeed, as we shall see, aesthetics is a discourse fundamentally *about* modernity.[16] The term *aesthetic* itself is of relatively modern coinage—the Greek word that Alexander Baumgarten appropriated for the title of his *Aesthetica* (1750) simply means sense perception (we preserve this classical meaning in the privative *anaesthesia*). Friedrich Schlegel's grumble in the fragment I have posted as an epigraph partly registers a classicist's annoyance that the root meaning of *aesthetic* was not being kept in mind as the word became increasingly popular in late eighteenth-century Germany as a name for judgments about the beautiful.[17] In Britain, the word shows up rarely—and then usually only in order to be mocked as Germanic philosophical jargon—until the late nineteenth century, though the discourse that we now call aesthetics became separated out from poetics, rhetoric, and moral philosophy in Britain over the course of the eighteenth century. The history of a term cannot, of course, tell us anything directly about the history of the phenomenon to which it refers. But the emergence of new meanings and newly prominent roles for several charged words, all intimately connected with each other and with the term and the notion of aesthetics—such "keywords," as Raymond Williams calls them, as *art, artist, literature, culture*—suggests the usefulness of thinking of aesthetics as a specifically modern discourse.[18] All modernities are porous, especially in the present case: reflection on the beautiful and on the role of art goes back as far as Western philosophy itself, as do relations between art and pedagogy, and among art, politics, and technics; and we shall need to trace a few of these filiations.[19] But as many scholars have pointed out, only over the last two hundred fifty years or so has there been a space more or less clearly marked out in Western societies for a special kind of object, judgment, activity, or experience that the term *aesthetic* has come to define. At least it is *supposed* to be clearly marked out. Our brief initial consideration of aesthetics and politics has already suggested that aesthetics is a discourse of framing that violates its own frame and that, in consequence, a historical narrative such as the one I am about to provide will need to rely on thoroughly heuristic, and potentially quite unstable, distinctions.[20]

As a philosophical field, aesthetics forms part—a crucial, though, for reasons we shall encounter shortly, almost always subordinate, part—of modern philosophy's effort to ground itself in the subject and its perceptions. Though the German and British aesthetic traditions developed under quite different political and intellectual conditions, common to both was an effort to characterize forms of knowing inherent to sensory apprehension. With grave qualifications, we may offer here Terry Eagleton's memorable hyperbole that "aesthetics was born as a discourse of the body."[21] The qualifications are at least twofold: first, the body, as I suggest later in this introduction and argue more substantially in Chapter 2, is an extremely complex aesthetic trope; second—and this point is really only a restatement of the first—the aim of aesthetics is never simply to celebrate (or denigrate) pleasurable (or unpleasurable) sensation, but is rather to articulate sensory experience with supersensory harmony, form, or meaning. The conceptual metaphor "taste," the keystone of eighteenth-century aesthetic discourse, borrows the tongue's intimate and immediate sensuality in order to signify, in the words of Edmund Burke, "that faculty, or those faculties of the mind which are affected with, or which form a judgment of the works of imagination and the elegant arts."[22] Aesthetic judgment is judgment in advance of rule or precept, formed as naturally as a taste on the tongue—yet also, like the taste buds, capable of being educated: an important complication, to which we shall return in a moment. A judgment of taste judges the sensuous particular without recourse to any preexisting law or governing concept; in Howard Caygill's evocative phrase, it "give[s] itself law."[23] Through a sleight of hand that has always threatened to make aesthetics as suspect as it is seductive, aesthetic judgment claims simultaneously to produce and to discover the essential harmony of perceiving mind and perceived world, sensation and idea, phenomenality and cognition. In doing so, it inscribes the individual within the generality of human being. For the main point about taste is that all human beings have it. "As the conformation of their organs are nearly, or altogether the same in all men," Burke writes, "so the manner of perceiving external objects is in all men the same" (13); thus, "as the senses are the great originals of all our ideas, and consequently of all our pleasures, if they are not uncertain and arbitrary, the whole ground-work of Taste is common to all" (23). The body, in this empiricist aesthetic, serves as the formal outline of humanity. It tropes what Kant calls the *sensus communis*: the field of essential communicability to which aesthetic judgment testifies, and upon which it depends.

Aesthetics, therefore, unlike poetics or classical rhetoric, has relatively little to do with, for instance, technical aspects of literary composition, and everything to do with such large protopolitical matters as the definition of the human, the possibility of judgment without rule, or the perception of psychic, natural, social, and cosmic harmony. The political cast of aesthetics becomes yet more obvious if we return to the paradox that taste is simultaneously natural and educable. All of us have taste, just as we all have bodies; yet taste is "improved exactly as we improve our judgment, by extending our knowledge, by a steady attention to our object, and by frequent exercise" (Burke, 26). As aesthetics develops as a discourse, this paradox of taste becomes that of culture: all humanity is represented in and by aesthetic culture, though this culture actually achieves representation only in and as an acculturated minority.[24] Aesthetics thus unfolds as a pedagogical, political, and historical model. It is highly misleading to assert, as many do these days, that aesthetics is "ahistorical." Without question, a utopian sublimation of historical contingency into form constitutes the telos of aesthetic discourse, but much of the political force of aesthetics resides in its historicism, in its projection of a temporal line running from the primitive to the modern, and then onward to a futurity, an ever-deferred end of history, that aesthetic experience prefigures. Acculturated subjects, actualizing their human potential in aesthetic judgment, become capable of representing the less acculturated both in an aesthetic and a political sense precisely because the difference between representative and represented has a temporal dimension. Someday, humanity will achieve itself as a national, and in the end, global subject; in the meantime, an acculturated minority speaks for the collective.[25]

Aesthetics thus, on this level, exemplifies what we call "bourgeois ideology." The disinterestedness that marks judgments of taste represents the moment when the empirical subject transcends its class interests in a moment of contact with the formal identity—the transcendental body, as it were—of humanity. This formal identity, furthermore, has an empirical representative in mainstream aesthetic discourse: the state. "From the end of the eighteenth century to the late nineteenth century," David Lloyd and Paul Thomas observe, "a remarkable convergence takes place in Europe between theories of the modern state and theories of culture" (1). Both culture and the state function, at least in principle, as sites of imaginary reconciliation—imaginary in Lacan's or Althusser's sense—for an increasingly complex and fragmented social order. Schiller's influential rewriting of Kant, *Über die ästhetische Erziehung des Menschen* (*On the Aesthetic Education of*

Man; 1795), deserves a glance here, for Schiller anchors his claim that the "problem of politics" must be approached "through the problem of the aesthetic" to a pair of sentences that compose the most elegantly compact summation imaginable of aesthetics as a political model:

Every individual human being, one may say, carries within him, potentially and prescriptively [*der Anlage und Bestimmung nach*], a pure ideal man [*reinen idealischen Menschen*], and it is his life's task to be, through all his changing manifestations, in harmony with that unchanging unity. This pure man, which is to be discerned more or less clearly in every individual, is represented by the State, the objective and as it were canonical [*kanonische*] form in which all the diversity of individual subjects strive to unite.[26]

But we may take as our main example here the great manifesto of aesthetic ideology in the British tradition: Matthew Arnold's *Culture and Anarchy* (1869). Written directly in response to the Hyde Park riots, and more generally in response to working-class agitation for an extension of the franchise, Arnold's treatise makes no bones about its political intentions. Culture opposes anarchy, and anarchy threatens Britain because "we have not the notion, so familiar on the Continent and to antiquity, of *the State*,— the nation in its collective and corporate character."[27] As the "idea of the whole community," the State allows us to "rise above the idea of class" (98), and culture leads us inexorably toward the State because culture develops us toward our "best self":

By our *best self* we are united, impersonal, at harmony. We are in no peril from giving authority to this, because it is the truest friend we all of us can have; and when anarchy is a danger to us, to this authority we may turn with sure trust. Well, and this is the very self which culture, or the study of perfection, seeks to develop in us . . . ! So that our poor culture, which is flouted as so unpractical, leads us to the very ideas capable of meeting the great want of our present embarrassed times! We want an authority, and we find nothing but jealous classes, checks, and a deadlock; culture suggests the idea of *the State*. We find no basis for a firm State-power in our ordinary selves; culture suggests one to us in our *best self*. (99)

In an indirect way, as we shall see in Chapter 2, it is the function of Arnoldian criticism to help move the state toward its own idea of itself by pointing out imperfections. But aesthetic education implies the sanctity of the state, with the result that at times we find Arnold edging close to a blind bureaucratism. The "intolerableness of anarchy" is so compelling (because "without order there can be no society, and without society there can be no human perfection") that no act of civil disobedience is ever justifiable, no matter how good the cause or how pernicious the governmental authority: "In our eyes, the very framework and exterior order of the State, whoever may administer the State, is sacred" (181). Arnold's authoritarianism is by no means representative of British liberal opinion in the 1860s, but his position usefully illuminates one powerful drive within aesthetics: when the analogy between the state and the artwork is pushed to its limit, aesthetic politics becomes bureaucratic formalism as freedom becomes indistinguishable from the nihilism of absolute obedience.

Such texts provide fantasies, of course—fantasies that exist in dialectical relation with the institutional realities that both produce and are produced by aesthetic discourse. The evolution of theories and institutions of the modern democratic state—the state as the expression of the will of a people—was accompanied by the growth of institutions of culture and acculturation, institutions that set out, sometimes indirectly but often overtly, to form ethical, disciplined citizens.[28] We had occasion to remark at the beginning of this chapter that aesthetics is no simple mirage: the schools, museums, journals, and so on that form part of the infrastructure of the modern state and civil society testify to the importance and material impact of aesthetic narratives of culture and acculturation. Certain aspects of this history are well known[29]; less often remarked is the semi-covert, tense intimacy between aesthetics and technics to which the state's proliferating cultural institutions, after their fashion, bear witness.

Aesthetics, Technics

In the next chapter, I trace the uneasy mutual entanglement of aesthetic nationalism and the state's aesthetic–educational apparatus by examining Benedict Anderson's seminal account of the nation as an "imagined community," the imagining of which, according to Anderson, is made possible by the development of communicational technologies and practices. Let me here take a slightly different route and offer for inspection a recent meditation on the virtues of Western civil society by Ernest Gellner. For it is possible to overemphasize—as Lloyd and Thomas possibly do—the vector connecting aesthetics to the state; and Gellner, focusing on civil society as the state's counterweight in classic political theory, reminds us that aesthetic culture sets out to shape the social order in quotidian and unofficial ways. At the same time, Gellner helps us glimpse the cogs and cables of technical mediation at work under the skin of the aesthetic social body. He believes that civil society works to the extent that (Western) humanity has become "modular," characterized by a positive kind of mobility and substitutability that makes people "capable of performing highly diverse tasks in the same general cultural idiom":

This is indeed one of the most important general traits of a modern society: cultural homogeneity, the capacity for context-free communication, the standardization of expression and comprehension. Citizens must be equal in culture as well as in basic status. This is presupposed both by mobility and hence the substitutability of men, and by the constant communication in an anonymous mass society between individuals unfamiliar with one another.[30]

One hardly needs to be fresh from a reading of Marx's critique of Hegel to feel that Gellner's image of a transparent and egalitarian civil society, unmarked by class difference (or race, or gender, or any other marking category), is no less fantastic than Arnold's notion of the State as our "best self." And in fact, the two fantasies are related. Gellner confirms his aesthetic understanding of "culture" a few paragraphs later, when he returns to the notion of culture to aestheticize and nationalize it—and thus, inevitably, to return it to the State:

Modularity with its moral and intellectual pre-conditions makes Civil Society, the existence of non-suffocating, optional yet effective segments, possible; but it makes not only for a civil, but also for a nationalist society. In these circumstances, for the first time in world history a High Culture in this sense becomes the pervasive and operational culture of an entire society, rather than being at most the privilege and badge of a restricted social stratum. It is bound to define the limits of a society culturally and politically—for the enormous and costly educational machinery which makes all this possible also needs a political protector, paymaster, and quality-controller. The state has not merely the monopoly of legitimate violence, but also of the accreditation of educational qualification. So the marriage of state and culture takes place, and we find ourselves in the Age of Nationalism. (106–7)

It may seem counterintuitive to equate "High Culture" with "the pervasive and operational culture of an entire society"; but in conflating the aesthetic and anthropological senses of culture, Gellner is simply following out the inflationary spiral of aesthetic discourse: culture ascends, sooner or later, to the human itself as a totalizing formal category. As we shall see in the next chapter, this is why *aesthetic* nationalism (and all European-style nationalisms have an aesthetic component) exists in a sustainable, if fraught, dialectic with globalism (and, for that matter, imperialism). Gellner's focus on civil society, however, allows us to invert our telescope and watch aesthetics inflate in, as it were, the opposite direction as well—not, this time, upward to include all of humanity at the end of history, but downward to include all of humanity at the origin of aesthetic society's possibility. That is, civil society depends on the fundamental perceptual, communicational, and referential harmony, the *sensus communis*, to which aesthetic judgment testifies and that it works to produce. Training us for life in the nation-state, aesthetic education presupposes its own accomplishment as the foundation of the social itself.[31]

And at work within this fundamental fantasy of a transparent "cultural idiom" are processes of mediation and reproduction that we may properly style *technical*. Idiosyncratic though some of Gellner's formulations may sound, they help us toward an understanding of the peculiar intimacy between aestheticism and technophilism. The "enormous and costly educational machinery" that enables aesthetic education as a political program is not an accidental appendage, prosthesis, or supplement to an essentially spiritual process of *Bildung*; rather, "machinery" (for all Matthew Arnold's protests to the contrary) inheres within aesthetic culture as its most intimate condition of possibility. We may take a moment to recall the common root of our notions of art and technology in the complex Greek word *techne* (a work of art; a craft or trade; a skill or way of making something; cunning devices or wiles). Modern aesthetics comes into being by separating itself from handicraft on the one hand and mass (or technically reproduced) culture on the other, but these acts of separation are endlessly inconclusive because a radical inconclusivity haunts the act of aesthetic formalization that would constitute aesthetics as a discipline or discourse (and would mark it off from, say, handicraft, or from processes of mechanical reproduction). For aesthetics, as we have noted, cannot afford and has no wish to cut itself off entirely from the world. Or rather, it must and also must not cut itself off; the aesthetic frame must be both absolute and permeable—a pure cut, yet a suspended one, as Jacques

Derrida puts it in his reading of Kant's *Critique of Judgment.*[32] Interest thus infiltrates and contains disinterestedness, which for its part remains a detour or vacation: a moment of freedom determined by, at the very least, an interest in returning to interestedness. Aesthetics bleeds into technics at the very point where it establishes its difference from technics. Its reliance on framing or formalization both constitutes and destroys its identity as a distinct, separate domain.

It is therefore necessary to pursue the paradox of the aesthetic frame or form a little further. In Kant, an aesthetic judgment of taste claims universal validity despite the fact that it bears on a singular event and has no conceptual status. Judgment here becomes reflexive rather than determining, which is to say that it reflects back on itself: the judgment is made *as if* it were a cognitive judgment. As Samuel Weber puts it, judgment "imitates itself": it projects onto the world the purposiveness that judgment must presuppose in order to occur.[33] This projection, however, requires some sort of referential anchor, which Kant locates in the difficult notion of form. Though form defines the aesthetic object of judgment, "the effort to purify [form] from every vestige of conceptual or material determination," Weber notes, "tends at the same time to undercut the minimal unity required to distinguish form from mere projection" (22). Form constantly threatens to unravel; it belongs yet does not belong to the object it enframes and (aesthetically) defines. Any frame continuous with the object would itself require a frame. Yet a frame discontinuous with its object could not frame it—could not, that is, provide the referential anchor that reflective judgment needs. The status of the frame as *parergon* or ornament is fundamentally ambiguous: "Even what we call ornaments [*parerga*]," Kant writes, "i.e., what does not belong to the whole presentation of the object as an intrinsic constituent, but is only an extrinsic addition, increases our taste's liking, and yet it too does so only by its form, as in the case of picture frames, or drapery on statues, or colonnades around magnificent buildings" (*Critique of Judgment*, sect. 14). Thus aesthetic form becomes, under pressure, a figure for difference and for the (necessary, but uncertain) phenomenalization of difference. The frame must in some fashion be perceived if the object is to be judged aesthetically; yet as a principle of articulation, the (im)pure cut of the frame slips away from perception and toward the realm of the inscription—the mark, work, or institution of difference that Derrida tropes as writing. Alternatively, we may say that it drifts into the orbit of what de Man understands as rhetoric. Form, crumbling into outline, becomes catachresis and projection—a projection of purposiveness upon a mark that may not be purposive, and a projection of phenomenality upon differences that cannot themselves be perceived or conceived.[34]

Aesthetics, Technics, Theory

Many consequences result from this aesthetic–linguistic problematic, the delineation of which has landed us on the crosshairs of the intersection between aesthetics and theory. Traditional philosophical systems always subordinate the category of the aesthetic to reason and ethics because aesthetic judgment contains within it a critical thrust powerful enough to threaten understanding. If form is a radically unstable figure, aesthetics becomes an ideology that propagates itself on the strength of a process that destroys the ideology it enables. This predicament affects not just our conception of aesthetics itself, but also our understanding of the relationship between aesthetics, on the one hand, and technics or politics on the other. For aesthetics can at this point no longer be imagined as a mere detour, a risk-free vacation from securely referential discourses such as politics or technics; instead, aesthetics, as a discourse inhabited by—indeed, defined by—a risk it flaunts and hides, becomes a privileged site of ideological critique as well as ideological mystification. Pushing to the limit the problem of judgment or reading in advance of rule or guarantee, aesthetics renders legible a dimension of signification that in Chapter 3 we shall define as *material*. Aesthetics becomes theory: theory as a critical narrative that tells the story of the nonaesthetic, nonphenomenal ontology of aesthetics. According to this narrative, the harmony of aesthetic play conceals even as it reveals a radically arbitrary moment at the origin of signification, and the referential spillage of aesthetics into politics and technics must be derived from this peculiar sort of materiality—one name for which in de Man's work is "literariness" as the "autonomous potential of language"—rather than the other way around.

We shall say more about reference and about the project and predicament of theory as a reflection on literariness in a moment. First, let me recall that both writing and rhetoric have classic associations with *techne* and the technical in order to risk the claim that the question concerning technology intersects, at certain points in its trajectory, the problem of aesthetic form as that of the inscription. Of all the topics that a critique of aesthetics drives one to engage, this one is perhaps the most egregiously vast, but even the briefest surveys of the history of reflection on technics suggests its importance for our project. One of the richest words in the classical lexicon, *techne* is the "inventive craft [*mechanoen technas*] that drives man to well or ill."[35] It defines humanity's difference from and dominance over the natural world and includes within its purview not just agriculture and the crafts, but language and everything we would now call culture. In its highest capacity, it is the supplement necessary for the fulfillment of nature (*physis*); for this reason, as Philippe Lacoue-Labarthe has stressed, the technical can never be entirely distinguished from the organic.[36] Yet as supplement, the essence of *techne* is lack. Unlike the productions of nature, according to Aristotle, "no product of art [*poiouménon*] has within itself the principle of its own making" (*Physics*, II, 1 [192b]). Technics is a prosthesis appended to the body of nature, and its presence potentially does damage: as writing, it vitiates living memory in the *Phaedrus*; as rhetoric, it instrumentalizes the *logos* and must be expelled from true philosophical thought. A dangerous supplement, technics is simultaneously a source of power and contagion: a form of mastery that threatens to wound or even destroy the human subject it defines.[37]

Told thus, the story of technics lends support to Samuel Weber's suggestion that we translate as "goings on" the *Wesen* ("essence") of technics in Heidegger's analysis: "as something that *goes on*, technics moves *away* from itself in being what it is."[38] Heidegger's reflections on modern technology turn on this self-difference. Technics appears to be an expression of humanity's will-to-power over a world of objects, and this instrumentalist and humanist conception of technics, Heidegger emphasizes, is correct and even in some ways inevitable. Yet the essence or goings-on of modern technics is something else. It is the order of *Gestell* ("enframing," though Weber suggests "emplacement"), under which the world becomes *Bestand*, or "standing-reserve." The world is put on order, transformed into that which can be extracted and stored; objects and places cease to exist as such, insofar as they are placed on call and become standing-reserve—nodes within a network, we might say now in the Internet age. Modern technics is driven by the goal of regulating and securing (*Steuerung und Sicherung*), and as Weber emphasizes, "the obsession with securing, with placing into safety, can be seen as a response to the unchanged unsecuring in which technics as such continues to take part" (69). He goes on to observe that the decisive issue that emerges from Heidegger's inquiry is "how a movement of unsecuring comes to evoke as response its diametrical opposite—the frantic effort to establish control and security" (70). And if we read that double movement as a version of the rhetorical predicament uncovered by aesthetic judgment, we begin to understand why, in so-called postmodern culture, mass-produced varieties of aesthetic experience proliferate with the proliferation of media technologies. The challenge left by Walter Benjamin, no doubt somewhat surreptitiously, in his great essay, "The Work of Art in the Age of Mechanical Reproduction," is that it is *precisely* in the era of mechanical reproduction that the "aura" flourishes. Or rather, the aura flourishes as it withers: it blossoms in and as the reproducibility of the image within global communicational technological networks. A movement of unsecuring accompanies and conditions the production of these sensuous intensities. Weber observes that the medium of television, for instance, overcomes distance and separation "only because it also *becomes* separation"; unlike film or photography, television transmits not images but rather "the semblance of presentation as such," and in the process, splits the unity of place, events, bodies, and subjects (116–17). This splitting "camouflages itself by taking the form of a visible *image*" (120); but the structuring ambiguity remains: we can never know whether or not what we are seeing is "live." The deeper the penetration of technology into the real, the more manipulable as image the real becomes—yet at the price of a constitutive uncertainty. The aesthetic effect conceals yet depends on "what Derrida has called the irreducible iterability of the mark—that repeatability that both allows a trait to constitute its identity while splitting it at the same time" (Weber, 121).[39]

Always at stake in these various yet interrelated formulations is the status of the human. Aesthetics, which risks everything on its phenomenalization of form, discovers the essence of humanity in our ability to play freely—though for reasons we have begun to detail, free play, in the Schillerian tradition, must never become too free. "Man" must remain the paragon, as Derrida puts it, who suspends within himself the "pure cut" of the *parergon* or frame: as the subject of judgment and the ideal of beauty, man returns aesthetics to itself by leading it away from itself.[40] This role has its dangers. One way to sum up the arguments and readings I shall be offering in this book would be to say that they characterize aesthetics as a necessary peril, not unlike the character modern technics bears in Heidegger's later writings. That technology is potentially dangerous has been a commonplace since the Industrial Revolution—and indeed, as we have seen, since the classical era: a theme that has all the more power, of course, at a point in history when, for some decades, the destruction of humanity and its entire historical archive has been a quotidian possibility; when organic life is being reconceived as a species of cybernetic information, animals are being cloned, the literal manufacture of humans is on the horizon; and so on. "So long as we represent technology as an instrument, we remain held fast in the will [*im Willen hängen*] to master it," Heidegger writes.[41] Imagining itself a subject willing itself into being through technology, humanity becomes human resources, just as the natural world becomes natural resources—becomes, that is, another element to be processed, stockpiled, and circulated within the economy of the modern technical order. Such claims have considerable persuasive power. It is less clear, perhaps, that aesthetics should threaten in any significant way the humanness it celebrates. Yet one would be hard put to imagine a more thoroughgoing transformation of humanity into human resources than one finds in Gellner's aestheticized model of civil society as a totality of modular, mobile, and substitutable human units. Gellner explicitly borrows his notion of the "modular" from the world of mass-produced furniture (97), but his idea of aesthetic society as a technical accomplishment is of older provenance and returns us to the figure of the dance that Schiller, in a well-known letter to Körner, uses to represent the harmonious movement of aesthetic society:

I know of no better image for the ideal of a beautiful society than a well-executed English dance, composed of many complicated turns. A spectator located on the balcony observes innumerable criss-crossing motions which keep decisively but arbitrarily changing directions *without ever colliding with each other.* Everything is so ordered that each dancer has already vacated his position by the time the other arrives. Everything fits so skillfully, yet so artlessly, that everyone seems to be following his own lead, without getting into anyone's way. Such a dance is the perfect symbol of one's own individually asserted freedom as well as of one's respect for the freedom of the other.[42]

In their monumental edition of Schiller's *Aesthetic Education*, Elizabeth M. Wilkinson and L. A. Willoughby gloss the figure of the dance ("the most apposite metaphor for the form of [Schiller's] treatise") in ways that elicit the technical gleam of aesthetic formalization: "the perpetually repeated figures—so highly formalized that they can easily be recorded in notation—admit of only as much individuality in their successive execution by the different dancers as can be expressed through the grace of bodily movement" (cxxxi).[43] Like Schiller and his editors, and like Matthew Arnold and so many others in this aesthetic–political tradition, Gellner imagines a recovery of human freedom in and as the formal beauty of the dance; but the potentially dehumanizing thrust of aesthetic formalization, already legible in Schiller's vision of marionette-like dancers, becomes more pressing as Gellner translates this dance into the idiom and era of mechanical reproduction. Humanity, aestheticized, turns into machinery. The machine, which seems the opposite of the organic work of art, is in fact its double, and the elegant turns of this technopolis simultaneously reveal and ward off the inhumanity and incoherence of the process by which humanity is being affirmed. Aestheticized political models not only conceal real social injustice; as we shall note in various contexts over the course of this book, they actively produce violence as a by-product of their own impossible reliance on, and projection of, sociopolitical homogeneity and transparency.

The Resistance to Theory

Given that it transforms the iterability of the mark into the illusion, never fully sustained, of sensuous presence, aesthetics is fundamentally about, and implicated in, questions of language. It is "part of a universal system of philosophy rather than a specific theory," de Man writes, insofar as it seeks to phenomenalize the difference and deferral of the sign ("Resistance," 8). Aesthetics is consequently an unstable discourse, uncontainable within the bounds of a philosophical subcategory or a historically delimited period. It violates its own frame because its frame depends on unacknowledged and ongoing violation, and that skewed interplay constitutes the kind of predicament that theory, in its radical or de Manian sense, identifies as linguistic. Language has clearly been at issue for some time in the foregoing presentation of aesthetic politics. Gellner's technophilic fantasy lauds civil society's "capacity for context-free communication," a state of transparency achieved through "the standardization of expression and comprehension." Formalization is supposed to serve transparency—and it does, yet with a residue: the residue of technics itself as mediation. As we know from the ever-increasing memory requirements of our personal computers, the more immediate the image, the more elaborate the processes of its production. The fully standardized civil society, in the Gellnerian sense, is the fully televised and commodified society. And because transparency is not itself transparent, a cult of transparency inevitably fetishizes and aestheticizes the technology of transparency's production. Yet these proliferating acts of aestheticization necessarily repeat, of course, the instability at the origin of aesthetic effect. To term this instability *linguistic* is to understand language as our richest, most difficult term for mediation. Language is the Western tradition's master trope for that which must become transparency: to be itself, language must efface itself before objects and concepts, "dissolve," as Daniel Heller-Roazen puts it, "into those things of which it speaks."[44] Language exists in order to be obliterated. And where language persists not as meaning, not as semantic or intersubjective communication, but as an opacity, a stumbling, a transport or drift or mutation irreducible to meaning or intention, then language may be said, oxymoronically, to persist *as language*, as the technical supplement that in itself can never properly exist.

Aesthetics moves away from itself in being what it is, and so does theory: theory reflects on this—its own—self-difference but cannot overcome it. Before theory can get going, it is in debt to an error that has already begun and that can be named but not avoided: the error of language itself. Let us reinspect, a little more carefully this time, de Man's characterization of theory's linguistic orientation:

> Literary theory can be said to come into being when the approach to literary texts is no longer based on non-linguistic, that is to say, historical and aesthetic, considerations, or, to put it somewhat less crudely, when the object of discussion is no longer the meaning or the value but the modalities of production and of reception of meaning and value prior to their establishment—the implication being that this establishment is problematic enough to require an autonomous discipline of critical investigation to consider its possibility and its status. . . . The advent of theory, the break that is now so often being deplored and that sets it aside from literary history and from literary criticism, occurs with the introduction of linguistic terminology in the metalanguage about literature. By linguistic terminology is meant a terminology that designates reference prior to designating the referent

and takes into account, in the consideration of the world, the referential function of language or, to be somewhat more specific, that considers reference as a function of language and not necessarily as an intuition. (7–8)

To consider "reference as a function of language" is not to deny that language refers: "In a genuine semiology as well as in other linguistically oriented theories, the referential function of language is not being denied— far from it; what is in question is its authority as a model for natural or phenomenal cognition" (11). Language refers all the time; indeed, as we shall see in Chapter 3, de Man's studies of rhetorical language take as their starting point language's referential drive. Language *must* refer: in order to be itself, it must point to that which it is not. Language becomes language insofar as it is radically exposed to otherness; by tearing language apart, referentiality makes language what it is. But this referential drive cannot necessarily be intuited or known, in the same way that we can know mental or worldly phenomena. We must in consequence, and quite counterintuitively, seek to understand reference as a dimension of what de Man calls "literariness" or the "autonomous potential of language." Reference happens, constantly, but not in ways that can finally be rendered reliable or predictable. The event of reference exceeds the possibility of its being formalized as knowledge. Rhetorical reading thematizes this problem in the idiom of rhetoric (our culture's oldest term for the systematic use of language to refer to language). The process of formalization whereby the mark is determined as *meaningful* form is rendered as a performative trope, an act of prosopopoeia or giving face that, impossibly, posits what it claims to discover and transforms difference into phenomenal form.

It is from this standpoint that de Man offers his well-known definition of ideology: "What we call ideology is precisely the confusion of linguistic with natural reality, of reference with phenomenalism" (11). Thus defined, ideology becomes that which the "linguistics of literariness" critiques:

It follows that, more than any other mode of inquiry, including economics, the linguistics of literariness is a powerful and indispensable tool in the unmasking of ideological aberrations, as well as a determining factor in accounting for their occurrence. Those who reproach literary theory for being oblivious to social and historical (that is to say ideological) reality are merely stating their fear at having their own ideological mystifications exposed by the tool they are trying to discredit. (11)

It is frequently noted of this dense passage that it generalizes ideology across the social and historical field: ideology, that is, becomes constitutive of all social and historical "reality." The definition follows from and accords with the critique of aesthetics in which theory is always engaged. For as we have seen, aesthetics models the work of ideology per se. By universalizing the singularity, the radical particularity, of the here and now of judgment, aesthetics exemplifies the naturalizing and universalizing operations of any system of ideas worthy of the name "ideology." Aesthetics, as the phenomenalization of difference, is the ideology of ideology. Two aspects of de Man's argument here bear emphasis: first, that his text does not in the least deny the gravity of social and historical experience, and in fact dignifies these spheres of life with the resonant noun: social and historical *reality*. And second, that the theorist and his theory are caught up in this reality. If "the resistance to theory is a resistance to the use of language about language" (12), then the resistance to theory is internal to theory. No stable positive knowledge emerges from theory's linguistic focus, both because the entity being studied, "language," is an uncertain catachresis ("there is probably no word to be found in the language that is as overdetermined, self-evasive, disfigured and disfiguring as 'language'" [13]), and because theory repeats the aesthetic error it critiques, formalizing its particular acts of reading into universal statements ("To the extent . . . that they are theory, that is to say teachable, generalizable and highly responsive to systematization, rhetorical readings, like the other kinds, still avoid and resist the reading they advocate" [19]). One may say that theory lives a cycle of demystification and resistance, but it would be equally true to say that theory negotiates its own constant imbrication in social and historical reality. Like all other kinds of aesthetic discourse, theory is always also about politics.

Theoretical reflection, however, underscores the impossibility of discovering a stable metalanguage with which to pursue a critique of aesthetics. Aesthetics, despite its constitutive disavowals, is in the end a dimension of rhetoric, and it forces us to use terminology one can never entirely rely on, as I have been doing throughout these pages and shall continue to do in what follows. The pleonasm "aesthetic ideology," for instance, offers a useful term to denote highly aestheticized political systems in which human and state identity is overtly modeled on the artwork or aesthetic experience. The more modest-sounding "aesthetic discourse," a favored phrase in the preceding paragraphs (and in those that follow), can helpfully suggest a kind of talk recognizable both by its terminology (beauty and sublimity, genius, imagination, etc.) and the web of meanings, relations, and presuppositions that these terms imply. But aesthetics violates its own frame too fundamentally for terms such as *ideology* or *discourse* to have more than provisional purchase on their putative objects.[45] Theory is always also aesthetics, ideology, the resistance to theory. This economy of infection and implication does not render all statements equivalently mystified or insightful, since theory's negative epistemological thrust is not disqualified by the fact that theory repeats the error it critiques. All repetitions are, after all, different. But the mutual implication of aesthetics and theory accounts for the endless back and forth of criticism, whereby literary or other aesthetic works are by turns judged ideologically complicit and subversive. This ambivalence can never come to rest because ambivalence launches the possibility of critique.[46] Thus theory will always be accusable of being an aestheticism, just as aesthetics will always remain a resource and a trap for criticism.[47] And by the same token, theory will always be accusable of being a technologism—a fetishization of "rigor" that serves to "model the intellectual work of the theorist on the new social form of intellectual work, the technobureaucratic labor of the new professional-managerial class," as John Guillory's influential argument has it (181). No genuine critique of aesthetics, however, can occur without exposing itself to such risks.

It remains to consider, finally, the role of literature and the valence of the term "literariness" in de Man's discourse and in the general aesthetic–political–technical–theoretical problematic we have outlined here. Literature is of course an aesthetic institution. As a cultural space preserved, however imperfectly, for uses of language that are understood to be, at least in principle, sheerly formal and without immediate consequence—in a word, *fictional*—literature arguably represents the epitome, the most remarkable accomplishment, of modern aesthetics.[48] This notion of literature, which begins to take shape in the latter half of the eighteenth century and finds its first fully modern expression in the writings of the Jena romantics, compresses the tensions of aesthetic discourse into a tightly wound paradox.[49] For on the one hand, literature is the mainstay of aesthetic education, the hard currency of bourgeois cultural capital, and the model of the self-reflexive subject of *Bildung.* More than any other art, lit-erature has served the schools as the aesthetic experience that teaches morality and political wisdom and leads the student toward humanity and the state.[50] For reasons we are now prepared to appreciate, there have been very few thoroughgoing "formalisms" in criticism's historical record, either before or after literature became an object to be studied and taught at the university level in the last years of the nineteenth century. Because earlier we glanced at Harold Bloom's invocation of the aestheticist tradition, we may recall here that, though Wildean aestheticism pleasures itself with witty reversals of Arnoldian pieties ("the primary aim of the critic is to see the object as in itself it really is not"), a thematic reading of "The Critic as Artist" willing to accept Gilbert's authority in the dialogue will emerge with familiar truisms: "the most perfect art is that which most fully mirrors man in all his infinite variety." Because art is mimetic of, and grounded in, man, its nonreferentiality is finally a total referentiality. One may or may not want to trust Gilbert, but it is fair to say that he offers us a version of the fundamental promise of all aesthetic discourse: "Beauty has as many meanings as man has moods. Beauty is the symbol of symbols. Beauty re-veals everything, because it expresses nothing."[51]

Yet on the other hand—and Wilde and his texts are, of course, as good an example of this as any—literature, like the visual and plastic arts in the nineteenth and twentieth centuries, comes into its own as rebellion, subversion, and letters from exile; as the scandal of Friedrich Schlegel's *Lu-cinde* and, decades later, the trials of *Madame Bovary* and the *Fleurs du mal;* as the negativity of Mallarmé and the strange, impersonal agony of Kafka; as avant-garde movements of various stripe, in flight from the museums and classrooms to which they are ultimately doomed. In some respects, the great adventure of modern art will always seem futile: aesthetic edu-cation—or, in the case of the visual and plastic arts, the art market—has no difficulty absorbing these performances. For one thing, they can always be understood as representations and enactments of the human condition in all its negativity, complexity, or perversion; for another, they provide thematic elaborations of the self-critical, even self-destructive drive of all art in its relation to the aesthetic expectations that define it; and we have seen that aesthetic institutions are perfectly capable of celebrating art's critical power. Indeed, these institutions rely on this power to construe differences between high and low art, or between insight and ideology.

Aesthetic education, even in its most Arnoldian versions, always pays homage (if only the barest lip service) to the artwork's critical thrust. Theory and aesthetics are intertwined from the outset. Rhetorical reading, as de Man notes, certainly does not escape this dialectic, but nor do the Marxist or feminist or Foucauldian critical performances that circulate in late twentieth-century and early twenty-first-century scholarly journals, classrooms, and conferences. Rhetorical reading does, however, open for inspection fault lines of aesthetic culture that cut across the ideological—social and historical—differences between high literature and the technoaesthetic world of mass culture and mass communications. When de Man claims that theory "upsets the established canon of literary works and blurs the borderlines between literary and non-literary discourse" (11), this is no idle boast, superficial appearances to the contrary. There is a sense in which de Man's brief, famous riff on Archie Bunker and the bowling shoes at the beginning of *Allegories of Reading* is as exemplary of the reach of theory as are the book's subsequent readings of European literary and philosophical texts, just as there is a sense in which the journalistic conviction that "deconstruction" lies at the heart of multiculturalism, canon reform, the politicization of the aesthetic, and so on, is not entirely wrong. In their literariness, the works of Kafka or Proust or Joyce attend to the deferral and difference—the "mediatedness"—that composes and enables, yet also haunts and at times troubles all media technology. The strange anonymity of literature is at work, however silently and unexpectedly, in the goings-on of television and the Internet.[52] For, as language about language, literature exemplifies and enacts the contradictions of aesthetics in an era of technical reproducibility. It is for this reason that critics have at times been drawn to characterize postmodernity, approvingly or not, as a proliferation of literary techniques and effects.[53]

When theory is "high," it is literary; and high theory retains an abiding interest in, even loyalty to, literature. If the conservative or journalistic characterization of deconstruction as antiaestheticist is not simply wrong, neither is the hasty "left-wing" characterization of deconstruction as aestheticist. Literariness, to be sure, hardly remains a stable term under such pressures. It, too, according to de Man, resists itself: the autonomous potential of language flips over into the Cratylean promise that the phenomenality and referential functioning of the signifier may converge. On the one hand, "whenever this autonomous potential of language can be revealed by analysis, we are dealing with literariness"; on the other hand, "the ensuing foregrounding of material, phenomenal aspects of the signifier creates a strong illusion of aesthetic seduction at the very moment when the actual aesthetic function has been, at the very least, suspended" (10). Literariness is only seemingly an end-of-the-line term in de Man; it is in fact caught up in a larger economy of conceptual displacement from which no stable metalanguage can be extracted. Yet the discursive and institutional development of aesthetics has made literature and literariness inescapable terms for any critique of aesthetics willing to assume the burden of its own historical and theoretical possibility. And the problem of this strange, exemplary aesthetic institution, literature, is of course inextricable from political issues. If we ask what Gellner's transparent civil society ought to be least able to tolerate—what one would think it would need above all to expel—it is linguistic opacity and surprise. Yet his modern technorepublic can no more exile its poets than it can protect itself against literariness: Gellner's global village depends on literature and literariness for the "culture" that provides a founding illusion of homogeneity.

Romanticism

Up to this point, I have sought to provide a historical and conceptual narrative that steers away from literary–historical periodization; but few if any statements in the foregoing pages would be much altered if before the noun *aesthetics* one pencilled in the adjective *romantic*. Our modern notions of culture, art, and literature are, we say easily, romantic ones; they emerge during the romantic era; and if the emergence of these notions involves multiple genealogies and if the "romantic era" proves hard to circumscribe, this does not really matter. The relationship between romanticism and aesthetics is elastically pleonastic and can survive all sorts of conflicting historical tugs and jerks. Eighteenth-century authors, scenes, or themes are "preromantic" to the extent that they emphasize a modern aesthetic idiom; nineteenth- and twentieth-century writers become "late romantics" on similar grounds. Indeed, the entire literary production of the last two centuries has not infrequently been characterized as a development internal to romanticism, to the extent that our contemporary ideas of literature, art, criticism, imagination, nationalism, revolution, human rights, and so on remain fundamentally romantic. It has become a commonplace of scholarship that the retrospective, academic construction of romanticism and a "romantic period" in the late nineteenth and early twentieth century occurred as an act of aestheticization, whereby certain writers, texts, and genres were privileged at the expense of others, the importance of the French Revolution was downplayed, Novalis and Shelley were rendered luminous, ineffective angels, and so on.[54] When, for instance, in the postwar era that witnessed the definitive professionalization and bureaucratization of American scholarship, René Wellek sought to fence off a normative field within which to contain A. O. Lovejoy's prolifically multiple romanticisms, he used for his bricks and mortar selective commonplaces of post-Kantian and Coleridgean aesthetic discourse ("imagination for the view of poetry, nature for the view of the world, and symbol and myth for poetic style").[55] It thus became possible to claim, in circular fashion, that romanticism had been constructed romantically, fifty to a hundred years after the "romantic era"—especially in Britain—was supposed to have ended: when Jerome McGann published the book often credited with having spurred into prominence the recent "historicist" turn in romantic studies in North America, he opened it with the claim—a more paradoxical claim than he saw fit to admit—that the "scholarship and criticism of romanticism and its works are dominated by a Romantic Ideology."[56] The equation romantic = aesthetic here acquires the supplemental correlative aesthetic = ideology, and the defining characteristics of romanticism become a litany of specifically aesthetic errors; for example, "the ideals of creative imagination, artistic autonomy, and poetic wholeness" (48). As ideology, McGann suggests, romanticism lives on past its death and dictates its own construction, to the point of being if anything more tenacious in the era of Wellek and Abrams or Hartman and Bloom than in that of Wordsworth or Keats. And McGann's own claim to stand outside this ideology rapidly becomes tendentious, as our foregoing discussion of aesthetics might lead us to suspect. Before the demystifying critic has gotten two pages into his argument, romanticism has split into a good and a bad half, and the ideology has incorporated a reflection on its own contradictions, while McGann himself has begun to sound remarkably "romantic":

Romantic poetry occupies an implicit—sometimes even an explicit—critical position toward its subject matter. The works of romantic art, like the works of any historical moment, "transcend" their particular sociohistorical position only because they are completely incorporated to that position, only because they have localized themselves. In this fact we observe that paradox fundamental to all works of art which is best revealed through an historical method of criticism: that such works transcend their age and speak to alien cultures because they are so completely true to themselves, because they are time and place specific, because they are—from our point of view—*different*. (2)

If one removes the scare quotes and a brace of "only"s from its second sentence, the citation becomes practically indistinguishable from much of the academic writing that a "New Historicism" wishes to reject as ideological. The work of art transcends its context in and through its historicity, its sensuous presence-to-self: McGann's comments do not deviate in any significant way from the main current of aesthetic–humanist thought. Somewhat against its own intention, *The Romantic Ideology* offers an exemplary demonstration of the persistence of the ideology it sets out to critique. Indeed, we might wonder why its author feels so strongly that in order to "return poetry to a human form" (160)—surely a romantic ambition if there ever was one—a denunciation of romanticism is required.

Yet precisely because it is a trope for aesthetics, romanticism must turn on itself. It splits into error and critique, with the critique turning out to be another version of what was denounced as error. This spiral, particularly legible in McGann, can be read back through the romantic–aesthetic tradition to the romantics "themselves."[57] The peculiarities of the romantic academic tradition ultimately derive from this predicament. An early symptom was the bifurcation of romanticism into a style or set of themes, on the one hand, and a historical slice of time on the other: certain exemplary performances then needed to become, in properly aesthetic fashion, representative of the "period."[58] The case of British romanticism is peculiarly extreme: its six exemplary poets had to be airlifted out of several discrete and often ambiguous contexts (the Lake Poets; the Cockney School; the Satanic School—and even these designations, of course, are labels originally affixed to certain groups of poets by hostile reviewers) in order to form a visionary company that could embody the spirit of the age. The result was a unique brace of nominalizations. From the point of view of nomenclature, "the Romantics"—that is, the six exemplary poets—represent "the Romantic era" as no other canonical British authors represent theirs (in ordinary literary–historical usage, "Elizabethans" or "Victorians" refer more broadly to historical populations; "Augustans" has about it a touch of the coterie; only "modernists" comes close to the synecdochic aestheticism of "romantics"). A certain tension between spirit and age, however, laces even the most celebratory accounts of romanticism. It is, after all, a movement destined to die young or end badly, bequeathing only its promise to us as our own utopian possibility—and when a critic puts pressure on the synecdochical–aesthetic model, the fracture within romanticism develops according to whatever direction the critic happens to take. The difference between the thematic and historical definitions of romanticism can be exacerbated ("Not every artistic production in the romantic period is a romantic one" [McGann, 19]); rhetorical or generic elements can come into play (symbol and allegory; romantic and Gothic).[59] In various ways, these binary oppositions all offer a version of the difference between aesthetic illusion and critical insight, and whenever the critique is pursued with any seriousness, the binary opposition collapses at the point when, haunted by its other, the aesthetic text becomes its own critical commentary. Any entity marked as romantic will turn out to resist its own romanticism. Such, to be sure, is the general predicament of critical reading: acts of demystification discover their possibility in the text being read. But romanticism exacerbates the addictive cycle of interpretation—the ironic spiral of ideology and critique—to the extent that romanticism and aesthetics are overlapping figures for each other. Romanticism thus becomes the home turf of aesthetic ideology, on the one hand, and high theory on the other.[60] Appropriating a Heideggerian phrase, Maurice Blanchot writes of "the non-romantic essence of romanticism."[61] If romanticism is the self as creative impulse and will to power, the goings-on of romanticism are something else entirely and have more to do with literariness, in the sense sketched earlier, than with literature as a cultural form.

Thus, like aesthetics, technics, literature, and theory, romanticism is a conceptual node fractured by self-difference and self-resistance. It is both ideological fantasy and critical demystification; historical object and present concern; reactionary and revolutionary; naive and satanic; religious and secular; the locus of ambivalence and of utopian hope. It is the product of an "academic ideology" as much as of an aesthetic one, as John Rieder comments; yet it excites desires and anxieties as no other period term can.[62] We shall consider further the political complications of romanticism in Chapter 5; here it will suffice to observe that, even in an era of routinized, bureaucratic–professional scholarship, "whenever romantic

attitudes are implicitly or explicitly under discussion, a certain heightening
of tone takes place, an increase of polemical tension develops, as if something of immediate concern to all were at stake," as de Man observed in his
1967 Gauss lectures.[63] (He himself was to serve as an occasion for height-
ened tone and polemical tension in subsequent years, for reasons directly
related, as we have seen, to the romantic–aesthetic problematic.) Romanticism still matters, still occasions surprising displays of passion or anxiety:
the investment in aesthetics that critics may no longer wish to recognize or
confess finds displaced expression in, for instance, ecocritical movements,
or the kind of principled cultural critique that understands its task as little
short of redemptive.[64] Alternatively, appalled by the dizzying turns of romantic self-resistance, critics react negatively, denounce romanticism as a
pernicious ideology, a *mensonge romantique*, and seek to get rid of it.[65]
Lovejoy's famous proposal that, given the unlikelihood that "we should all
cease talking about Romanticism," we should at least "learn to use the
word Romanticism in the plural" (234–35) has a postmodern equivalent in
the odd contemporary spectacle of professional interpreters of British romanticism (I shall return shortly to the peculiarities of the British tradition) writing articles for each other's consumption that anxiously recon-
sider, and not infrequently excoriate, the very idea of "romanticism."[66]
Such doubts, of course, do not in the least prevent business from going on
as usual, any more than the coeval rejection and "politicization" of aesthetics prevents business from going on as usual in professional humanistic
studies generally. As we have seen, aesthetic institutions necessarily incorporate, however uneasily, a critical, theoretical element, and do their work
all the more handily for being pressured by self-resistance.

   In the orbit of romanticism, however, these contradictions become
visible. All periodizing terms are arbitrary, disputable, and occasionally the
subject of dispute; but romanticism names the historical emergence of the
very idea of aesthetic–historical periodization. We are being romantic when
we seek out the historical identity or *Zeitgeist* of romanticism, or the Renaissance, or, for that matter, "modernity" itself as a cultural development;
hence the impulse, shared by critics of remarkably different backgrounds—
from James Chandler to Philippe Lacoue-Labarthe and Jean-Luc Nancy—
to declare that we are all in some sense still romantic, or still within the
horizon of a romantic era.[67] Yet romanticism also brings to our representation of aesthetics the character of an *event*. Romanticism occurred—when,

exactly, is forever uncertain, because romanticism altered our understanding of temporality. It occurred with the violence and promise of the Revolution with which it has always been associated, as an event that implicates and constitutes us as historical entities and as subjects of historical understanding. Romanticism is "uncontainable," as Carol Jacobs puts it; and that uncontainability is nothing more or less than a predicament of reading—reading a text within which we are inscribed, and an event that claims us.[68]

Gender

It remains to say a word about the focus on gender announced in this book's subtitle. A study of aesthetics—let alone the politics of aesthetics—encounters figures, effects, and questions of gender at every turn, and on every level of analysis. Though it would be pointless to claim that aesthetics has had a more substantial role to play in the history of gender politics than in the history of class warfare or racial stereotyping, figures of gender and gendered difference can nonetheless be said to play a particularly prominent role in the constitution of aesthetic discourse.[69] Modern aesthetics begins its development in an era when gender and sexual difference were accruing new ideological importance as Western European societies shifted, slowly and unevenly, and at times violently, from a rank to a class-based political order under the impact of capitalism, with the concomitant production of a bourgeois culture predicated on the separation of domestic and economic spheres, and powerful enough to produce and impose new normative conceptions of gentility, maternity, and so on. Ambitious scholarly analyses, in many cases exploring lines of inquiry opened by the work of Michel Foucault, have drawn attention to the prominence and ideological force of the discourse of sexuality in the modern era and have tracked the development of an increasingly binary model of sexual difference over the course of the seventeenth and eighteenth centuries. Whether or not one is persuaded that "in or about the late eighteenth [century] . . . human sexual nature changed," as Thomas Laqueur suggests, his history of the shift in European science from a Galenic, one-sex anatomical model (according to which the female is an inverted and lower version of the male) to a two-sex model (according to which the sexes are radically distinct) provides a usefully concrete example of a diffuse and widespread

historical phenomenon.[70] The binary opposition of male and female—
legible, according to some late nineteenth-century accounts, on the most
microscopic level of the body's constitution—granted sexual difference the
status of a major ideological fulcrum during the era that witnessed the full
development of aesthetics. "Because of the place that woman occupied in
the symbolic order, she was the guarantor of truth, legitimacy, property,
and male identity," Mary Poovey writes, targeting mid-nineteenth-century
British middle-class culture here, though her generalization would arguably hold good for the century and a half or so between Edmund Burke
and Oscar Wilde, at the very least.[71] Poovey has in fact argued that sexual
difference "becomes the fundamental organizing dichotomy" in British
eighteenth-century aesthetic discourse; and Kathy Alexis Psomiades, focusing on late nineteenth-century British aestheticism, argues that "the
category of the aesthetic in bourgeois culture is itself predicated upon the
figuration of art as a beautiful feminine body, whether that body is characterized by its presence or its absence."[72] Figures of gender obviously function differently in different historical and cultural contexts, but even in the
twentieth century, aesthetic discourse bears legible traces of these gendered
histories, particularly when distinctions between high and popular culture
are in play.[73]

As a discourse involving the senses, and thus a subordinate helpmeet
to the sterner realms of ethics and epistemology, aesthetics has enduring associations with femininity in the history of metaphysics and has specific
historical ties to the ambiguously gendered eighteenth-century discourse of
sensibility.[74] The imperative to (re)masculinize aesthetics is one of Western
high culture's leitmotivs over the past two centuries, and the binary opposition masculine/feminine maps onto any number of forks and folds
within aesthetic discourse: high art, and a properly formal identification
with humanity, are masculine; popular culture, Gothic romances, and the
mass-produced work in the age of mechanical reproduction, are feminine—though the binary opposition immediately splits and redoubles
under inspection, and, as in all other spheres of aesthetic discourse, critical
readings of literary texts that are keyed to gender oppositions circle through
an endless dialectic whereby the text is alternately, or simultaneously, subversive of and complicit with gendered expectations.[75] Here, our example
of the moment is, of course, romanticism. Romanticism has no doubt
tended to be marked as masculine and represented by male writers in

Western Europe, but even the most austerely male and heterosexual major figures in these various romanticisms (and there are not very many such figures; Wordsworth is probably one's best candidate, unless Goethe is allowed honorary status as a romantic) know contexts in which they can be read as deviant, whereas romanticism as a whole has, of course, a long history of being received as a sexual as well as political and aesthetic scandal— as a bevy of authors and texts that are perverted, dangerously effeminate, and generally in need of control.[76]

Gender is thus a constitutive, though not entirely reliable, element in the construction of academic and literary–historical romanticism; and though feminist and gender criticism has not transformed romantic studies any more thoroughly than other areas of the humanities, such criticism has in at least one case had the power to bruise the operations of academic canonization in ways unimaginable in other fields. Once again, we encounter the peculiar vicissitudes of British romanticism. Here, the exaggerated aesthetic screening that produced a period represented by six lyric poets resulted in a situation in which the mere expansion of the canon—in itself a perfectly unremarkable aesthetic operation—was able to throw the notion of "romanticism" and its era into a degree of disarray. In German studies, where romanticism names a movement within a larger literary context and has been treated more as a "school" than an "era," renewed interest in, say, Dorothea Schlegel provokes no equivalent crisis; the same goes, *mutatis mutandis*, for the recovery of women or otherwise marginalized writers in British eighteenth-century or Victorian studies. But the peculiarly forceful aesthetic exemplarity of the "romantics" in British romanticism meant that scholars who recovered for analysis or aesthetic appreciation poets and writers such as Felicia Hemans, Anna Barbauld, Charlotte Smith, or Joanna Baillie were also immediately driving a wedge between the romantics and their period, drawing attention to the contingencies of canonization and to romanticism's historical and institutional construction, and marking off as "romantic" a particular, if exemplary, aesthetic illusion. What is then said about Hemans or Barbauld is often as aesthetic–humanist as anything ever said about Wordsworth or Coleridge; but the boat rocks anyway—gently, but visibly: hence the ongoing, if in no way incapacitating, identity crisis within British romantic studies.[77]

This book makes no claim to contribute directly to the richly complex field of gender theory, and it certainly offers no systematic historical treatment of the complex role of gender and sexual difference within aesthetic discourse. The three principal points are made over the course of this study: that aesthetic discourse often seeks, at moments of stress, to anchor the turns of figurative language to the putative naturalness of sexual difference; that the favored figure for natural figuration is the mother, who suffers "abjection," in Julia Kristeva's sense, proportionate to her inability to allay anxieties about language; that, in consequence, gender and sexual differences become *non*-natural in aesthetic and romantic contexts and become thinkable as performed or posited differences that are ultimately unreliable.[78] The binary opposition male/female, which—particularly during this era, as we have seen—looks so promising as a natural ground for the difference between literal and figurative meaning, crumbles into an anxious (or exhilarating or even humorous, and not infrequently violent) scene of fetishism.[79] Gender turns ambiguous, volatile, fictional. Aesthetics as a discourse and a field of social activity has always been sexually ambiguous, uncertainly androgynous, sliding toward decadence, dangerously homoerotic. These thematic complications respond to the radical uncertainty of gender as an aesthetic figure.

Different aspects of these claims are worked out over the course of this book. Here, let me close with a brief comment on rhetoric and gender, along with a review of the gendered body's rhetorical complexity. The readings that unfold in subsequent chapters lend support to Lee Edelman's claim that "sexuality is constituted through operations as much rhetorical as psychological," and they elicit from that interpretive predicament the lesson that although a particular trope for the rhetoricity of the sexual will always do analytic and political work within the context of its deployment, no metaterm will ever definitively control the field of sexual and gender difference. To propose, as Edelman does, that the category of "homosexuality" has been "constructed to bear the cultural burden of the rhetoricity inherent in 'sexuality' itself," is to open space for invaluable, historically situated cultural critique; but in other interpretive contexts, other terms will impose themselves with equal historical and theoretical necessity: woman; the feminine; the lesbian; or alternative, less nominalized queer identifications.[80] Edelman's finely grained readings point toward the interplay of such tropes insofar as they repeatedly allow the figure of the homosexual to drift into alignment with "woman" as "the figure associated in the popular mind with specularity or narcissism and in psychoanalytic discourse with the lure of the imaginary as manifested in that figure's identification with the mother" (196). Such overlaps produce dense textual knots where, as Edelman emphasizes, the rhetorical slippage of sexual identification is negotiated as an economy of writing and erasure, face-giving and effacement. The fetishistic question par excellence—"What's the difference"— is asked and erased as difference is given face as the homosexual (or—or also—as woman): a figure of facelessness, a scapegoat by means of which the rhetoricity of sexuality can be rhetorically expelled.

Another way to approach this question is as a matter of the body—a body that matters, in Judith Butler's phrase, which is also to say a body that must be read. The body is one of the master tropes of aesthetic discourse, and we shall be tracking some of its vicissitudes over the course of the next four chapters. It promises a totality that it undermines, because no aesthetic embodiment can occur without the risk of oversignification or overfigurativeness. Lacan-inflected psychoanalytic thought often renders this tension as one between imaginary and symbolic registers, but the notion of a symbolic order arguably does not do justice to the body's rhetorical volatility in such contexts. If, as Lacan comments, "the image of [man]'s body is the principle of every unity he perceives in objects," not only is the body an imaginary unity requiring constant reconstitution and renegotiation, but the same is true for any "body part" that receives recognition and significance as such.[81] Following this line of reasoning, Judith Butler argues that the Lacanian discourse of the phallus unwittingly recapitulates the phantasmatics of the Lacanian mirror stage by idealizing an anatomical part—the penis—into a whole: the whole, in this case, of a constitutive lack. "As imaginary effect," Butler concludes, "the phallus would be as decentered and tenuous as the ego"—hence her iconoclastic proposal of "the lesbian phallus" as the specter of the phallus's arbitrariness and transferability.[82] I would take from that discussion a sense of the overlap between, on the one hand, the constitutive instability of gender as a bodily code, and, on the other hand, the "materiality" of the body as a fragmenting, inscriptive force prior to and at work in the castrated, meaningful body of the symbolic order. Marked by the law of sexual difference and given over to the play of symbolic substitutions, the body remains a body because of the persistence or reiteration of imaginary acts of totalization, yet in its bodiliness remains irreducible to the meanings it generates. Gender identity thus always involves an act of reading. The phallus of psychoanalysis—

the mark of sexual difference—must be *read* as such, *taken* as such, and a touch of arbitrariness and uncertainty will always cling to such performative acts of interpretation, putting them in need of constant reiteration and renegotiation and opening them to citation, parody, and figurative displacement. In consequence, aesthetics, as a "discourse of the body," has been a discourse obsessively respectful of sexual difference *and* a place where gender turns ambiguous—where the codes governing middle-class sexual behaviors and identities are exposed to the possibility of being cited, undermined, parodied, reperformed.

An archaic trope for these uncertainties, I suggest in Chapter 3, is the Medusa as the face of terror and the consolation of face. In the Greek myth, she is both a petrifying otherness and a trophy bagged (and later a weapon used) by Perseus, a killing gaze objectified through technical stratagems (sandals, a helmet, a mirror) and transformed thereby into a technical resource. In his famous unpublished paper on the Medusa, Freud associates her with the horror (*Grauen*) of the mother's genitals and suggests that the sight of her decapitated head functions on two levels at once: as trauma, and as defense.

The hair upon Medusa's head is frequently represented in works of art in the form of snakes, and these once again are derived from the castration complex. It is a remarkable fact that, however frightening they may be in themselves, they nevertheless serve actually as a mitigation of the horror, for they replace the penis, the absence of which is the cause of the horror. . . . The sight of Medusa's head makes the spectator stiff with terror, turns him to stone. Observe that we have here once again the same origin from the castration complex and the same transformation of affect! For becoming stiff [*das Starrwerden*] means an erection. Thus in the original situation it offers a consolation to the spectator: he is still in possession of a penis, and the stiffening reassures him of the fact.[83]

The snakes, then, in this allegorical reading, figure both the absence and presence of the penis, and their petrifying power simultaneously conveys death and life, castration and restitution. Such is the doubleness of the fetish, which substitutes for the missing maternal phallus only by erecting a memorial, a *Denkmal*, to the fact that a substitution has been performed. Hence the mix of love and aggressivity that fetishes inspire. And at work in the fetish's doubleness is a radical uncertainty that this doubleness disguises and repeats. "Dissemination will always have threatened signification there," Derrida writes.[84] For an "absence" (of, say, the phallus) must, once again, be *read* as "absence" before the agitated uncertainties of fetishism can get underway. Medusa gives to that performative linguistic moment a terrifying, consoling, gendered face.

Envoi: Readings in the Politics of Aesthetics

The chapters that follow seek to document this introduction's basic claim, which is that the romantic and aesthetic tradition, in its reach as ideology and its fractured self-doubling as literary theory, offers our culture's most substantial elaboration of the question that has been posed with characteristic precision and economy by Barbara Johnson: "What are the political consequences of the fact that language is not a transparently expressive medium?"[85] Part I of this book, "The Aesthetic National Body," has a theme: I seek here to develop a critique of aesthetics as political model and gendered discourse by examining aspects of the rhetoric of aesthetic nationalism. Chapter 1 pursues the interplay between aesthetics and technics a little further by scrutinizing Benedict Anderson's influential definition of the nation as an "imagined community" and Johann Gottlieb Fichte's efforts to imagine Germany in *Reden an die deutsche Nation* (*Addresses to the German Nation*; 1807–8). We shall see that this act of imagining, which involves an aestheticization of the nation-state's technical–communicational condition of possibility, generates figures of mourning, and above all figures of mourning mothers, a trope examined from a somewhat different angle in Chapter 2, which reads closely Matthew Arnold's seminal essay, "The Function of Criticism" (1864) in order to explain why, at precisely the moment in his text in which the aesthetic embodiment of British culture is at stake, Arnold conjures into existence "a girl named Wragg"—an abject, murderous mother who represents the gap between Britain's present condition and the aesthetic state toward which Arnoldian criticism strives. As a discourse of the body that cannot help disclosing its radical figurativeness, aesthetics, in this text, both evades and reveals the arbitrariness of our culture's long-standing association between materiality and the maternal and in the process discloses a literal materiality—a materiality of the letter—at work in the name of the figure who, giving face to difference, pays with her abjection the wages of aesthetic nationalism.

As my summary of Part I makes clear, this book deliberately transgresses the conventional borders of "romanticism" as a literary–historical period or movement; and these introductory pages have tried to provide context for an interpretive effort that, if not entirely averse to risk, certainly has no desire to be judged scattered or willful, or self-indulgently unobservant of academic pieties. The romanticism that interests me here is a romanticism inseparable from aesthetics—and correspondingly uncontainable. Yet such a romanticism is not without relation to the academic field that has grown up around this term. Part II, "Radical Figures of Romanticism," offers three chapters focused on writers in the romantic tradition— two bona fide romantics, plus a twentieth-century romanticist—who push conventions of the aesthetic institution they inhabit to the breaking point: Paul de Man, Friedrich Schlegel, and Percy Shelley. These authors and texts do not, it should be stressed, represent a norm, whether of an age, a movement, or a particular aesthetic. I offer them rather as extravagantly exemplary figures. They are canonical, male, and (with the partial exception of de Man) entirely conventional and proper objects of a critical study featuring the word *romanticism* in its subtitle, yet they expose romanticism to its nonromantic nonessence. Chapter 3 is obviously in a sense this book's theory chapter: de Man's work provides a theoretical account of the linguistic materiality that Arnold's text associates with its girl named Wragg. But this chapter, like the others, aspires to the status of a reading: my main purpose here is to account for the gestures of monumentalization and sacrifice that mark the reception of de Man's work by pursuing ways in which history, politics, and pathos are linked in his writing. The monumentalization of de Man as a sublimely self-knowing superreader eventually lends itself to being figuratively aligned with Schiller's vision, about halfway through the *Aesthetic Education of Man*, of the face of the Juno Ludovisi— an aestheticized Medusa face that serves to some extent as an end-of-the-line figure, in Neil Hertz's phrase, for the maternalist and fetishistic fantasies encountered in the previous two chapters.

Finally, Chapters 4 and 5 seek to extend our appreciation of the degree to which romantic literary writing at times radically displaces and rewrites the politics of aesthetics. Chapter 4 brings into full focus this book's thematization of gender as an unstable, performative difference within aesthetics: Friedrich Schlegel's pseudo roman à clef *Lucinde* (1799) ironizes gender difference to the point that the body's materiality can be grasped in linguistic terms as the constitutive uncertainty that makes figuration possible. Chapter 5 returns to questions of aesthetics, politics, and romanticism broached in this introduction and discovers in various texts by Percy Shelley a systematic, rigorous attention to the problem of political agency. A state of uncertainty, Shelley suggests, conditions and opens up the possibility of all political and ethical engagement. A poetics attentive to and performative of such uncertainty does not constitute an apolitical aestheticism, but in fact relays a fundamental ethical attentiveness and an openness to future possibility. Arguing along these lines, I offer, near the end of this book's winding road, an interpretation of the Shelleyan assertion that "poets are the unacknowledged legislators of the world" that will at least have the virtue of being relatively uncommon: I shall read it as an affirmation of history's resistance to form and thus as a rebuttal of the aesthetic politics it seems to exemplify. Romanticism holds open the possibility that things will be different someday, because they are in fact different now. The politics of aesthetics are ongoing, and unguaranteed.

PART I

THE AESTHETIC NATIONAL BODY

Imagi-Nation: The Imagined Community
and the Aesthetics of Mourning

> The essence of a nation is that all individuals have many things in common and
> also that they have forgotten many things.
> —Ernest Renan, "What is a Nation?"

Of the many relics of the romantic era that continue to shape our
(post)modernity, the nation-state surely ranks among the most significant.
Two decades ago, Benedict Anderson commented that "'the end of the
era of nationalism,' so long prophesied, is not remotely in sight" (*IC*, 3),
and the intervening years have made it increasingly clear that the developments and processes we summarize as "globalization" operate in mingled synchrony and tension with the political form of the nation-state.[1]
That the nation-state should remain the premier vehicle of political and
economic legitimation in an era dominated by American imperialism and
international capital—forces that, of course, regularly and flagrantly vio-
late the sovereignty of disadvantaged nations—is unsurprising if one ac-
cepts the continuing pertinency and power of a Western master narrative
of modernity, according to which the nation represents the emergence of
a people into history and prefigures the global achievement of universal
human concord. As the proper subject of history, the nation-state can prefigure history's end because, as David Lloyd writes, "the particularism of
[nationalism's] contents, potentially in contradiction with the universal-
ism of modernity, is subsumed in the *formal* congruence between its own
narratives of identity, directed at one people, and the narrative of identity
that universal history represents for humanity in general."[2] Lloyd goes on
to note that the nation's intermediate status in this narrative—halfway
between primitive tribalism and modernity's ever-deferred perpetual

peace—accounts for nationalism's irreducibly double association with modernization and atavism. In consequence, the modernist paradigm continues to rule many skeptical or hostile accounts of nationalism, for as long as the nation-state is taken to supersede other political or social formations, the cosmopolitan critique fails to challenge "the fundamental philosophy of universal history that underwrites nationalism's inscription in modernity" (177). Indeed, both in the corporate media and in mainstream Western political discourse generally, nations and nationalisms are commonly treated as atavistic or progressive, depending on the degree to which their behavior harmonizes with globalizing imperatives. That these imperatives emanate quite blatantly from Wall Street in no way seriously troubles the effectiveness of modernity as a narrative paradigm.[3]

Seeking to discredit universalizing narrative, much cultural criticism in recent years has exchanged cosmopolitanism and the abstract question of "nationalism" for an emphasis on the contextual construction of national movements or identities.[4] This valuable body of work has sought to recover the particularity of cultural and socioeconomic circumstance, stressed the fundamental role of racism in colonialist contexts, and noted ways in which nationalist movements draw on or unleash forms of resistance that challenge representationalist politics. The pages that follow, however, remain focused on the nationalist fantasy proper to the discourse of modernity. Cultural critique can only profit from knowing as much as possible about the favored turns of the universal–historicist model, particularly since this model is an aesthetic one that grants a world-historical role to "culture." The state, in a tradition that in its main lines runs from Schiller through Hegel and Matthew Arnold and is still very much alive today, *represents* the community to itself, thereby giving the community form and in a certain sense giving it an ethical imperative and a future; as we saw in the Introduction, the state represents "our best self" (Arnold), "the archetype of a human being" (Schiller), because it signifies the formal unification both of the citizen with the community and of the community with universal humanity.[5] Because this unification is ideal rather than actual, it can be projected as the ethical terminus of history (that is, as the ideal of an accomplished modernity). The state's core mission thus becomes pedagogical: its job is to acculturate its subjects into citizens. The production of a docile citizenry thereby obtains an ethical aura and an aesthetic character, insofar as the artwork—and the domain of aesthetic or "cultural" experience generally—become imaginable as disinterested spaces in which the subject of aesthetic education achieves a proleptic, formal moment of identification with humanity per se. The retooling of liberal education that resulted in the creation of national literature departments in universities at the end of the nineteenth century would have been inconceivable in the absence of this aesthetic model of culture.[6]

The aesthetic substratum of state-oriented nationalism helps account, perhaps, for the fact that the title of Benedict Anderson's *Imagined Communities* has become a tag phrase—almost a mantra—in academic and para-academic discussions of nationalism. Particularly within that amorphous field we call cultural studies, a powerful set of expectations seems to hold sway: no matter what the critic's agenda or methodology, she or he can usually be counted on to affirm—usually more or less in passing, with a bare nod at Anderson's actual arguments—that nations are "imagined communities." The affinity between nation and imagination is incessantly noted and rarely interrogated. It has about it, in other words, something of the force of the "imaginary" in Lacan's sense as well as Anderson's.[7] No less than that of the nation, the notion of the imagination maintains a tenacious purchase on "our models of culture, interpretation, and evaluation."[8] And the roots of the association between these two romantic inventions—imagination and nation—run very deep indeed, at least if one credits Philippe Lacoue-Labarthe's archaeology of "the fiction of the political" in the Western tradition:

The political (the City) belongs to a form of plastic art, formation and information, *fiction* in the strict sense. This is a deep theme which derives from Plato's politico-pedagogical writings (especially *The Republic*) and reappears in the guise of such concepts as *Gestaltung* (configuration, fashioning) or *Bildung*, a term with a revealingly polysemic character (formation, constitution, organization, education, culture, etc.). The fact that the political is a form of plastic art in no way means that the *polis* is an artificial or conventional formation, but that the political belongs to the sphere of *techne* in the highest sense of the term, that is to say in the sense in which *techne* is conceived as the accomplishment and revelation of *physis* itself. This is why the *polis* is also "natural": it is the "beautiful formation" that has spontaneously sprung from the "genius of a people" (the Greek genius) according to the modern—but in fact very ancient—interpretation of Aristotelian mimetology.[9]

Our itinerary will be more circumscribed than that recommended by Lacoue-Labarthe, but we shall be engaging a similar cluster of themes. I propose first to recall a few passages from Anderson's *Imagined Communities* in order to remark on ways in which this text both opens up and veers away from a critique of aesthetic nationalism. Anderson makes legible the nation's inseparability from questions of language and technics. Furthermore, without necessarily meaning to, he allows us to locate the possibility of aesthetic formalization—the engine of modernity's aesthetic narrative—in a "prior" condition of anonymity, contamination, and loss, a predicament that aesthetic narrative both forecloses and records. Anderson's text suggests that the "imagined community" of the nation develops in productive tension with the conditions of mechanical reproduction that make it possible, and that imagining the nation entails fantasies about communication and technology, and the production of gendered and irretrievably mournful scenes of pedagogy.

In the second part of this chapter, I turn to a text by Fichte, one of the romantic era's great theorists of the imagination, *Addresses to the German Nation* (1807–8). Counterintuitive though it may seem, such a trajectory has unexpected advantages. In a rather broad sense, it might be said that Anderson writes as a late romantic, not just because he invokes the creative imagination but because, in doing so, he sets out to rescue nationalism from the condescension of an enlightened cosmopolitanism. Identifying nationalism—particularly in the wake of the Indochinese conflicts of the late 1970s—as "an uncomfortable *anomaly* for Marxist theory" (*IC*, 3), Anderson proposes to reclassify it "with 'kinship' and 'religion' rather than with 'liberalism' or 'fascism'" (5)—to understand nationalism, that is, as an expression of fundamental human needs (for continuity, for affective bonds) in an age of mechanical reproduction. Anderson thus positions nationalism at a remove from the state: its roots are different from the state's and run deeper, ultimately tapping into the substratum of the imagination itself. That no doubt sounds like a romantic preoccupation, as does Anderson's interest in drawing sharp distinctions between authentic, popular nationalism and the mass-produced icons and manipulative strategizing of "official" nationalisms. But it is an equally "romantic" characteristic of Anderson's text that, to some extent despite itself, it also suggests the impossibility of keeping nation and state from blurring into each other, precisely because the nation, *as* "imagined," inevitably becomes the object of aesthetic pedagogy. For a dramatic instance of this slippage between nation and state, one can scarcely do better than consult Fichte's *Addresses*, a work so famous for its ethnolinguistic celebration of "Germanness" that readers routinely underestimate its central theme of mass national (state) education and often overlook entirely the fact that Fichte's ethnolinguistic nation is also, fundamentally and crucially, an *imagined* community. My point throughout will not be to suggest that we can or ought to do without the notion of the imagination in thinking about nationalism. As Anderson so brilliantly shows, that would be tantamount to not thinking about nationalism at all. I am rather proposing that we understand both imagination and nation as figures inextricable from aesthetic discourse, which is another way of saying that they are fictions possessed of great referential force and chronic referential instability—fictions of an impossible, ineradicable mourning.

I

All communities, as Anderson points out, are in some sense imagined. Even the members of a hamlet or a family (and we shall be returning to the family) relate to each other with "an element of fond imagining," as Anderson rather optimistically puts it (*IC*, 154), and any political unit larger than a hamlet or possessed of a sense of history longer than a generation necessarily requires its constituents to partake of a collective identity irreducible to a face-to-face encounter. But the nation is *radically* imagined: it cannot be experienced immediately as a perception. The subject of a kingdom can at least in principle perceive the monarch, and willy-nilly has face-to-face encounters with the monarch's bureaucratic or feudal representatives. But a nation-state is fundamentally and irretrievably faceless, even when a king or a charismatic dictator rules it. Elaborating with his own inimitable brio on this Andersonian theme, Franco Moretti remarks that one can imagine or visualize a town, valley, or city, even the universe itself ("a starry sky, after all, is not a bad image of it"). "But the nation-state? 'Where' is it? What does it look like? How can one *see* it?"[10] The nation can only be visualized—imagined—through the mediation of a catachresis, an arbitrary sign. It is no coincidence that in Hegel's famous account of the difference between signs and symbols in his *Enzyklopädie der philosophischen Wissenschaften* (*Encyclopedia of the Philosophical Sciences*; 1817), one of his three exemplary examples of the sign is the flag (the two others are the cockade and the gravestone; we shall shortly reencounter the matter of gravestones), or that his discussion of the sign occurs as part of a section of the *Encyclopedia* devoted to "imagination" (*Einbildungskraft*). As Paul de Man comments, "although it would not be correct to say that Hegel valorizes the sign over the symbol, the reverse would be even less true"—for, precisely because it is arbitrary, "the sign illustrates the capacity of the intellect to 'use' the perceived world for its own purposes."[11] The sign results from the imagination's ability to posit what cannot simply be perceived. Hence the abstract forms and solid colors favored by the flags of modern nation-states; unlike the detailed fretwork of heraldry, these aggressively simple bars and stars testify to the arbitrariness of a sign that has been posited, not inherited or found. The nation, like one's own death, cannot be imagined and can only be imagined; inevitably—if often in banal and prefabricated ways—it partakes of the discourse of the sublime.[12]

Anderson's great Benjaminian argument in *Imagined Communities* derives the possibility of this imaginative act out of developments in reproductive and communicational technologies. The modernity of the nation is that of the Gutenberg revolution: as language becomes mechanically reproducible in Walter Benjamin's sense and print-capitalism begins to create markets, the fundamentally anonymous community of the nation-state becomes imaginable. Anderson hypothesizes that novels and newspapers "provided the technical means for 're-presenting' the *kind* of imagined community that is the nation" because they exploited and reinforced a perception of time as "homogenous, empty time"—a temporal field "in which simultaneity is, as it were, transverse, cross-time, marked not by prefiguration and fulfilment, but by temporal coincidence, and measured by clock and calendar" (*IC*, 24). Homogenous, empty time opens the possibility of the anonymous community ("An American will never meet, or even know the names of more than a handful of his 240,000,000-odd fellow Americans. . . . But he has complete confidence in their steady, anonymous, simultaneous activity" [26]). Far more than the novel, the newspaper is Anderson's exemplary cultural form ("What more vivid figure for the secular, historically-clocked, imagined community can be envisioned?" [35]).[13] A commodity that expires within twenty-four hours or less, the newspaper summons its reader to a "mass ceremony" predicated on the simultaneous participation of uncountable other readers, elsewhere. Furthermore, "the newspaper reader, observing exact replicas of his own paper being consumed by his subway, barbershop, or residential neighbors, is continually reassured that the imagined world is visibly rooted in everyday life." Thus, "fiction seeps quietly and continuously into reality, creating that remarkable confidence of community in anonymity which is the hallmark of modern nations" (36).

Anderson's argument retains a cagily respectful relation to Marxist etiological narrative. Claiming that the book is "the first modern-style mass-produced, industrial commodity," he suggests that print-capitalism laid "the bases for national consciousness" in three ways: it produced "unified fields of exchange and communication below Latin and above the spoken vernaculars"; it gave "a new fixity to language, which in the long run helped to build that image of antiquity so central to the subjective idea of the nation"; and it created new "languages of power" as certain dialects, closer to the print-language, gained prestige and ground over others (*IC*, 34). Anderson goes so far as to credit print-capitalism with fundamentally contributing to the emergence of the bourgeoisie as a self-conscious class:

> Here was a class which, figuratively speaking, came into being as a class only in so many replications. Factory-owner in Lille was connected to factory-owner in Lyon only by reverberation. They had no necessary reason to know of one another's existence; they did not typically marry each other's daughters or inherit each other's property. But they did come to visualize in a general way the existence of thousands and thousands like themselves through print-language. For an illiterate bourgeoisie is scarcely imaginable. Thus in world-historical terms bourgeoisies were the first classes to achieve solidarities on an essentially imagined basis. (*IC*, 77)

The material production of class consciousness and national consciousness here remains inseparable from capitalism as a mode of production, but it is equally inseparable from the shock of print technology. Anderson does not write about shock, preferring to allow Benjamin's phrase "homogenous, empty time" to float free of complication; but in his own British commonsensical way, he subtly defamiliarizes and repositions the question of technology. Without ever becoming personified as an independently determining force, technics nonetheless ceases to be conceivable simply as congealed labor—that is, as an externalization of an originating, self-producing human identity—and becomes a version of the question of "language," a question that then in its turn undergoes complications. The nation's material base is language; and language, for Anderson, means neither this or that so-called natural language (the modern ones, in any case, are products of print-capitalism's intervention into a heterogenous field of vernaculars) nor a formal interplay of *langue* and *parole*. Rather (though Anderson certainly never puts it this way), language appears here as what Jacques Derrida calls a tele-technics, bound up with and in excess of the materiality and historicity of its occurrence.[14] "Print-language," Anderson emphasizes, "is what invents nationalism, not *a* particular language per se" (*IC*, 134). Indeed, he notes, twentieth-century communicational technologies "made it possible and practical to 'represent' the imagined community in ways that did not require linguistic uniformity" (139). If nationalism is inherently an affair of language, language is a question of technics, and technics a matter of inscription, communication, dissemination, reserve.[15]

It is at this point, however, that we may begin to remark Anderson's resistance to his own insight, and as a first step toward getting myself back to the topic of the imagination, let me return to Anderson's homogenizing presentation of "homogenous, empty time." If *Imagined Communities* makes legible a tele-technics of language, it nonetheless labors to efface its own accomplishment by characterizing the homogeneity and emptiness of the time of capitalism, modern technology, and modernity as *fundamentally* homogenous. Hence, perhaps, Anderson's elision of Benjamin's account of the shock experience, the shattering of the aura, and all the other dislocations proper to "the age of mechanical reproduction." For surely "homogenous, empty time" is always also fracture and rupture. It is capitalism's inhuman accumulative rhythms; modernity's unnerving acceleration; "the virtualization of space and time, the possibility of virtual events whose movement and speed prohibit us more than ever . . . from opposing presence to its representation, 'real time' to 'deferred time,' effectivity to its simulacrum, the living to the non-living, in short, the living to the living-dead of its ghosts" (Derrida, 169). We may briefly recall that Benjamin defined the shock experience by drawing on Freud's counterintuitive proposal that one of consciousness' functions is to ward off stimuli and that, consequently, becoming-conscious works against the formation of a memory trace: "The greater the share of the shock factor in particular impressions, the more consciousness has to be on alert as a screen against stimuli; the more efficiently it does so, the less do these impressions enter experience [*Erfahrung*], tending to remain in the sphere of a certain hour of one's life [*Erlebnis*]."[16] Anderson, in his essay "Memory and Forgetting," which he appended to the revised edition of *Imagined Communities*, touches on this

Benjaminian theme, but he leaves unstated the ways in which it might complicate time's homogeneity:

> How strange it is to need another's help to learn that this naked baby in the yellowed photograph, sprawled happily on rug or cot, is you. The photograph, fine child of the age of mechanical reproduction, is only the most peremptory of a huge modern accumulation of documentary evidence (birth certificates, diaries, report cards, letters, medical records, and the like) which simultaneously records a certain apparent continuity and emphasizes its loss from memory. Out of this estrangement comes a conception of personhood, identity (yes, you and that naked baby are identical) which, because it cannot be "remembered," must be narrated. . . . These narratives, like . . . novels and newspapers . . . are set in homogenous, empty time. (*IC*, 204)

Yet what bears emphasis is that the amnesia conditioning these narratives, these everyday identity effects, is structurally irreducible to the subject's biological or psychological existence. Even the photograph taken yesterday, at my behest, captures me in a way irreducible to perception or recollection. It can circulate beyond my knowledge or life span, and it can be altered, spliced, remade; as in Ridley Scott's film *Blade Runner*, it and the identity narrative it generates can always possibly be fakes, because technical reproduction captures its referent thanks to procedures that are inherently and essentially iterable, alien to the identity they construct and document. An irreducible anonymity laces our technonarratives of self-formation, and the impact of this anonymity is precisely what Benjamin calls shock. The homogenous empty time in which these narratives unfold corrodes the identities it enables. Benjamin consistently emphasizes that the disruption of *Erfahrung* goes hand in hand with the "homogenizing" force of capitalist and mechanical reproduction: the shock experience of the crowd, the photograph, the film, and so on "corresponds to what the worker 'experiences' at his machine"—the numbing drill of a reiterated present tense, "sealed off from experience" (176). Homogenous, empty time's field of the "meanwhile" generates not just the imagined certainties of Balzacian or scientific or nationalist narrative, but also Emma Bovary's shattering boredom—her inability to live in time.[17] It is possible that the time of modernity necessitates "imaginative" operations such as, for instance, the production of the sort of container-like trope that undergirds Anderson's account of homogenous temporality. Yet Anderson's own narrative of nationalism's origins deconstructs that trope, suggesting the inextricability of homogenous, empty time from the operations of print-capitalism, which is to say from the mechanical exploitation of the iterability of the sign. The newspaper can always in principle be read *elsewhere*: the community of its readers is irretrievably exposed to an alterity that is never unreservedly "outside" the community, but labors at its heart, constituting its intimacy. This predicament names the condition of possibility of any linguistic event, as Jacques Derrida has shown; Derrida's most famous name for this fundamental tele-technics of the sign is, of course, "writing." The homogenous time of modernity emerges out of print-capitalism's exploitation of writing as *différance*.[18]

Anderson's narrative about nationalism thus encourages us to understand the experience of the nation as grounded in and produced by a systematic misrecognition of its origins. The nation is a hallucinated limit to iterability. Made possible by difference, deferral, and technological shock, the nation homogenizes time and space, draws and polices borders, historicizes itself as the continuous arc of an unfolding identity. (Furthermore, since every border presupposes an outside, outside the nation lies more space, occupied by other nations and by atavistic entities that ought to become nations. The globe—as in "globalization"—figures the totality of nation-space as imagined community.) Originating in an anonymity "prior" to any identity—an anonymity constitutive of the possibility of imagining an identity—the nation imagines anonymity *as* identity, as an essentialized formal abstraction. The nature of this imaginative act becomes correspondingly complex. It is frequently characterized in nationalist discourse as an act of will—of a will capable of willing itself, as national will, into existence.[19] Anderson's phrase "imagined community" draws on this tradition. He intends it to capture the romantic theme of the "creative" imagination (*IC*, 6), and this notion of the imagination goes along with his running emphasis on the positive aspects of nationalism—so long as nationalism is understood as an authentic impulse toward continuity and meaning, rather than as the instrumentalism and bad faith of "all those nationalisms which, by the late twentieth century, have got married to states" (*S*, 47). Yet if the nation as "imagined community" is always fundamentally irreducible to the state, the difference between spontaneous and "official" nationalism nonetheless becomes, under the impact of Anderson's narrative of nationalism's origins, as unstable as it is necessary. Enabled, even in its most affirmative manifestations, by the dislocations of technical reproduction, the "imagination" ceases to be a psychological faculty and becomes an aesthetic, unstable figure that tropes anonymity as identity and difference as homogeneity. The signs of nationhood—the flags and emblems that, according to Hegel, in their sheer arbitrariness demonstrate the mind's creative power—serve the cause of misrecognition insofar as they transform a semiotic function (linguistic arbitrariness) into an *image*—an image of the nation as will, or, better, of the nation as imagi-nation. The arbitrariness of the sign and the radical anonymity that marks the possibility of the sign's apprehension are thus figured as a sensuous experience and become a sublime intuition of the nation as *this* flag, anthem, building, cultural monument. Sensuous tokens of lack, mechanically produced substitutes for what Benjamin calls *Erfahrung*, these signs are in a quite precise sense the fetishes of an imagined nation.

They are aesthetic fetishes not just because they transform the super-sensuous into the perceivable, but because they interpellate the national subject as the subject of a national culture. In his most extended discussion of how nations "transform fatality into continuity" and "turn chance into destiny" (*IC*, 11, 12), Anderson—facing the challenge of explaining why people should be willing to die for the sake of a community composed of mutually anonymous readers of the same newspaper—inevitably slips into an aesthetic terminology:

In everything "natural" there is always something unchosen. In this way, nation-ness is assimilated to skin-colour, gender, parentage, and birth-era—all those things one cannot help. And in these "natural ties" one senses what one might call "the beauty of gemeinschaft." To put it another way, precisely because such ties are not chosen, they have about them a halo of disinterestedness. (*IC*, 143)

I would suggest that "disinterestedness" bears its full Arnoldian burden in that last sentence, and I would also stress that here, as in his account of nationalism's origins, Anderson willy-nilly blurs the difference between popular, affective nationalism, on the one hand, and the "official" nationalism that can be associated with a state's educational apparatus, on the other. For as his subsequent discussion shows, the natural is naturalized by way of a culture that manifests itself as canonical texts, symbols, and touchstones—a culture that is in fact, once again, "language," language as a naturalized technics, humanized and homogenized as voice:

No one can give the date of birth of any language. Each looms up impeceptibly out of a horizonless past. (Insofar as *homo sapiens* is *homo dicens*, it can seem diffi-cult to imagine an origin of language newer than the species itself.) Languages thus appear rooted beyond almost anything else in contemporary societies. At the same time, nothing connects us affectively to the dead more than language. If English-speakers hear the words "Earth to earth, ashes to ashes, dust to dust"—created almost four and a half centuries ago—they get a ghostly intimation of si-multaneity across homogenous, empty time. (*IC*, 144–45)

The words of the Anglican burial service occasion here the diachronic equivalent of the "unisonance" that, according to Anderson, singers of na-tional anthems experience as they imagine a nation of anonymous others singing along. Unisonance (or "imagined sound") is nothing less than "the echoed physical realization of the imagined community. . . . How selfless this unisonance feels!" (*IC*, 145). Anderson rightly describes these English-language speakers as "hearing" (rather than, say, "reading") the burial ser-vice. Like the anthem singers, they are hearing imagined voices. In this hal-lucinated moment of unisonance, they identify with the totality of a nation and, at the globe's horizon, with the universality of *homo dicens*. These in-stances of logocentric interpellation constitute the national subject's prop-erly *aesthetic* education. Culture, that is, names the subject's identification with anonymity as "disinterestedness"—with anonymity as the formal, ab-stract identity of the nation and the human, as mediated by the national state. Anderson's account of the "eerie splendor" that characterizes these moments—as anonymity is aestheticized as voice and image—appropri-ately strings together scraps of canonical and subcanonical national culture, which is to say, school texts: lines from the *Book of Common Prayer*, a sen-tence of Thomas Browne's, Charles Wolfe's patriotic elegy entitled "The Burial of Sir John Moore" (*IC*, 145–47).

Without exception, all of these exemplary scraps are about death, and in one case, about death in war. No doubt it is hardly occasion for sur-prise that imagined communities—many sorts, if not all sorts, of imagined communities for that matter, not just the nation per se—should foster their sense of themselves by invoking death's universality and by represent-ing death as enemy action. But in what is perhaps his text's most resonant paragraph, Anderson suggests that imagining the nation entails a scene of mourning unlike those of earlier societies:

No more arresting emblems of the modern culture of nationalism exist than cenotaphs and tombs of Unknown Soldiers. The public ceremonial reverence accorded these monuments precisely *because* they are either deliberately empty or no one knows who lies inside them, has no true precedents in earlier times. To feel the force of this modernity one has only to imagine the general reaction to the busybody who "discovered" the Unknown Soldier's name or insisted on filling the cenotaph with some real bones. Sacrilege of a strange, contemporary kind! Yet void as these tombs are of identifiable mortal remains or immortal souls, they are nonetheless saturated with ghostly *national* imaginings. (*IC*, 9)

The funereal and thanophilic character of much official Western national culture has often been noted, but Anderson's brilliant commentary on the cenotaph reveals nationalism's peculiarly absolute *abstraction* of death. The abstraction is, or pretends to be, "at the origin": no corpse ever was or ever could be buried under this gravestone. Indeed, as Anderson suggests, burying a corpse under the monument would pollute it as perhaps no other act of sacrilege would. The corpse, then, may be read as the remainder, the excess that nationalism's official scene of mourning excludes. The corpse marks death's resistance to its own universality, recalling the inassimilable particularity and finitude of *this* death, the absoluteness of an irrecuperable loss. In the terminology we have been working with, the corpse marks the resistance of anonymity to abstraction or formalization. From a national perspective, it is the *unimaginable*. Yet without it—without, that is, the possibility of the radically other death that it represents—the Tomb could not exist. And if we understand the irrecuperability of loss as a restatement of the essential drift of "writing" in a Derridean sense, we may say that the nation itself as imagined community comes into existence thanks to a death it cannot mourn, a corpse it cannot bury—a corpse that must be foreclosed, expelled from the nation's abstracted, aestheticized anonymity.

But if we interpret the Tomb of the Unknown Soldier's exclusion of the *identifiable* corpse as a symptom of the fundamental instability of an identity predicated on anonymity, we also need to underscore the ideological power of such monuments.[20] The Tomb's scene of interpellation can have very powerful effects, for it permits the mourning subject to transform a particular loss—real or imagined—into the general loss suffered by the nation. Because the absolute singularity and irreparability of loss is thereby foreclosed, a sheen of hypocrisy inevitably clings to official acts of mourning, however passionately felt or well intended. Yet this halo of bad faith, which registers the ontological instability of official nationalism, does not necessarily impede the production of nationalistic pathos. It is no coincidence, I think, that the most memorable paragraph in *Imagined Communities* should invoke the Tomb of the Unknown Soldier—an invention of "official nationalism" if there ever was one, and the exemplary emblem of the aesthetic culture of nationalism, insofar as it stages the subject's identification with the nation as formalized anonymity. Official nationalism constantly infiltrates Anderson's account of the "imagined community" because the state's aesthetic–pedagogic project, or work or mourning, exploits the same processes of technical reproduction that makes the imagining of the nation possible in the first place.

In closing, we may remark one final complication: the Unknown Soldier's tomb commemorates a death that is not, after all, entirely abstract. The death it remembers, mourns, and celebrates is a male death, suffered in war—war with some other, anonymous, abstract nation. From the perspective of nationalism per se, only male citizens can die, and they can only die in war. All other kinds of loss or damage are to be sublated into this death, to the extent that national identity succeeds in trumping all other forms of identity.[21] The mourners are thus in principle both male and female, for they are the entire people of the nation; but the feminine position in this scene is immutable, for all a woman will ever be able to do is mourn. She mourns, furthermore, above all as a mother, as Anderson hints at the end of his penultimate chapter as he rapidly and tacitly sets another scene of mourning:

It may indeed appear paradoxical that the objects of all these attachments are "imagined". . . . But *amor patriae* does not differ in this respect from the other affections, in which there is always an element of fond imagining. (This is why looking at the photo-albums of strangers' weddings is like studying the archaeologist's ground plan of the Hanging Gardens of Babylon.) What the eye is to the lover—that particular, ordinary eye he or she is born with—language—whatever language history has made his or her mother-tongue—is to the patriot. Through that language, encountered at mother's knee and parted with only at the grave, pasts are restored, fellowships are imagined, and futures dreamed. (*IC*, 154)

Throughout his discussion of the role of aesthetic culture in national consciousness, Anderson tends to drift somewhat leeward of his historicist argument. In the passage I quoted earlier, for instance, he writes of nationalism's seeming "disinterestedness" without noting that, historically speaking, aesthetic disinterestedness is a rather recent notion—a notion more or less coeval with that of the nation-state, uncoincidentally. And his supple blend of distance from and sympathy with aesthetic nationalism yields to a more pressing rhetoric of pathos as he discovers similarities between nationalism and familial sentiment, identifies *amor patriae* with a heterosexual passion that leads straight to a wedding (albeit that of strangers), and finally inscribes it within a domestic scene, figuring language as a "mother-tongue" that accompanies the male nationalist in his itinerary from "mother's knee" to "the grave." We know, of course, that this grave cannot be that of the Unknown Soldier, for no mother's son can be buried there. But the mother can mourn there; mourning is her destiny, as Anderson's sentence suggests (the patriot was first at her knee, then in the grave), and this because continuity is her function.[22] Sheltered within her domestic space, anonymity becomes familiarity. She provides a "natural" origin not just for the male patriot, but for language itself, and thus for the (imagi)nation itself.[23] Summarizing a good deal of feminist work on nationalism, the editors of the collection *Between Woman and Nation* comment that "the 'essential woman' (raced or not) becomes the national iconic signifier for the material, the passive, and the corporeal, to be worshipped, protected, and controlled by those with the power to remember and to forget, to guard, to define, and redefine." It is part of the achievement of *Imagined Communities* to have shown how poorly grounded, yet also how insistent, that patriarchal fantasy is.[24]

II

In the foregoing pages, I have argued two principal points: that the imagination of the nation responds to and to some extent cushions or wards off the shock of modernity, and that in doing so, it constructs an imagined community at once irreducible to the state and fundamentally tangled up with the state's aesthetic–cultural project. These two points are interrelated. Because processes of mechanical replication constitute the material condition of possibility of imagining the nation, this imagination's spontaneous force is haunted by a technically enhanced iterability that also serves—and exceeds, and at times destabilizes—state power.

The imaginative transformation of this iterability into sensuous tokens of abstract anonymity and unisonance generates a sense of the collective that no state can embody or entirely control, yet that also animates the movement of aesthetic education. The "crisis of the hyphen," Anderson's witty phrase for the morphings of the late twentieth-century nation-state, originates in tensions that the nation-state has to some degree always known.[25] I should perhaps reemphasize that I am not proposing that we ignore the difference between nation and state or between popular and official nationalisms; a great deal, both hermeneutically and politically, frequently hangs on that difference. But it will never be an absolute or stable difference. Anderson hesitates between a keen awareness of this dilemma and a reluctance to confront it: he writes powerfully of the role of the "replica" in official nationalism, a replica for which *"there is no original"* (S, 48, Anderson's italics), but he overforcefully associates such originary replication with an "imaginative impasse" and a lack of what Walter Benjamin called aura, the better to contrast official nationalism with more genuine expressions of national feeling (S, 47, 49). We would rather insist, with Samuel Weber, that *"aura thrives in its decline,* and that the reproductive media are particularly conducive to this thriving."[26] The national flag, as Anderson says, is the ultimate model of a replica without original (S, 48 n. 6); it is always ready to become sheer kitsch, yet it cannot be entirely dissociated from the stranger movement of what Weber calls "mediauratic" happenings: "auratic flashes and shadows that are not just produced and reproduced by the media but which *are* themselves the media, since they come to pass in places that are literally inter-mediary, in the interstices of a process of reproduction and recording . . . that is above all a mass movement of collection and dispersion, of banding together and disbanding" (106).[27] The (national) imagination caught up in that mediation is perhaps best thought of neither as a simple victim of state manipulation nor as Hegel's pure act of mind, but rather as a figure for the ambivalence at the heart of nationalism's relation to the state and to modernity. Imagining difference as unisonance, the imagination presents itself both as a spontaneous force and as a faculty to be tended, disciplined, and trained—in other words, as a faculty dependent for its realization on those exemplary imaginative acts that, since the romantic era, we have called aesthetic culture.

It will be interesting at this point to return to a text written quite early in the history of nationalist discourse and test the reach of some of these generalizations within an aesthetic–nationalist tradition. Johann Gottlieb Fichte gave his *Addresses to the German Nation* at the Academy of Sciences in Berlin during the winter of 1807–8, in the wake of Napoleon's crushing defeat of Prussia. Throughout that winter, French troops continued to patrol Berlin; the era of the Holy Roman Empire was over, and Prussia's future in the new world order was by no means assured. Modernity had arrived with a shock. Fichte, opening his lectures, speaks of the giant steps, the *Riesenschritte*, with which time had begun to move.²⁸ In this exigency, addressing himself to a "German nation" that did not yet exist, vacillating between prudence and pugnacity as he walked a fine line between sedition and patriotism, fighting the censor (the Prussian authorities, not the French, who seem to have ignored him entirely) for the right to publish each lecture in the series, Fichte provided a text that eventually became a classic within the German tradition, one that in its own time knew a degree of influence: old-fashioned histories of Germany often characterize the *Addresses* as the first significant and fully developed expression of German nationalism and as an event that helped prepare, in some small and hard-to-define fashion, for the so-called war of national liberation in 1813–15 and the development of more properly nationalist movements in subsequent decades.²⁹ What "influence" means, however, is complicated by the fact that Fichte's text was misread, or read selectively, from the start. Even today, his text is still often assimilated to "romantic" celebrations of *Volk*, *Vaterland*, and the German language, themes that unquestionably loom large in the *Addresses* but that undergo fundamental reorientation under the pressure of Fichte's theories of imagination and will.³⁰ A close reading of the *Addresses* uncovers a complex, conflicted text, one that, for present purposes, I shall represent as forcefully replaying some of the tensions we have remarked in Anderson's *Imagined Communities*. Basking in "the devouring flame of a higher patriotism [*Vaterlandsliebe*]" that transcends loyalty to the state (135/141), Fichte's text nonetheless takes as its main theme the necessity of a state-run educational program, a proposal that I shall suggest we understand as the Fichtean version of aesthetic pedagogy.

One can hardly blame Fichte's readers for having tended to privilege his ethnolinguistic theme. Language, in the *Addresses*, plays so leading a role that its story is that of modernity itself. According to Fichte, language, in its essence, is "in no way dependent on arbitrary decisions and agreements" but is rather governed by "a fundamental law, in accordance with which every idea becomes in the human organs of speech one particular sound and no other" (61/56). All languages are thus originally one language, though Fichte's version of this Adamic fantasy understands the original unity as a transcendental model that may never have existed in reality. From the beginning, different environments and experiences would have influenced the original language, deflecting it into particular phonetic and semantic channels.[31] Nevertheless, such deviations from "the one pure human language" are to be understood as governed by "strict law" (62/56). As languages change over time, they remain organically continuous and in conformity with their particular and proper deviation, so long as the people (*Volk*) continues to speak the language. Even though "after some centuries have passed the descendants do not understand the language of their ancestors," their language remains fundamentally the same language, because at any one time its speakers never cease understanding each other, and "their eternal go-between and interpreter always was, and continues to be, the common power of nature speaking through all" (63/57).

In the modern world, however, only the Germans can claim to be in touch with this natural power. Fichte's argument here relies on an implicit limitation of the modern world to Northern Europe and on an explicit affirmation of the common origin of all northern European peoples: "The German [*der Deutsche*] is in the first instance a branch of the Teutons [*ein Stamm der Germanier*]. Of the Teutons it suffices here to define them as those who were to unite the social order of ancient Europe with the true religion of ancient Asia, and thereby develop in and out of themselves a new age, opposed to the fallen ancient world" (58/52). Yet in the struggle to produce this new age, certain Teutons fell away from the source. In conquering Rome, they gained the ancient world and lost their Teutonic soul precisely to the extent that they lost their language. Because all abstractions, concepts, or ideas, according to Fichte, are produced as figurative displacements of sensuous perceptions, the meanings of a culture's language are all ultimately rooted in concrete experience. So long as a people retains its original language, it remains connected to "the root where concepts [*Begriffe*] stream forth from spiritual nature herself" (86/86). When a people forgets its language and adopts a foreign one, it inherits meanings irreducibly foreign to its experience. The aesthetic link between perception and cognition breaks, and with it the natural continuity of a language and thus of a people. Despite their appearance of being alive, Romance languages and cultures (including post–Norman Invasion English, presumably, though Fichte, obsessed with France, rather surprisingly says nothing at all about Britain) bear within them "a dead element deeper down" (68/64). Indeed, Romance cultures "are entirely without a mother tongue [*Muttersprache*]" (71/67).

It follows that the Germans are the only people who are genuinely a *people*: they are "quite simply *the* people [*das Volk schlechtweg*]" (106/108), having remained "in the stream of original culture [*ursprünglicher Bildung*]" (87/87). The task of modernity itself—the destiny proper to the Teutons—belongs to them. Defeated in war, the Germans now have the chance to rise above selfishness, assume the mantle of nationality, and achieve a genuine, spiritual, rather than martial, conquest of history. Fichte points out that it is in the world's interest that Germany should fulfill its destiny. For, in that happy event, even the Franks' self-loss in their encounter with Rome becomes a fortunate fall: the Romance cultures will then have achieved their proper historical role of serving as mediators or buffers between Germany and antiquity. The Franks, overwhelmed by Roman culture, allow the Germans, secure in their Teutonic modernity, to absorb antiquity "after their own nature . . . as an element in their own life" (88/88). "In this way, both parts of the common nation [*gemeinsamen Nation*; that is, the original Teutons] remained one, and only in this simultaneous separation and unity do they form a graft on the stem of the culture of antiquity, which otherwise would have been broken off by the new age, and so humanity would have begun again from the beginning" (88/88). With Germany's emergence as a nation, history itself will be healed. On the other hand, if Germany is destroyed, Europe will fall into "spiritual death" (89/89), its last living cultural–historical–linguistic root having been severed. And Europe's fate is the world's fate: "If you perish in this your essential nature," Fichte tells his audience (that is, the "German nation") at the end of the *Addresses*, "then there perishes with you every hope of the whole human race for salvation from the depths of its miseries. . . . If you go under, all humanity goes under with you, without hope of future restoration" (246/269).

Such, in its main lines, is Fichte's version of a narrative one encounters periodically throughout nineteenth- and early twentieth-century German letters: a story often and famously cast as one of Germany's affinity with Greece, which is to say with a pre-Roman antiquity that promises to underwrite Europe's true renaissance as a postcapitalist, postimperialist— post-Spanish, -British, or -Napoleonic—modernity. Fichte's version of this story appears simple only as long as we fail to ask after the central matter at hand—the text's definition of Germanness. Etienne Balibar rightly emphasizes that Fichte rejects protoracist possibilities: "even as Fichte places himself in opposition to Kant by granting an ethical importance to language and linguistic unity, he follows him in completely dissociating the notions of stock and people, and opposes the idea that there would be a historical link between linguistic continuity and biological continuity" ("Fichte," 76–77). What makes a *Volk* a *Volk* is not blood descent but linguistic continuity.[32] Nor, in principle, is Fichte interested in the objective characteristics of this or that language. German has nothing special about it grammatically, semantically, or phonetically; all that matters is that it has been continuously spoken (61/55). As Balibar says, language, for Fichte, is an ethical attitude, "a way of 'living' a language" ("Fichte," 78). And while that claim needs nuancing—Fichte's notorious (indeed, at times inadvertently comical) concern for linguistic purity suggests the difficulty of maintaining a steady distinction between "objective" and "subjective" aspects of language, or between speech acts and linguistic structures[33]—it pays to attend to the Fichtean homology between language and ethical action, for at one point in the *Addresses*, this homology stiffens to the point of damaging the linguistic theme. In the seventh Address, we encounter the unambiguous claim that "whoever believes in spirituality and in the freedom of this spirituality, and who wills the eternal development of this spirituality by freedom, *wherever he may have been born and whatever language he speaks*, is of our people [*unsers Geschlechts*]; he is one of us, and will come over to our side." Whoever believes the opposite, "*wherever he may have been born and whatever language he speaks*, is non-German [*undeutsch*] and a stranger to us; and it is to be wished that he would separate himself from us completely, and the sooner the better" (122/127, my italics).

For though at various points in Fichte's *Addresses* the continuous and living German language seems the precondition of such belief in spirituality and freedom, Fichte's definition of Germanness has so much to do with belief that he is able, at least on occasion, to abandon the linguistic theme as a merely external, disposable *sign* of belief. If one were to try to sum up his definition of Germanness, one would have to venture something like the following: Germanness is an imaginative act that imagines itself as the (national) repetition of itself. The question of *address* is fundamental: as Fichte emphasizes, he speaks to a German nation that in certain crucial respects does not yet exist and must be posited:

> I speak for Germans simply [*schlechtweg*], of Germans simply, not recognizing, but setting aside completely and rejecting, all the dissociating distinctions which for centuries unhappy events have caused in this nation. . . . In the spirit of which these addresses are the expression, I perceive that organic unity [*durcheinander verwachsene Einheit*] in which no member [*Glied*] regards the fate of another as the fate of a stranger, and which must and shall arise, if we are not to perish altogether—I see this unity already achieved, completed, and existing. (14/4)

Fichte further defines his audience under two more headings: first, he assumes (*voraussetzt*) "such German listeners as have not given themselves over in their entire being to a feeling of pain at the loss they have suffered, who take comfort in this pain, luxuriate in their disconsolate grief . . . but rather such as have already risen, or are at least capable of rising, above this justifiable pain to clear thought and meditation" (14/4–5). Second, he assumes "such hearers as are disposed to see things through their own eyes" rather than through "a strange and foreign eyeglass" (15/6). Listeners not meeting these criteria are repeatedly invited to leave. In the seventh Address, as we saw, Fichte declares the pessimist "non-German and a stranger to us"; in the twelfth Address, he proposes as "the certain characteristic [*festen Grundzug*] of the German" the desire to "form an opinion for himself about that which concerns Germans," whereas "a man who does not want to hear or to think about this subject may rightly be regarded, from now on, as not belonging to us" (197/212). The German is he who can posit Germany. If he cannot—being overly mournful, or being equipped with a "foreign eyeglass," or pessimistic, or insouciant—he is not *deutsch*, not genuinely of the *Volk*, though he be a Teuton and a native speaker. To be German is to repeat Fichte's own imaginative act in listening to or reading Fichte. To listen—to really hear—Fichte is to imagine Germany and thereby to begin to enact or realize Germany. The Lutheran note is explicit: "He who has ears, let him hear" (122/127).[34] The language to be heard is that of intuitive experience: "Whoever feels this within him will be convinced; whoever does not feel it cannot be convinced, since my proof rests entirely on that supposition [*Voraussetzung*]: on him my words are lost; but who would not risk [*auf das Spiel setzen*] something so trivial as words?"

(146–47/156). Words can be squandered; they are spirit's inessential, if necessary, supplement. What matters is the act of speaking and listening, a communicational circuit that is in itself the imagining of Germany.

The imagined community thus entails an act of positing that at first glance might look like a tautology. If you are truly hearing Fichte, you are German by definition; it might seem, therefore, that you didn't need to hear him in the first place—except that it is precisely in the hearing that Germanness constitutes itself as its own future possibility. When Fichte posits as his addressee the German nation ("I see this unity already achieved, completed, and existing") he speaks with the voice of imagination. Imagination (*Einbildungskraft*) is "the power spontaneously to create images [*Bilder*] that are independent of reality and in no way imitations of it [*Nachbilder*], but are rather prefigurations of it [*Vorbilder*]" (31/23). The *Addresses* are proleptic: they address the future; they aim their spirit-charged words at an ear to come. In the aiming or speaking or imagining, the addressee comes into being *as* a future. As is always the case in Fichte, a nontemporal act of positing opens up temporality—here, the time of nation building—thanks to the power of imagination.[35] When Fichte writes that "We must become on the spot [*zur Stelle*] what we should be in any case: Germans" (193/207), he compacts into an instant the temporality of *Bildung*: we who hear Fichte are being educated, albeit in the momentary flame of an inspiration. And the work before us is pedagogical: "most citizens [*Bürger*] must be educated to a sense of fatherland" (145/154). The imagination both enables *Bildung* and constitutes *Bildung*'s object. For in order to imagine the nation, the imagination must be trained:

The external eye, when accustomed to cleanliness and order, is troubled and distressed, as though actually hurt, by a stain [*einen Flecken*] which indeed causes the body no actual injury, or by the sight of objects lying in chaotic confusion; while the eye accustomed to dirt and disorder is quite comfortable under such circumstances. So too the inner spiritual eye of man can be so accustomed and trained [*gebildet*] that the mere sight of a muddled and disorderly, unworthy and dishonorable existence of its own or a kindred people [*verbrüderten Stammes*] causes it internal pain, apart from anything there may be to fear or to hope from this for its own material welfare. This pain, apart again from any material fear or hope, permits the possessor of such an eye no rest until he has removed, in so far as he can, this condition which displeases him, and has set in its place that which alone can please him. For the possessor of such an eye, because of this stimulating feeling of approval or disapproval, the welfare of his whole environment is bound up inextricably with the welfare of his own self, which is conscious of itself only as part of the whole and can endure itself only when the whole is pleasing. To educate itself to possess such an eye [*Die Sichbildung zu einem solchen Auge*] will therefore be a sure means, and indeed the only means left to a nation which has lost its independence, and with it all influence over public fear and hope, of rising again into life from the destruction it has suffered. (20–21/12)

The subject of this education is being trained to feel pain, and to feel it as an aesthetic experience that is equally an ethical imperative. The unaesthetic nation can be perceived—as pain—in and through the imagining of the nation that one then inevitably works to realize precisely as the national imagining of the nation. For if the nation can be brought to imagine itself, this imagining will itself be the nation's *Sichbildung.* No longer the proleptic vision of an educated, privileged, Fichtean few, the nation will be realized.

The task ahead thus consists "in the fashioning of an entirely new, universal and national self—one that may have existed before in individuals as an exception, but never as a national self—and in the education of the nation [*in der Bildung zu einem durchaus neuen, und bisher vielleicht als Ausnahme bei einzelnen, niemals als allgemeines und nationales Selbst, dagewesenen Selbst, und in der Erziehung der Nation*]" (21/13). The heart and soul of Fichte's *Addresses* is his educational plan. Designed to result in the production of a nation, it is a vision of *mass* education. All classes and both sexes are to be educated together; "the subjects of instruction are the same for both sexes" (in this respect, Fichte's solitary concession to the sexism of his time takes the form of the pronouncement that "the general relation of the two sexes to each other, stout-hearted protection on the one side and loving help on the other, must appear in the educational institution and be fostered in the pupils" [169–70/180–81]). Nowhere is Fichte's Jacobin side so visible as in these sections of the *Addresses.* Not only is national education to be radically democratic in its generality, but it is to intervene in civil society with the full force of the state. Children, if at all possible, are to be taken from their families and educated in isolation from adult society in state-funded coeducational boarding schools. We may skip over here the details of Fichte's educational theories, many of which derive from Pestalozzi[36]; for our present purposes, the important point is that Fichte's plan aims at a *total* education, an utter making—or breaking and remaking—of human being: "den Menschen selbst zu bilden" (23/15). Children are to be extracted from the familial unit and educated apart because this new sort of *Bildung* is to reach the very roots (*Wurzeln*) of the subject; it will "completely destroy freedom of will in the soil it undertakes to cultivate" (28/20), so as to produce a new freedom, training the imagination, the foundation of this new *Bildung*, through procedures that stimulate the pupil's own self-determination (32/24). The educated imagination serves a pure moral will: the pupil freely creates, through the proleptic power of imagination, the image of a moral order; he (or, as we have seen, she) then cathects this image and seeks to realize it (39/32). This image is "Germany." The patriotism that results from such *Bildung* transcends the state, for this *Vaterlandsliebe* amounts to nothing less than the love of humanity and the desire for "the blossoming of the eternal and the divine in the world" (131/138). This desire for the eternal "unites first [the patriot's] own nation, and then, through his own nation, the whole human race" (129/136). And despite the small to nonexistent role Fichte gives to the "humanities" (indeed, even to reading and writing) in his educational system, we need to recognize his plan as a program of *aesthetic* education precisely insofar as it sets out to shape the creative faculty it presupposes.[37] For though Fichte's is not a program of acculturation in an Arnoldian sense, it is no less an aesthetic education turned "NATIONAL EDUCATION, the *nisus formativus* of the body politic," as Coleridge would put it twenty years later—"the shaping and informing spirit, which *educing*, i.e., eliciting, the latent *man* in all the natives of the soil, *trains them up* to citizens of the country, free subjects of the realm."[38] The subject is "trained up" to perceive the unperceivable Nation: a nation that is at once Germany and humanity itself. The state is thus in a sense being asked to submit to nationalism, to transcend itself by funding a pedagogical project that exceeds it. ("But that love of fatherland ought above all to inspire the German State, wherever Germans are governed, and take the lead, and be the motive power in all its decisions" [175/187].) Yet it would be more accurate, here and elsewhere in Fichte's text, to speak of an unsteady interplay between nation and state. The state's interests persist: "As to the State's doubt whether it can meet the costs of a national education, would that one could convince it that by this one expenditure it will provide for most of the others in the most economical way . . . !" Above all, the state would save on military expenses: it would have "an army such as no age has yet seen" in its fit, utterly selfless and self-sacrificing citizen–soldiers (178/190). Fichte's vision of the ethical, pacifist, cosmopolitan nation is always also a vision of total mobilization, and that ambiguity, I suggest, inheres in the very grain of aesthetic nationalism.

Yet for the present, all depends on an exemplary performance— Fichte's. "I was the first one to see it vividly; therefore it fell to me to take the first step. . . . There must always be one who is first; then let him be first who can!" (232/252). His exemplarity resides in his ability to speak with the voice, the living force, of the German language; his exemplarity also hangs, as we have seen, on a structure of address, an ability to image "the German nation" as a receptive ear. And we may return at this point to Benedict Anderson's great insight and ask after the technical precondition of such an address. For Fichte's task is to communicate his imaginative vision not just to a circle of auditors, but to a nation to be that can *only* be imagined:

You, worthy gathering, are indeed to my bodily eye the first and immediate representatives who make present to me the beloved national traits, and are the visible spark at which the flame of my address kindles itself. But my spirit gathers round it the educated part of the whole German nation, from all the lands over which it is spread; . . . it longs that part of the living force with which these lectures may grip you, may also remain in and breathe from the dumb printed page which alone will come to the eyes of the absent, and may in all places kindle German hearts to decision and deed. (13/3–4)

In his final lecture, Fichte returns to this theme: "I have had in view the whole German nation, and my intention has been to gather around me, in the room in which you are bodily present, everyone in the domain of the German language who is able to understand me." Once again he expresses the hope that he has thrown out sparks that will be gathered, "so that at this central point a single, continuous, and unceasing flame of patriotic disposition may be kindled, which will spread over the whole soil of the fatherland to its uttermost boundaries" (228/248). Fichte's reiterated figures of spark and flame, voice and breath, communicate his understanding of language as spiritual force. Yet in an Andersonian spirit, we may also remark how irreducible the supplemental role of "the dumb printed page" is in this scene of address. To address the nation is to assemble it "around a speaker by the means of a printed book [*durch den Bücherdruck um sich zu versammeln*]" (195/209).[39] The imagination of the nation presupposes print

FIGURE I. *Fichte's Address to the German Nation.* Wall painting, 1913/14, by Arthur Kampf. Used by permission of AKG London.

technology; and as both Anderson and Fichte suggest in their different ways, the imagined nation equally demands the subordination of technics to a trope of "unisonance." A text, in aesthetic–nationalist discourse, must function as technically extended voice. One could say, perhaps a little overimaginatively, that in imagining the aesthetic nation, Fichte necessarily imagines the possibility of radio—a haunted radio attuned, like all national transmitters, to the transmissions of the dead and the unborn: "Your forefathers unite themselves with these addresses, and make a solemn appeal to you"; "There comes a solemn appeal to you from your descendants not yet born"; "A solemn appeal comes to you even from foreign countries, insofar as they still understand themselves" (242–44/264–66).[40] It is the function of nationalist kitsch to imagine haunting as presence and to imagine broadcasting as voice, such that the nation can be imagined as rippling outward from the face-to-face intimacy and presence-to-self that the nation's imagining has in fact rendered impossible. Arthur Kampf's pictorial version of this fantasy, composed on the eve of World War I (Figure 1), may be read as having driven its truth literally underground: the Seuss-like carpeted tufts on which the orator stands and various listeners sit, together with the columnar trees, the exaggerated lighting, and the figures' theatrical gestures and costumes, suggest the superficiality—the desperate inauthenticity—of this bucolic national assembly. The painting's real, unacknowledged subject is the mechanical generation of nationalist fantasy *as* kitsch, which is to say as the aestheticization of an unassimilated modernity.[41]

To the extent that its unisonance depends on a misrecognition of its own predicament, aesthetic nationalism needs to be able to acknowledge and quarantine loss. Nationalisms typically cultivate sites and occasions of mourning; Fichtean nationalism—understandably, under the circumstances—begins in mourning. The fundamental task of Fichtean aesthetic education, as we saw, is to teach its national subjects how to mourn the figurative wound, the stain or *Fleck*, on the phantasmatic national body. But too much mourning would be crippling. Germans who have become possessed by mourning, who "take comfort in this pain, luxuriate in their disconsolate grief, and think thereby to compromise with the call that summons them to action," are not true Germans, and Fichte posits them out of existence (14/4). The difference between German and not-German might even be said to turn on the question of proper and excessive mourning. Yet in closing his first Address, Fichte stages a remarkable scene:

The age [*Die Zeit*] seems to me a shade [*ein Schatten*] that stands over his own corpse [*Leichname*], out of which he has been driven by a host of diseases, and weeps, and cannot tear his gaze from the form so beloved of old, and tries in despair every means to enter again the home of pestilence. Already, indeed, the quickening breezes of that other world, which the departed has entered, have taken her [that is, *die Zeit*] unto themselves and are surrounding her with the warm breath of love; the whispering voices of her sisters greet her with joy and bid her welcome; and already inside her there is stir and growth in all directions toward the more glorious form into which she will develop. But as yet she has no feeling for these breezes or ear for these voices—or if she had them, they have disappeared in the pain of her loss, with which she thinks she has lost herself as well. What is to be done with her? Already the dawn of the new world has broken and gilds the mountain-tops, and figures forth the coming day. I wish, so far as I can, to seize the rays of this dawn and weave them into a mirror, in which our grief-stricken age [*trostlose Zeit*] may see herself, so that she may believe she is still there, perceive her true identity, and see as in prophetic vision her own development and forms. In the contemplation of this, the picture of her former life will doubtless sink and vanish, and the dead body [*der Tote*] may be borne to its resting place without undue lamenting. (26/18)

I have forced the passage a bit by translating the pronouns literally. In the first sentence "the age" (a feminine noun in German, *die Zeit*) is a "shade" (a masculine noun, *Schatten*) who stands and weeps; but after the first sentence, Fichte reverts to the feminine pronoun—to, that is, the figure of "die Zeit" herself. The otherworldly "sisters" who greet this mourner lend additional momentum to her personification as feminine, as does the association of long standing between mothers and mourning that we noted earlier in connection with Benedict Anderson's text. Fichte imagines himself weaving the light of the future into a mirror: in this imaginary, specular, and solar moment, the Age will imagine herself back into existence ("believe she is still there"), forget her loss, moderate her grief, and allow her body to be buried. I say "her" body out of respect for the scene's personifying momentum, though the body she mourns is of course grammatically male (*der Leichnam*; *der Tote*).

It is possible, I think, to read this scene as an allegory that speaks to the ambivalence of national mourning. Just as the Tomb of the Unknown Soldier remains forever a tomb, marked by the death it abstracts and forecloses, so the Age, in Fichte's scenario, remains bending over her corpse, a Niobe petrified by grief, untouched by the orator's resurrectional rhetoric.

She is the modernity that is Germany, but Fichte's living words have not yet reached her, and, like figures on a Grecian urn, they never will. She is the Nation divided from itself, split into soul and body by the mark of difference and death; but the mark is singular and uncertain, the difference between life and death undecidable, and the work of mourning as irreducible as the gap between an allegorical sign and its meaning. The task of nationalism, particularly of what Anderson calls "official nationalism," is to monumentalize such scenes and fence them off. They record, and thus to some extent compensate for, the imagined community's dependence on the unimaginable.

2

"A Girl Named Wragg": The Body of Aesthetics and the Function of Criticism

> Look closely at the letters. Can you see,
> entering (stage right), then floating full,
> then heading off—so soon—
> how like a little kohl-rimmed moon
> *o* plots her course from *b* to *d*
>
> as y, unanswered, knocks at the stage door?
> Looked at too long, words fail,
> phase out. Ask, now that *body* shines
> no longer, by what light you learn these lines,
> and what the *b* and *d* stood for.
> —James Merrill, "b o d y"

Despite their constitutive anonymity, their reliance on communicational technologies, and their penchant for abstract symbols, modern nation-states are often represented figuratively as organic bodies. Rarely, however, in nationalist or protonationalist writing does one encounter the classical anthropomorphic trope of a body politic with head, arms, and legs. This articulated figure disappears in favor of a more abstract organicism under the terms of which, as one critic puts it, "no class of individuals need represent the foot."[1] A body without organs has clear rhetorical advantages in an era of mass politics and population management. Mary Poovey has recently contrasted seventeenth-century uses of the phrase *body politic* that excluded the poor altogether (or, rather, saw the poor as parasitic on, and dangerous to, the body politic), with the late eighteenth-century notion of the *great body of the people*:

As Adam Smith used this phrase in the *Wealth of Nations*, it referred not to the well-to-do but to the mass of laboring poor. By the early nineteenth century, both of these phrases were joined by the image of the social body, which was used in two quite different ways: it referred either to the poor in isolation from the rest of the population, or to British (or English) society as an organic whole. The ambiguity that this double usage produced . . . allowed social analysts to treat one segment of the population as a special problem at the same time that they could gesture toward the mutual interests that (theoretically) united all parts of the social whole. The phrase *social body* therefore promised full membership in a whole (and held out the image *of* that whole) to a part identified as needing both discipline and care.[2]

The trope of the social body organizes a rhetoric of health and hygiene that one encounters constantly in the discourses and practices that went into the making of the domain of the "social" during the nineteenth century. The groundwork of mass culture, Poovey suggests, is being laid through such developments: the disciplinary appurtenances of modernity emerge in and as the production of a social and epistemological field supportive of the atomizing and homogenizing work of the twentieth-century culture industry. The image of the social body in this sense ultimately prefigures the rule of the image per se in postmodern society, though more immediately it provides the organic analogue for the abstract, technically propagated unity of the nation-state as imagined community.[3]

Arguably the most important discourse contributing to the production of the social body's imagined unity during the century or so between Smith's *Wealth of Nations* (1776) and Matthew Arnold's *Culture and Anarchy* (1869) was the discourse of aesthetics. As we have seen in previous chapters, aesthetics, which developed as a distinct philosophical enterprise out of eighteenth-century moral philosophy in Britain and Wolffian rationalism in Germany as an attempt to characterize a mode of knowledge inherent in sensory perception, was never just one more philosophical category among others. Rather, it provided a vocabulary for the secular self-production of the subject, of the state, and thus finally of modernity itself. The harmony among mental faculties produced during an aesthetic judgment modeled the potential harmony of the social order because this act of judgment, in its disinterestedness, positioned the judging subject as representative of the fundamental unity of humanity itself. Aesthetics is thus always a historicism, where history is the temporality of an educative process that fuels itself on examples from the past in order to progress toward an ever-deferred ideal future. Such is the tacit logic girding Victorian middle-class discussions of the desirability of *acculturating* the working class. To acculturate does not mean to educate in the sense of imparting knowledge or skills; rather, it means to produce a subject capable of transcending class identity by identifying with what Arnold famously called "our best self," which is to say "the idea of the whole community, *the State.*"[4] Representing "the nation in its collective and corporate character" ("Democracy," 22–23), the state finally stands in for the corporate body of humanity itself, toward which culture beckons. Though Arnold's Germanic fondness for the idea of "the State," capitalized, was doubtless somewhat idiosyncratic, his understanding of the political stakes of acculturation was a Victorian commonplace.[5] Culture serves the state by forming subjects capable of disinterested reflection who can recapitulate the state's universality. Culture, that is, produces the consensual grounds for representative democracy. Hence the emphasis, in middle-class Victorian political writings, on education as a prerequisite for political enfranchisement. Few discourses have in the end shaped the social field more profoundly than has aesthetics. The development of "English" as a school subject forms only a small part of the story of the emergence of the various institutional and discursive apparatuses of "culture" that make up the fabric of modern life.

Because aesthetics always involves sensuous manifestation, which is to say figuration, it has always been a volatile discourse as well as a powerful one. At the very point where aesthetic ideology exerts maximum force—let us say in promising, and performing, the totality of a national body—the discourse's reliance on figuration becomes obvious, and potentially anxious. Gestures of denegation and abjection often follow. If Terry Eagleton is right to claim that aesthetics is "a discourse of the body," then we stand to learn something about the instability as well as the rhetorical power of the figure of the body if we examine closely a fully developed aesthetic model of culture and society such as Matthew Arnold's.[6] The following discussion has as its main object a reading of Arnold's classic essay "The Function of Criticism at the Present Time"; but first, because the complexity of the trope of the body, particularly in its interplay with aesthetics, is rarely granted more than a nod of acknowledgment in contemporary cultural criticism, I shall spend a few pages summarizing the alluring trickiness of this metaphor.

I

During its two and a half centuries of formal existence, modern aesthetics has been inseparable from themes and figures of embodiment. The subject of aesthetics is an embodied subject, attentive and responsive to sensuous things. Judgments of taste imply a functional if metaphorical tongue, and something specific on the palate. The point of such judgments, to be sure, is to disclose a supersensory harmony or truth, or ground for judgment without rule—at the limit, to transcend the body's vulnerability through a sublime intuition of one's supersensible destiny. Yet in this endeavor an embodied perspective is all important: the sublime thrill degrades into simple terror as soon as danger comes too close, whereas the beautiful, stripped of its frame, becomes what Kant calls the merely agreeable—"what the senses like in sensation."[7] To perceive beauty is to transcend one's limited, embodied perspective *from* that perspective. Disinterestedness begins with the body and after its fashion remains faithful to it, just as the artwork remains faithful to sensuous appearance, or what the German tradition calls *Schein*. Both art and the aesthetic subject transcend the corporeal only in and through the corporeal. In consequence, the historicist and anthropomorphic myth at the heart of postromantic aesthetics—the narrative of human and national self-creation that leads from savagery to culture and that, in Matthew Arnold's idiom, will persist "until the raw and unkindled masses of humanity are touched with sweetness and light" (*Culture and Anarchy*, 79)— usually offers as the figure of its telos a (male, white) human body: Kant's "model image" of man as the "ideal of beauty" (81); Blake's Albion; or, somewhat closer to home, Northrop Frye's Blakean vision of apocalypse as "the imaginative conception of the whole of nature as the content of an infinite and eternal living body which, if not human, is closer to being human than to being inanimate."[8]

Even this thumbnail sketch, however, reveals that the body is the site of considerable semantic tension in aesthetic discourse. If the beautiful must be distinguished—fundamentally and absolutely, thanks to the pure, parergonal cut of a framing disinterestedness—from "what the senses like in sensation," this is to say that aesthetics, discourse of the body though it be, must never become too much wrapped up in the body.[9] The body is weak, leaky, given over to degradation, death, and corruption; it is ungovernably desirous and fallible—in romantic writing, the locus of "dire forces," as David Farrell Krell has shown.[10] Even at the best of times, some of its parts and functions require veiling. Unsurprisingly, according to a tradition with ancient comic, cynical, and materialist roots, the body is that which *resists* the aesthetic—that which chastises and debunks aesthetic (or "German," or "romantic") ideology. The nature of this resistance, however, is complex. On the one hand, there exists an almost irresistible temptation to understand this resistance as the pressure of necessity, or of "the real." On the other hand, as soon as one takes "the body" as "real," one repeats a version of the aesthetic illusion: the body reacquires an imaginary totality—often in the guise of sensuous plenitude—at the same time that it demands to be read as "constructed." The constructedness of the body is of course one of the great themes of many of the last century's innovative intellectual trends: psychoanalysis, phenomenology, histories of manners, and more recent Marxist, feminist, or Foucault-inspired historicisms. That bodies are in some sense made, not born—that they exist not as answers, but as questions, or tangles of questions, questions of form and knowledge, power, discipline, gender, figurative language—has become one of the commonplaces of cultural scholarship. Yet equally commonplace is the rhetorical elevation of the body into a sign of the plenitude of the real. A recent *PMLA* essay on Thomas de Quincey has even managed the trick of having its constructionism and essentialism serially while remaining seemingly oblivious to any potential contradiction: "Both bodies and signs are material, social artifacts. By relating them de Quincey simply lives, without reference to anything beyond his embodiment."[11] On the one hand, the artificiality of a construct that necessarily refers elsewhere for its grounds of existence; on the other hand, a plenitude of self-reference in which one "simply lives," as though the body were capable of embodying referentiality itself.

The resistance that the body offers to aesthetics, therefore, may be thought as the force of fatality, but this force turns out to involve a reinscription, as well as a demystification, of the body's aesthetic illusion. The question of the body thus inevitably becomes a version of the problem of the rhetorical construction of meaning, where meaning is conceived, in Nietzschean fashion, as an effaced figure. Without quite saying so, Judith Butler presses her definition of the "materiality" of the body in this direction:

It must be possible to concede and affirm an array of "materialities" that pertain to the body, that which is signified by the domains of biology, anatomy, physiology, hormonal and chemical composition, illness, age, weight, metabolism, life and death. None of this can be denied. But the undeniability of these "materialities" in no way implies what it means to affirm them, indeed, what interpretive matrices condition, enable, and limit that necessary affirmation. That each of these categories has a history and a historicity . . . implies that they are *both* persistent and contested regions.

We might want to claim that what persists within these contested domains is the "materiality" of the body. But perhaps we will have fulfilled the same function, and opened up some others, if we claim that what persists here is a *demand in and for language*, a "that which" which prompts and occasions, say, within the domain of science, calls to be explained, described, diagnosed, altered or within the cultural fabric of lived experience, fed, exercised, mobilized, put to sleep, a site of enactments and passions of various kinds.[12]

As a "demand in and for language," the material body would be a referential imperative rather than a proper referent—a wound in language rather than an entity toward which language would simply point. Butler's definition emerges in the wake of a dense discussion of the Freudian and Lacanian allegory of the "bodily ego," according to which the ego is "the projection of a [bodily] surface."[13] The ego constitutes itself through a proleptic fiction, and this fiction props itself up on the materiality of the body prior to its figuration *as* body; for if the ego forms itself as a projection of body surfaces, those surfaces themselves must first be construed or taken as such. The "surface" of the body becomes at once the site and the *nachträglich* effect of the occurrence or positing of figure or form.[14] "Materiality" would thus seek to name a force or performance of formalization through which figure—the body, the mirrored ego—emerges in its phenomenality. The fatality of the body is then thinkable as a linguistic predicament: as a referential and historical force inseparable from the ungroundedness—the radical figurativeness or impropriety—of the meanings and images through which bodies and selves come into being.[15]

Certainly from the point of view of aesthetic discourse, the body's power to cause trouble may be couched in terms of figurative language. Within the high aesthetic tradition, the body is that which is negated in order to be preserved, and preserved in order to be negated. One way to characterize the body's resistance to this dialectical role is to say that *as* a figure, it figures too much and too little—too much and too little unity, reference, specificity. Discussions of organic form inevitably turn into potentially unstable discussions of figurative language. "What are the foot, body and head of a poem?" as William K. Wimsatt puts it, worrying the turns of a Platonic simile that seems constantly in danger of being "carr[ied] too far."[16] Wimsatt's solution, in fact, is to reverse the poles of the trope: the artwork, he suggests, has *literal* organic form—a synthetic unity in multiplicity—whereas "the merely physical organism," vulnerable to contingency, prosthetic supplementation, and other sorts of inadequacy and damage, "enjoys this character only by metaphoric extension and hence in a less exact degree" (25).[17] The "body," in this remarkable New Critical meditation, becomes a catachresis, a fundamentally improper or incomplete, and correspondingly unruly trope. It will always be carried "too far," for the body here figures an aesthetic totality that its own bodiliness undermines.

Questions about the head or feet of a poem (as opposed to a body politic) may seem merely absurd. But other sorts of literalization have clearer ideological purchase, even within the genteel orbit of literary argument: If a poem is organic, does it have a gender? Does aesthetics as a "discourse of the body" necessarily at some point become a story about sexual difference and desire? And once the body is in play as a figure, is there really any way to prevent such questions from occurring? Terry Eagleton's attempt to ground aesthetics in bodily experience offers an instructive example. In its main lines of argument *The Ideology of the Aesthetic* pursues a Foucaultian suggestion that eighteenth-century aesthetics inscribed social power—the rule of habit, sentiment, and affection—on and in the bodily sensorium, as authoritarian forms of political subordination mutated into the ruses of modern biopower. Yet as is so often the case, the critic, feeling the tug of the body's referential imperative, transforms the socially constructed body into a sensuous reservoir of being—with the result, according to Kathy Alexis Psomiades, that Eagleton "returns again and again to the lovely feminine body of the art object, a body his text figures as 'the body of the mother.'"[18] Psomiades cites and examines a number of passages. Here is one from Eagleton's final chapter:

[Human] creative self-making is carried out within given limits, which are finally those of the body itself. . . . Because human beings are weak and unprotected, especially in their infancy, they are in biological need of the care and emotional sustenance of others. It is here, as Freud recognized, that the first glimmerings of morality are to be found. (*Ideology*, 410)

Putting this passage into relation with similar claims elsewhere in Eagleton's *The Ideology of the Aesthetic*, Psomiades discerns a fantasy at work:

"the body of the mother marks a constant, a truth that is not relative, the truth of the body and the flesh, the truth of a real subject" (19).[19] One can imagine Eagleton's response: he did not intend this fundamental body to be a sexed body, let alone a maternal one; he was rather—in good aesthetic fashion—invoking the body of a common humanity. Yet as soon as the trope of the body is in play, it goes too far. It doesn't necessarily acquire a determinate gender, but it elicits *questions* of gender, sex, race, and so on— not because these categories are grounded in "the body" as a determinate entity, but rather because there is no such entity: "the body" is not a ground.[20] The radical figurativeness of the body, that is, is precisely what renders it historical. If we turn now to a moment in the history of aesthetics in which organic metaphor plays an exceptionally prominent role, we may expect to encounter anxieties about language marking moments of ideological stress.

II

Almost a century and a half after its first publication in 1864, Matthew Arnold's "The Function of Criticism at the Present Time" remains one of the most compact and influential documents in the history of aesthetic humanism. Several of its memorable turns of phrase are insistently echoed in the conservative cultural press. Its most famous sentence, for instance, reappeared, shorn of its elegance, during the Reagan era as William Bennett's demand that scholars pursue "the best that has been said, thought, written, and otherwise expressed about the human experience," and similar near-quotations or echoes would certainly not be difficult to obtain.[21] Particularly since the fabled incursion of "theory" into the literary academy, antitheoretical scholarly position papers have invoked "The Function of Criticism" with an air of beleaguered sanctity.[22] But as Gerald Graff notes, the habit of invoking Arnold in something like this gloomy fashion goes back to the struggles between generalists and philologists during the earliest years of the professional study of English at the university. "The Function of Criticism" has played a totemic role for a long time in the academy[23]; and this is partly, I think, because the essay is poised on the threshold of professional literary culture, preceding by a decade or two the earliest systematic teaching of "literature" in the schools, yet written at a time when the recreational and pedagogical spaces of what we now—partly because of Arnold's influence—call "culture" had achieved critical ideological mass. "Criticism," for Arnold, is a cultural, political, and epistemological activity, and its ambition to "know the best that is known and thought in the world" (36)—we may say, in our contemporary idiom, to establish and know the canon—is a literary–critical ambition only insofar as literature is taken to represent the epitome of a nation's spiritual accomplishment. For Arnold, as we shall see, the critic is nothing less than the unacknowledged legislator of the world. His essay has thus served as a nostalgic *point de repère* for cultural bureaucrats of a later era, and perhaps for that reason it has almost never, to my knowledge, been read closely, either by traditionalists or by anti-Arnoldian cultural theorists. It is *the* canonical text about criticism as canon formation, yet it is also a considerably stranger work than is frequently assumed.

There is, to begin with, Arnold's peculiarly epistemological characterization of "literature"—a word he generally uses in the modern sense to mean creative or imaginative writing, but with shades of the older, broader meaning of "learning; skill in letters" (to cite the four-word entry that Samuel Johnson found sufficient as a definition of "literature" in his *Dictionary* of 1757). Literature attaches to epistemology by way of criticism, criticism being "the endeavor, in all branches of knowledge, theology, philosophy, history, art, science, to see the object as in itself it really is" (26). Criticism, however, also shares in the "free creative activity" that is "the highest function of man" and that "great works of literature or art" epitomize (28). Literature, for its part, shares criticism's concern for ideas but lacks criticism's epistemological drive. As a consequence of these assertions, Arnold, in the opening pages of his essay, is able to claim that criticism renders literature possible, by generating a world of ideas to which literature can refer:

Now in literature—I will limit myself to literature, for it is about literature that the question arises—the elements with which the creative power works are ideas; the best ideas, on every matter which literature touches, current at the time. At any rate we may lay it down as certain that in modern literature no manifestation of the creative power not working with these can be very important or fruitful. And I say *current* at the time, not merely accessible at the time; for creative literary genius does not principally show itself in discovering new ideas, that is rather the business of the philosopher. The grand work of literary genius is a work of synthesis and exposition, not of analysis and discovery; its gift lies in the faculty of being happily inspired by a certain intellectual and spiritual atmosphere. (28)

Literature "must have" this "atmosphere," and some atmospheres are more sustaining than others: "for the creation of a masterwork of literature two powers must concur: the power of the man and the power of the moment" (29), and those historical periods that best nourish genius produce, of course, the greatest art. Literature has no control over its ideational context. But criticism to some extent does: criticism has a grip on history denied to literature because criticism has epistemological and referential purchase on the world, its central task being to "see the object as in itself it really is":

> Thus [criticism] tends, at last, to make an intellectual situation of which the creative power can profitably avail itself. It tends to establish an order of ideas, if not absolutely true, yet true by comparison with that which it displaces; to make the best ideas prevail. Presently these new ideas reach society, the touch of truth is the touch of life, and there is a stir and growth everywhere; out of this stir and growth come the creative epochs of literature. (29)

Criticism's epistemological acts of judgment, in other words, have performative consequences. With qualifications that I'll mention later, we may say that Arnold is claiming that criticism is the engine of history. Criticism renders the world ever more complex, causing poets to need to know more and more criticism before they can write poetry: "the creation of a modern poet, to be worth much, implies a great critical effort behind it; else it must be a comparatively poor, barren, and short-lived affair" (29). I shall shortly be examining the figures of animation and birth that condition an epistemological drive for which "the touch of truth is the touch of life"; for the moment, we may simply note that modernity is difficult, a theme Arnold inherits from Schiller and forwards on to the twentieth century while giving it—in these opening pages of his essay, at least—an epistemological-scientific spin that Arnold's heirs, burdened with the need to distinguish culture from science, have had to abjure or rephrase.[24]

Arnold is in fact, however, juggling two incompatible models of literary achievement. There is the epistemological model that I have thus far emphasized, according to which literature, synthesizing the ideas that criticism discerns or discovers, grows more complex as the world grows more complex, and thus logically ought to grow better as criticism approaches closer and closer to the truth of "the object as in itself it really is," through the process of repeatedly "establish[ing] an order of ideas, if not absolutely true, yet true by comparison with that which it displaces." Yet this narrative of scientific progress runs counter to the monumentalizing imperative of aesthetic canonization, and Arnold, having just told us that Wordsworth would have been a greater poet if he had read more books, pulls himself up short: "Coleridge had immense reading," after all; but the comparatively unlettered and scientifically unenlightened Pindar, Sophocles, and Shakespeare are nonetheless greater than any modern writers, because in their various eras "the poet lived in a current of ideas in the highest degree animating and nourishing to the creative power; society was, in the fullest measure, permeated by fresh thought, intelligent and alive" (30). Books and reading only provide a "semblance" of this organic "complete culture" (31), this "quickening and sustaining atmosphere" (30). The second model of literary accomplishment is that of the culture as a self-referential living body or ecosystem. If on the one hand criticism drives forward toward the *Ding an sich* (the body as referent), approaching truth asymptotically as history unfolds, on the other hand, aesthetic achievement depends on the internal integrity and health of a cultural, contextual body (the body as form). The two models appear to converge because, as noted a moment ago, the epistemological drive poses as the "touch of life"—it provides, as it were, for the care and feeding of the cultural body and its representative, the artwork. Yet these models are in fact sharply at odds. The first generates history as a drive toward a nourishing truth located in the future; the second looks backward to exemplary classical and Elizabethan texts and has no referential target external to the self-referring activity of the cultural and national ecosystem. The first's is a meliorist and the second's a nostalgic and canonizing narrative. Displaced into the terminology of the twentieth-century university, one could say that the first is like research—like an imperative to publish something new or perish—and the second is like teaching, to the extent that the teacher is an aesthetic educator, presiding over the ritualized worship of a secular text. It is typical of the rhetorical economy of aesthetic culture that over the course of Arnold's essay the second model tends to displace the first. As we have seen, Arnold begins by emphasizing criticism's epistemologic–scientific quest, but he closes his essay with pathos-laden sentences that stress the exemplariness of the canon:

The epochs of Aeschylus and Shakespeare make us feel their pre-eminence. In an epoch like those is, no doubt, the true life of literature; there is the promised land, toward which criticism can only beckon. That promised land it will not be ours to enter, and we shall die in the wilderness: but to have desired to enter it, to have saluted it from afar, is already, perhaps, the best distinction among contemporaries; it will certainly be the best title to esteem with posterity. (51)

Thus the naturalizing and formalist language of the ecosystem conveys the nonlinear time of the example, which leads us forward by *promising* from the past.

Yet if we ask how the canonical example leads us forward, we find ourselves returned to the epistemologic–scientific model: Arnold, who knows very well that the aesthetic is responsible in the end for epistemological questions, needs both narratives. The epistemological narrative, turned toward the futurity of the ideal, lacks duration, for like a shark, it must always keep moving forward in order to stay alive: "thus knowledge, and ever-fresh knowledge, must be the critic's great concern for himself" (49). The formal ecosystem of the example provides an enduring canon and the duration of cultural history, but it lacks forward momentum or an orientation toward truth as an external referent. Arnold's rhetorical challenge, as we have seen, is to blend epistemological and organic terminology so as to ensure that "the touch of truth is the touch of life" (29). In this, the adjective *fresh* and the noun and adjective *current* play important roles because they both suggest a forward-moving temporality while retaining organic associations, though Arnold usually retains the word *truth* for good measure (as in the repeated phrase "a current of true and fresh ideas" [37, 38] and its variants, "a current of fresh and true ideas" [49], "true and fresh ideas" [48]). In pursuing "true and fresh ideas," the critic pursues the true as a natural growth, and the fresh as an index of the true. Criticism is thus imaginable as the mother of literature and, more broadly, of history itself. Without criticism, poetry would be a "poor, barren, and short-lived affair" (29). If literature arrives too soon, it will be "premature," "doomed" (29); "a poor, starved, fragmentary, inadequate creation" (51). Deprived of "a free play of the mind," a nation's spirit would "die of inanition" (35). "What will nourish us in our growth toward perfection?" Arnold asks rhetorically (51). The answer is "a current of fresh and true ideas" (49), "a current of ideas . . . animating and nourishing" (30). The word *fresh* participates in a chain of images of liquid nourishment that in turn connects to a series of water-based metaphors of "mingling" and absorption, of a production of and passage into an "atmosphere." The *natural* referentiality or political functionality of criticism occurs in a sequence of tropes leading from osmosis through oral intake to mothering and birth.

The figure of the mother will shortly occupy center stage in Arnold's essay. For the present, we may note that the critic's maternal role is the matrix within which the competing models of organic self-reference and referential drive are to be harmonized. And since the referential thrust of criticism constitutes its performative, political power—its ability to leave a mark on the world—the trope of the mother will also shape Arnold's famous principle of disinterestedness. "The rule [of criticism] may be summed up in one word—*disinterestedness*" (37). Disinterestedness is defined in conventional, loosely post-Kantian fashion as "a free play of the mind" (37); but Arnold's emphasis falls not so much on the formality or purposive purposelessness of subjective judgment—here he tends simply to argue by way of negative example: we are to avoid "interested," politically purposive debate—but rather on the temporality of disinterestedness as an efficacious performative. For it is in and as disinterestedness that criticism obtains purchase on the world and drives history toward its ideal. The title of Arnold's essay, after all, is the *function* of criticism, and this functionality—this interested disinterest—occurs as the slow work of organic gestation or growth. Criticism's is a "slow and obscure work" (41); "Our ideas will, in the end, shape the world all the better for maturing a little" (48); "I say, the critic must keep out of the region of immediate practice in the political, social, humanitarian sphere, if he wants to make a beginning for that more free speculative treatment of things, which may perhaps one day make its benefits felt even in this sphere, but in a natural and thence irresistible manner" (42). From Schiller and Coleridge to the twentieth-century neohumanists and New Critics, to the cultural conservatives of our own present time, aesthetic temporality has been understood as a cure for that of revolution. Thus the contrast to aesthetic judgment's slow, organic process of gestation is the violent haste, the speed and immediacy, with which the French Revolution "transported" ideas "out of their own sphere" and had them "meddling rashly with practice" (35): "its movement of ideas, by quitting the intellectual sphere and rushing furiously into the political sphere . . . produced no such intellectual fruit as the movement of ideas of the Renascence" (33).

In the wake of his discussion of the French Revolution, Arnold offers us his first example of disinterested thinking: Edmund Burke, who allowed his writings to be "often disfigured by the violence and passion of the moment" (33–34), rose to greatness in transcending his hostility to the French Revolution.[25] Arnold quotes from the closing paragraph of *Thoughts on French Affairs*, where Burke wonders whether a "great change" is not after all in the air. If so, Burke concludes, "they who persist in opposing this mighty current of human affairs will appear rather to resist the decrees of Providence itself, than the mere designs of man." In Arnold's commentary, both the decrees of Providence and the "mighty current" reappear, in a passage dense enough to pose an interpretative challenge of a different order than we have yet encountered:

> That return of Burke upon himself has always seemed to me one of the finest things in English literature, or indeed in any literature. That is what I call living by ideas: when one side of a question has long had your earnest support, when all your feelings are engaged, when you hear all round you no language but one, when your party talks this language like a steam-engine and can imagine no other,—still to be able to think, still to be irresistibly carried, if so it be, by the current of thought to the opposite side of the question, and, like Balaam, to be unable to speak anything *but what the Lord has put in your mouth.* (35)

For a brief moment, the text leaves behind its humanist rhetoric of culture—"the mere designs of man," in Burke's phrase—and passes to the grander and more inhuman register of prophetic speech. We are at some distance here from "that full current of sympathetic motive" in which *Middlemarch's* Dorothea Brooke's "ideas and impulses were habitually swept along," and on which George Eliot, like Arnold, relied for her aesthetic historicism.[26] Here, the "current" that has meandered through Arnold's essay, promising organic wholeness, suddenly appears as a more turbulent force, possessed of some of the speed and fury of revolution, rebounding against "language like a steam-engine" with the power of a god speaking through a human vessel. Self-consciousness, or what Arnold describes as "that return of Burke upon himself," is the sign of properly disinterested mental activity. Indeed, historical progress, according to this broadly idealist model, is a progress from nature to self-consciousness (through a critical performativity that, as we have seen, must itself be *natural*), from the rule of force and necessity toward a state of "inward recognition, free assent of the will" (33). But Arnold's account of Burkean disinterestedness suggests the presence of a disturbing element in the organic model: a violence incompatible with the organic growth over time that is supposed to characterize the performative power of self-conscious, disinterested criticism. Embodied in the exemplary figure of Burke, the referential–epistemological drive becomes forceful to the point of resembling the inhumanity of divine language, and thus it potentially becomes alien to the organic register of freshness, or to the slow time of gestation. If this referential drive is what nourishes the national body, the national body is possibly in trouble—as is the organic–historical process of *Bildung* toward which disinterested aesthetic judgments contribute. Indeed, swept away by such a current, Arnoldian critics might find themselves having to begin rethinking *Bildung* along the lines of Friedrich Schlegel's definition of it as "a continuing chain of the most monstrous revolutions."[27]

Arnold, however, chooses another path: that of propitiative sacrifice. Inevitably, this means a return to the mother, the matrix within which form and formation are supposed to meet in organic harmony. Now, however, the mother must provide the counterexample and embody the "dire forces," as David Farrell Krell puts it, that threaten to disrupt the body as organic totality or form. Thus Arnold turns to an unnatural, murderous mother, "a girl named Wragg." Recent speeches by two opposed members of Parliament, Sir Charles Adderley and Mr. Roebuck, provide Arnold with his occasion. Adderley's and Roebuck's overpurposeful relationship to objects causes them to wax jingoistic about the state of the nation and the "old Anglo-Saxon breed," for, as interested philistines, they idealize the real immediately, with improper speed. The properly disinterested observer, however, reflecting on England, language, and aesthetics via the figure of Wragg, allows the gestational time of history to mediate between the real and the ideal toward which history strives:

But let criticism leave church-rates and the franchise alone, and in the most candid spirit, without a single lurking thought of practical innovation, confront with our dithyramb this paragraph on which I stumbled in a newspaper immediately after reading Mr. Roebuck:—

"A shocking child murder has just been committed at Nottingham. A girl named Wragg left the workhouse there on Saturday morning with her young illegitimate child. The child was soon afterwards found dead on Mapperly Hills, having been strangled. Wragg is in custody."

Nothing but that; but in juxtaposition with the absolute eulogies of Sir Charles Adderley and Mr. Roebuck, how eloquent, how suggestive are those few lines! "Our old Anglo-Saxon breed, the best in the whole world!"—how much there is harsh and ill-favoured there is in this best! *Wragg*! If we are to talk of ideal perfection, of the "best in the whole world," has anyone reflected what a touch of grossness in our race, what an original shortcoming in the more delicate spiritual perceptions, is shown by the natural growth amongst us of such hideous names,—Higginbottom, Stiggins, Bugg! In Ionia and Attica they were luckier in this respect than "the best race in the world;" by the Ilissus there was no Wragg, poor thing! And "our unrivaled happiness;"—what an element of grimness, bareness, and hideousness mixes with it and blurs it; the workhouse, the dismal Mapperly Hills,—how dismal those who have seen them will remember;—the gloom, the cold, the smoke, the strangled illegitimate child! "I ask you whether, the world over or in past history, there is anything like it?" Perhaps not, one is inclined to answer; but at any rate, in that case, the world is [not] very much to be pitied.[28] And the final touch,—short, bleak, and inhuman: *Wragg is in custody*. The sex lost in the confusion of our unrivalled happiness; or (shall I say?) the superfluous Christian name lopped off by the straightforward vigour of our old Anglo-Saxon breed! There is profit for the spirit in such contrasts as this; criticism serves the cause of perfection by establishing them. By eluding sterile conflict, by refusing to remain in the sphere where alone narrow and relative conceptions have any worth and validity, criticism may diminish its momentary importance, but only in this way has it a chance of gaining admittance for those wider and more perfect conceptions to which all its duty is really owed. Mr. Roebuck will have a poor opinion of an adversary who replies to his defiant songs of triumph only by murmuring under his breath, *Wragg is in custody*; but in no other way will these songs of triumph be induced gradually to moderate themselves, to get rid of what in them is excessive and offensive, and to fall into a softer and truer key. (40–41)

Arnold's invocation of Wragg constitutes a humanist's rebuke of vulgar jingoism and exemplifies the kind of moral attentiveness that Arnoldian culture seeks to cultivate. But it is also an odd, overcharged moment in the text. Arnold "stumbles" on Wragg as a paragraph in a newspaper; she comes to him as part of the rumble of the everyday, a rag of quotidian misery recorded in an ephemeral medium.[29] Yet she provides "The Function of Criticism" with its only practical example of disinterested aesthetic judgment because, paradoxically, she is the exemplary example: she embodies the very possibility of aesthetic example. For Wragg embodies the detritus of aesthetic history, and she thus represents the difference that makes the man of culture different from the philistine, and that makes the fallen world redeemable, at history's end, when difference will have fallen away and there will be no Wragg. By exemplifying the difference between the ideal and the real, Wragg makes aesthetic judgment necessary and possible, and referentially efficacious. Only by "murmuring under his breath, *Wragg is in custody*" does the disinterested critic begin to intervene in the world of politics as a "natural and thence irresistible" historical force (42); without the ground tone, the basso profundo of that murmur, all the fine judgments and discriminations of aesthetic judgment would make no difference at all. Neither "The Function of Criticism" nor its canonical objects of criticism—the "best that has been known and thought"—could exist without Wragg. If criticism, in this essay, is the mother of history and literature, Wragg is the mother of this mothering power.

We may thus begin to understand why Arnold trains such a fascinated, aggressive, cherishing gaze on Wragg; for, like a good Lacanian mother, she not only provides criticism with a body and an ego, but also threatens to shatter the mirror. Her threat takes both political and psychoanalytic form. The abject double of Britannia, Wragg embodies the ungovernable sexuality and productive power of a sub–working-class mother; "in custody" though she be, she nonetheless suggests the presence of disruptive, antiaesthetic forces within the national body. She is a counterexample intended to prove a rule—to reinforce the Victorian ideologeme that "morality and class stability will follow the expression of maternal instinct," as Mary Poovey puts it—but as a murderous mother occupying a sharply specular position vis-à-vis the narrator of "The Function of Criticism," she inspires lurid fantasies of castration and fragmentation, providing a mirror for symbolic mutilations that Arnold decries and excitedly repeats ("the sex lost"; "the superfluous Christian name lopped off").[30] One may even hear a flicker of fantasized anal rape in two of the names that Arnold conjures up to express his fascinated revulsion ("Higginbottom," "Bugg"), and that sadistic flourish suggests the degree to which a certain loss of control threatens the text here. "It will be remembered that the anal penis is also the phallus with which infantile imagination provides the feminine sex," Julia Kristeva tells us, adding in a somewhat more empirical vein that "maternal authority is experienced first and above all, after the first essentially oral frustrations, as sphincteral training."[31]

Whether or not one feels able to take such Freudian tropes literally, one might consider in this context Kristeva's speculations on maternal abjection: the formative psychic act that she proposes as a precondition of infantile narcissism—and as a source of terrors more archaic than the castration fantasies of an incest taboo. The self, according to this account, first comes into being by separating itself from an archaic maternality, a not-yet-object or "abject"—a potential chaos that Kristeva calls "the feminine" as "an 'other' without a name" (58); and this primal, ambivalent act of expulsion ("I expel *myself*, I spit *myself* out, I abject *myself* within the same motion through which 'I' claim to establish myself" [3]) haunts all future efforts to police the boundaries of bodies and selves. If the potential cruelty of aesthetic judgment becomes all too apparent in Arnold's greater readiness to lament Wragg's name than the society that produced and destroyed her, the mingled horror and satisfaction he feels for the name "Wragg" recalls the mood of the sort of scenarios to which Kristeva attends, as does his oddly compulsive attention to language in the first place: signs turn uncertain in the realm of abjection, as all borders and differences threaten to crumble.

Kristeva has frequently been criticized for reducing the feminine to the maternal ("the feminine, of which the maternal is the real support," etc. [71]); and at times her account of the prelinguistic, embodied character of maternal authority can read like a highly theorized version of the more modest fantasy by Terry Eagleton that we considered earlier. Arnold's abject and abjected Wragg, however, is nothing if not a linguistic entity. His essay's metaphors of natural temporality and performativity require that Wragg bear away language's figurative excess. Hers is the monstrous pregnancy, the *grossesse*, that enacts the "touch of grossness in our race"; an unnatural mother, she provides a maternal locus for "the natural growth amongst us of such hideous names." If language is the mother of abortive and ugly names, Wragg is the mother as language. Yet this nightmarish version of natural supernaturalism, whereby the production of language is naturalized by blaming the mother for unnatural language, cannot efface the pressure of a different sort of materiality. While reading, Arnold has been struck by a name, a fragmentary rag of a name. Punning backward to its appearance in newsprint and forward to its supererogatory mutilation at the hands of Arnoldian humanism, the name "Wragg" displays all the aesthetic charms of the signifier, but also all the volatility of a signifier cut off from meaning. A clutch of silent and redundant consonants that can be read but not heard, a homophone of its medium—of the kind of cheap paper newspapers use—it is an inherently *written*, perversely self-reflexive and literary name. And it fragments the proper and paternal name insofar as it suggests the possibility that Arnold's text is being generated by the arbitrary resources of a pun, and by random similarities or differences among words, such as the double-g catalogue of "Higginbottom, Stiggins, Bugg" that Arnold generates compulsively out of "Wragg."[32] If Wragg is the word made flesh and the unvirginal mother of the word, she is also a scapegoat who has been brought into the text in order to bear away the sins of language. She is a figure, a personification, imposed upon an unreliable play of letters; as such, she reveals the mother's abjection to be as arbitrary as the signs which maternal abjection underwrites. She is aesthetic disinterestedness as the uncertainly performative force of the letter, and thus she represents the end of the line for aesthetics as a "discourse of the body," or the canon as a corpus, or the nation as a body. It is to embody, and thus defend against, such material bodiliness that "a girl named Wragg" is summoned into the aesthetic realm under an ever-deferred sentence of expulsion.

PART II

RADICAL FIGURES OF ROMANTICISM

3

De Man, Schiller, and the
Politics of Reception

> What confronts fear in the character of meaningfulness is something *detrimental*,
> as Aristotle says, a *kakon*, *malum*, an evil. In particular, this detrimental thing is
> always something definite. If we already had the concept here, we would say some-
> thing historical, something definite breaking into the familiar world of concerned
> perception.
> —Martin Heidegger, *History of the Concept of Time: Prolegomena*

Particularly, though by no means only, in North America, the professional study of romantic literature finds itself having to negotiate, again and
again, its half-acknowledged obsession with Paul de Man. This predicament is most visible in those areas of scholarship where specific essays by
de Man have become canonical—discussions, say, of allegory and irony, or
of Shelley's *Triumph of Life*. But de Man haunts romantic studies in a way
that goes far beyond the ordinary workings of scholarly influence or professional filiation: he haunts romanticism as a figure rather than as a specific text or argument, a figure of "theory" always ready to emerge, once
again, from the wings—often, of course, simply in order to be rerebuked
and reexorcised, yet even in his briefest appearances conveying a reminder
of the vexed intimacy between romanticism and literary–theoretical reflection. In this respect romanticism is exemplary of a more general predicament. As I have argued both in this book's Introduction and elsewhere, de
Man serves contemporary American literary culture as a phantasmatic personification of "deconstruction" as "theory"; and if the phantom haunts
the field of professional romanticism more persistently than other reaches
of literary scholarship, this is only partly because de Man was a professional romanticist; it is also because romanticism epitomizes literary scholarship's deep and deeply problematic imbrication in aesthetic discourse.[1]

No serious study of the rhetoric and politics of aesthetics can avoid confronting de Man—though "confront" is a misleadingly specular trope for an engagement that is likely to be shot through with fantasy and repetitiveness and characterized by a particularly intense form of obsession. Twenty years and more after the publication of *Allegories of Reading*, de Man remains an influential yet never routine presence. His work continues to elicit intense acts of exegesis and to inspire critics in a variety of fields and traditions, yet because of his totemic association with theory, the mere mention of his name still has the power to raise the temperature of scholarly discussion.[2] Frank Lentricchia was clearly wide of the mark when in 1983 he predicted that the "war between traditionalists and deconstructors" would "draw to a close by the end of this decade," with de Man "rediscovered as the most brilliant hero of traditionalism."[3] Even if de Man's wartime contributions to *Le Soir* had remained hidden a few more years in the archive, Lentricchia would surely have lost his wager, as, in fact, the extraordinary proportions of the wartime journalism furor confirmed.[4] The acts of exorcism, of course, have been powerful and ongoing. One could with considerable justice invert Lentricchia's formulations and claim that the most significant realignments of institutional power in literary studies during the 1980s and 1990s amounted to a wholehearted endorsement of the rhetoric of *Criticism and Social Change*. Nothing, we have been told again and again, is more obvious than the political inadequacy of de Man's texts. The task of pursuing some form of "historicism," meanwhile, has taken on the self-evident necessity of an ethical imperative. "It is a fact," de Man wrote in 1972, "that this sort of thing happens, again and again, in literary studies."[5] What happens perhaps a little more rarely in literary studies is the event of an exemplary figure such as de Man, capable of inspiring such remarkable gestures of monumentalization and ritual sacrifice.

The pages that follow seek to articulate de Man's theoretical text with the politics of his reception and with the question of politics. I shall be pursuing the notions of history and politics that inform de Man's late texts, mounting an argument for their credibility and political usefulness, yet also seeking to account, by way of the same vocabulary, for the resistance his writing inspires. This topic acquires interest when, like de Man, we understand "resistance" as a necessary component of any act of reading. Overt displays of "resistance to theory," in other words, may be understood as spectacular versions of the subtler problematic posed by theory's "resistance"

to itself. The complement of fear and repression is idealization and identification. Both are predicated upon a monumentalizing gesture without
which no response to de Man seems able to come into being. The very act
of commenting, favorably or unfavorably, on his work draws one into a
network of effects characterizable in both institutional and libidinal terms.
The politics of criticism and the politics of charisma intersect within the
event of this fortuitously anthropomorphic proper name. One is thus led
to pursue what might otherwise seem a needless complication: the relation
in de Man's text among history, politics, and pathos. Further reasons for
privileging this cluster of issues will unfold as we negotiate de Man's theoretical propositions. But we can suggest the nature of this topic's interest,
and open the question of de Man's "own" resistance to ("de Manian") theory, by considering, in a somewhat naive and literalistic fashion, the affective career of the word *history* in his writing over thirty years.

De Man's essays tend to address the question of history in an elevated
tone. With surprising regularity, they seek closure in dramatic, aphoristic
invocations of the historical. Occasionally the mood is neutral or upbeat,
as when, at the end of his early essay on the theme of Faust, de Man writes
that a genuinely thematic reading must "pass from myth to idea, and from
idea to formal theme, before being able to become history" (*CW*, 88).[6]
More often, the tone is closer to that of the closing phrase of "The Dead-
End of Formalist Criticism," as it invokes "the sorrowful time of patience,
i.e., history" (*BI*, 245). The existential idiom of these early texts, their
thematization of history in terms of a nonnaturalistic, death-directed temporality, clearly favors but does not entirely explain the recurrence of such
a tone in essays so frequently marked by a refusal of pathetic language.[7]
The question is of interest because de Man's penchant for granting the
word *history* rhetorical charge does not disappear as his attention shifts to
rhetoric. His most famous, or infamous, aphorism on history is memorable
partly because it is—and has the ring of—a closing sentence: "the bases for
historical knowledge are not empirical facts but written texts, even if these
texts masquerade in the guise of wars or revolutions" (*BI*, 165). An essay devoted to themes of political action in Rousseau ends with the dramatic
proposition that "textual allegories on this level of rhetorical complexity
generate history" (*AR*, 277). And in the late essays that principally concern
us here, de Man's prose will often acquire extraordinary intensity at the
very moment when he is repudiating the pathos made available by notions

of historical time. In "Shelley Disfigured," an essay that bears on the historicity of an aesthetic object "that has been unearthed, edited, reconstructed, and much discussed" (*RR*, 93), de Man's tone, grimly elegiac throughout, rises memorably as he concludes the essay with a resurrection of Shelley's dead body—and finally, with a reintroduction of the charged word "history": "Reading as disfiguration, to the very extent that it resists historicism, turns out to be historically more reliable than the products of historical archeology" (*RR*, 123). But perhaps the most dramatic instance of such a deliberately pathetic renunciation of pathos occurs in the last sentence of "Anthropomorphism and Trope," where the work of "true 'mourning'" unrolls as a bleakly sublime list of deprivations: "The most *it* can do is enumerate non-anthropomorphic, non-elegiac, non-celebratory, non-lyrical, non-poetic, that is to say, prosaic, or better, *historical* modes of language power" (*RR*, 262, de Man's italics). The text performs what it denies, going to some length, in fact, to deliver a certain version of the elegiac satisfaction it is renouncing.

History is of course not by any means always, in de Man's work, the object of sibylline utterance or the cynosure of a concluding sentence. Essays such as "Literary History and Literary Modernity," which thematize history at length, are for that reason, in fact, more rather than less representative of an oeuvre that could with some justice be described as obsessed by the task of thinking romanticism, and literature in general, as historical events. But when the question of "distinguish[ing] rigorously between metaphorical and historical language," between a mystified and an authentic perception of the historical, appears with its full force (*BI*, 164), de Man writes more elliptically, and at a significantly higher pitch, than is usually the case. Clearly one purpose of these rhetorical performances is to exemplify the difficulty of rendering "true mourning," but the persistence with which the word *history* has attracted rhetorical energy in de Man's writing over three decades suggests the pressure of a pattern irreducible to what we ordinarily call the self-consciousness of an author or text. To interpret this disturbance in the de Manian text within the terms of that text is the burden of what follows.

For pragmatic reasons, I shall be centering attention on de Man's late essays on Kant and Schiller. With Kant, the aesthetic definitively enters the institution of philosophical discourse, and, according to de Man, the question of Kant's reception composes not just the philosophical possibility of aesthetic judgment, but also the political burden of critical thought: "For it is as a political force that the aesthetic still concerns us as one of the most powerful ideological drives to act upon the reality of history" (*RR*, 264). The late essays on German preromantic and romantic authors—on Kant, Schiller, Kleist, and Hegel—take as their target an understanding of romanticism deriving from Hegel, which situates Schiller's *Aesthetic Education of Man* ("the wellspring of romantic criticism," as René Wellek claims) on a path leading from subjective to objective idealism, from the *Critique of Judgment* to the *Lectures on Aesthetics*.[8] De Man refigures this teleological commonplace into an economy of demystification and regression in which the name "Schiller" operates as a personification of aesthetic ideology.[9] Produced by, and yet incommensurate with, the "historical" event of the *Critique of Judgment*, the "reception" of Kant takes its coordinates from Schiller's treatise, which in its turn figures the most disastrous of political possibilities. We are told at the end of de Man's late lecture draft, "Kant and Schiller," that Goebbels's misreading of Schiller in his 1929 novel *Michael* "does not differ essentially" from Schiller's misreading of Kant (*AI*, 155). In less dramatic, but perhaps equally significant ways, "Kant and Schiller" and "Kant's Materialism" also yield what are pretty much de Man's only explicit reflections on gender politics.

In negotiating de Man's invocation of Schiller, therefore, we engage the question of political criticism as a question of reception. That question returns upon itself as one of our reception of de Man, and of "de Man's" reception of "himself." The genial but genuine tone of accusation de Man adopts in "Kant and Schiller" as he reiterates one of the more venerable commonplaces of Schiller criticism—that Schiller lacks philosophical rigor, that he has misunderstood Kant, and so on—is not simply a pedagogical device designed to animate a semi-improvised lecture.[10] This personification is substituting for the dense pathos of essays like those on Kleist, Baudelaire, or Shelley and is ironically rehearsing the closure of reception: if Schiller anthropomorphizes the aesthetic, de Man anthropomorphizes the source of its error. The seductive promises of a certain monumental self-reflexivity are in place, as are those of more banal scenarios of naming and blaming. One will have no trouble imagining de Man exorcising his own Schillerian wartime journalism; and readers willing to repeat in full the Schillerian gesture will find in that image of human self-interrogation relief from the problem of figurative language to which de Man so ceaselessly attends. Our first task, therefore, is to gloss the shape and rationale of de Man's linguistic theme. To follow out that theme is to find ourselves entangled, before long, in questions of history, politics, and reception, and also to find ourselves poised for further reflection on the exemplary figure that, in the first part of this book, we found haunting the discourse of aesthetics and aesthetic nationalism: the figure of a (maternal) body, fragmenting into letters.

I

One tends to speak easily of the essential or radical figurativeness of language. The assumption often seems to be that this insight is easily borne, or even fundamentally inconsequent. Having renounced all metaphysical and representational naiveté, including, of course, the naiveté of believing that we could ever utterly renounce representational logic, metaphors of grounding, notions of truth and lie, and so on, we would, it seems, be in a position to forsake linguistic for other, more practical or obviously political topics. Versions of this pragmatic assurance surface repeatedly in contemporary criticism. And yet, if the radical figurativeness of language is suspected, or is even admitted as a possibility, all else in the de Manian narrative follows.

It follows, first, that the paradigmatic condition of reading is a condition of suspense between a literal and a figurative meaning. Since any literal meaning is vulnerable to being read as a figure for another meaning, itself a figure, and so on, language as trope must be understood as a process of circulation devoid of external support. Since, however, a meaning, in order to be read, must be taken in isolation from the possibility of tropological displacement, the condition of reading is structured by a double possibility: that of figuration, and that of propriety or reference. This difference—the difference between the figural and the proper—is itself that of figure. No external principle can regulate this difference a priori, since no referent can definitively ground tropological displacement. This is why de Man writes at the beginning of *Allegories of Reading* that "the grammatical model of the question becomes rhetorical not when we have, on the one hand, a literal meaning, and on the other hand a figural meaning, but when it is impossible to decide by grammatical or other linguistic devices which of the two meanings (that can be entirely incompatible) prevails"

(10). The figure that accounts for and describes the possibility of the difference between literal and figurative meaning is the figure of this difference's undecidability. Radical figuration implies the radical undecidability of figure. This undecidability defines, finally, the "text" (10) because there is no linguistic vantage point external to it. Undecidability is what is given to us to read, though by definition, it cannot necessarily be read. What is given to us to read is the possible impossibility of reading. This aporetic imperative generates the plot of de Man's theoretical text.

One consequence of rhetoric's radical suspension of meaning is that language can no longer be understood primarily as an intentional structure. The popular idea that deconstruction "makes no difference" because prejudices are irreducible and one has to make decisions anyway, forwards the kind of complacency that might be underwritten by substituting for rhetorical undecidability a phenomenological notion of "suspension" (*Aufhebung*), in which the referent is bracketed through an intentional act.[11] But intention directs itself toward meaning, and if all meaning is implicated in an undecidability of meaning arising from a process of semantic substitution, then this *process of substitution* is possibly indifferent to meaning and intention. Language as figuration cannot be reduced to a play of intentions because language's formal principle of articulation (or figuration) cannot be determinately motivated. We shall return to this problem in a moment—it is the problem of what de Man calls the materiality of language—but let us consider first another implication of radical figuration: the narrative or cognitive dimension of its error.

In order to be read, a figure must figure forth an aberrantly literal meaning. Rousseau's primitive man, on his way to language, sees another primitive man and experiences fear. Out of fear he exaggerates the other's size and invents a primitive metaphor, "giant." Since this metaphor has a proper meaning—fear—it is a proper metaphor, for all its referential inaccuracy. But fear is not actually a proper meaning, being "the result of a possible discrepancy between the outer and the inner properties of entities" (*AR*, 150). Metaphor, in coming into legibility, imposes meaning on undecidability (for "it remains an open question, for whoever is neither a paranoiac nor a fool, whether one can trust one's fellow man"): the metaphor "giant" "freezes hypothesis, or fiction, into fact and makes fear, itself a figural state of suspended meaning, into a definite, proper meaning devoid of alternatives" (*AR*, 151). This dense parable, which sets the stage for de Man's long and passionate engagement with Rousseau in *Allegories of Reading*, initiates figural narrative, the allegory of the (im)possibility of figure. An a priori condition of uncertainty has generated metaphor ("giant"), a reading self (by virtue of the internalized propriety of fear), and the possibility of referential denomination (the "giant" will be domesticated as a conceptual metaphor, "man"). Figuration betrays itself, obliterating its own radical figurativeness. Put slightly differently, the consequence of referential indetermination is insistent referentiality. Language, de Man insists, *must* refer. Like Marcel driven away from his books and out into the garden by his grandmother, like the critics who at the beginning of *Allegories of Reading* "cry out for the fresh air of referential meaning" (*AR*, 4), language turns away from its own figurativeness to produce literal meanings always marked in advance by the process of figuration that has produced them. Reference cannot be "avoided, bracketed, or reduced to being just one contingent property among others" (*AR*, 207). Werner Hamacher has thus been led to organize a powerful account of the de Manian system around the notion of an impossible and categorical referential imperative: "Language is imperative. It is imperative because its referential function gives the directions for possible reference, even if no referential meaning answers to it and though it corresponds to no referent."[12] One could supplement the imperative "Reference must occur" with a variant characterization: "Intentionality must occur." And the correlative of such imperatives is that "Reading must occur." The same principle of error that produces these effects of reference and intentionality also marks them with the necessary possibility of being read as mere figures. Referential indeterminacy "generates the illusion of a subject, a narrator, and a reader," and "the metaphor of temporality" (*AR*, 162). But since these illusions are figures of a figure, they bear within them their own critique. In this sense, they are self-deconstructive, but because the deconstruction cannot halt or avoid repeating the error it reads, "it engenders, in its turn, a supplementary figural superposition which narrates the unreadability of the prior narration" (*AR*, 205). This second-degree narrative is what de Man calls allegory. Of such narratives and their allegories, "one should remember that they are the unfolding and not the resolution of the chaotic uncertainty which Rousseau calls fear" (*AR*, 162).

Consequently, it is possible to think of critical philosophy as the thematic equivalent of allegory: a critique of trope that is enabled by the same spiral of error that produces referential illusion. The more rigorously the critique is pursued, the more surely it will reveal, unwittingly and to no epistemological profit to itself, the tropological process that enables it. And in the process, a certain limit to the notion of trope will appear:

> The passage from trope to performative . . . occurs always, and can only occur, by way of an epistemological critique of trope. The trope, the epistemology of tropes, allows for a critical discourse, a transcendental critical discourse, to emerge, which will push the notion of trope to an extreme, trying to saturate your whole field of language. But then certain linguistic elements will remain which the concept of trope cannot reach. (*AI*, 133)

The notion of the "performative" returns us to the topic we broached earlier: critical discourse's obligation to consider the possible indifference of substitutive pattern to semantic determination. Critical discourse is the critique of the possibility of trope—that is, of the figural structure that generates the epistemological field of truth and falsity as the task of judging literal and figural meaning. This narrative discovers undecidability as the condition of its possibility. Semantic undecidability implies the potential irrelevance of the principle of articulation to the meanings it articulates. Since "figure" names the conjunction of signification with a principle of substitution, the notion of figure must now be revised to signify "the alignment of a signification with any principle of linguistic articulation whatsoever, sensory or not. . . . The iconic, sensory, or, if one wishes, the aesthetic moment is not constitutive of figuration." Thus "the particular seduction of the figure is not necessarily that it creates an illusion of sensory pleasure, but that it creates an illusion of meaning" (*RR*, 115). Since the principle of articulation is possibly arbitrary, it becomes necessary to consider the role of a *performative* imposition of meaning on random difference. A catachretic prosopopoeia must "give face" to structural differences that can then be read as signs.[13] Figure must be figured. Such a collusion between figuration and positional power is not cognitively masterable, for it is radically inconsistent: "language posits and language means (since it articulates) but language cannot posit meaning; it can only reiterate (or reflect) it in its reconfirmed falsehood. Nor does the knowledge of this impossibility make it less possible" (*RR*, 117–18). The critique of trope finds its limit in its passage to a notion of language as performance. Twinned with that impossible performance is the possible randomness of the articulative patterns that will be yoked to meanings. This randomness of articulative pattern is what de Man, in his late texts, calls "materiality."

De Man's most elaborately showcased parable of the materiality of language is worth examining in some detail since it organizes his readings of Kant and, indirectly, his reading of Schiller. It is far beyond my means here to reproduce the dense argument of de Man's reading of the *Critique of Judgment* in "Phenomenality and Materiality in Kant" and in the short lecture "Kant's Materialism." For our purposes, it will suffice to note a few guiding themes, and "Kant's Materialism" holds particular interest for us, since in this text de Man sets out to correct a misreading of the role of the "empirical" in Kant by reevaluating the Kantian notion of affect. Kant seeks to resolve the divergence between form and content in the sublime by way of the affectivity of the subject. Thus, as Kant's rigorous transcendental critique of trope forces the emergence of a language of power (in his text's abrupt shift to a "dynamic" sublime), affective judgments take the place of rational judgments and we appear to reenter an empirical world of "assault, battle, and fright"—for in the dynamic sublime, mental faculties must struggle with nature, and an emotion such as admiration must do battle with another emotion, such as fear (*AI*, 122). However, this strategy is not entirely the "return of the empirical" it might seem. De Man claims that Kantian typologies of affect tend to take their organizing principle from the "dictionary" rather than from "experience," and that Kant is "often guided by external resemblances between words rather than by the inner resonances of emotion" (*AI*, 123). The Third *Critique's* elaborate contrast between surprise (*Verwunderung*) and admiration (*Bewunderung*), for instance, might well be underwritten by no better organizing principle than the accidental similarities and differences of signifiers (*AI*, 89). The dynamic sublime's concatenation of power and affect thus figures, as de Man reads it, language's performance of meaning.

The most sublime affect, Kant tells us, is in fact the absence of affect (*Affektlosigkeit*), a noble a-pathy linked in turn to the grandeur of architecture. This conclusion surfaces in the midst of a set of dictionary discriminations between sublime, active, male affects and beautiful, languorous, female ones. De Man remarks,

The interpretation of the architectonic as a principle of masculine virility, as pure macho of the German variety (whatever the word may be), seems inevitable. But to quote Derrida: "When erection is at stake, one should never be too much in a

hurry—one should let things take their course (*il faut laisser la chose se faire*)." . . .
If erection is indeed "la chose," then it is likely to be anything but what one—or
should I say men?—think(s) it to be. (*AI*, 126)

Eventually I shall be reinvoking these comments, but consider for now
their ultimate object, an extraordinary paragraph in which Kant illustrates
a general principle of aesthetic judgment: natural objects capable of producing sublime effects must be considered from a radically nonteleological
viewpoint. Kant provides as examples two landscapes and a human body:

Therefore, when we call the sight of the starry sky *sublime*, we must not base our
judgment upon any concepts of worlds that are inhabited by rational beings, and
then [conceive of] the bright dots that we see occupying the space above us as being these worlds' suns, moved in orbits prescribed for them with great purposiveness; but we must base our judgment regarding it merely on how we see it [*wie
man ihn sieht*], as a vast vault encompassing everything, and merely under this presentation may we posit the sublimity that a pure aesthetic judgment attributes to
this object. In the same way, when we judge the sight of the ocean we must not do
so on the basis of how we *think* it, enriched with all sorts of knowledge which we
possess (but which is not contained in the direct intuition), e.g., as a vast realm of
aquatic creatures, or as the great reservoir supplying the water for the vapors that
impregnate the air with clouds for the benefit of the land, or again as an element
that, while separating continents from one another, yet makes possible the greatest communication among them; for all such judgments will be teleological. Instead we must be able to view the ocean as poets do, merely in terms of what manifests itself to the eye [*was der Augenschein zeigt*]—e.g., if it is calm, as a clear
mirror of water bounded only by the sky; or, if it is turbulent, as being like an
abyss threatening to engulf everything—and yet find it sublime. The same applies
to the sublime and beautiful in the human figure. Here, too, we must not have in
mind, as bases determining our judgment, concepts of the purposes *for which* man
has all his limbs [*wozu alle seine Gliedmassen da sind*].[14]

If one takes this passage at its word, following its (impossible) injunction
to see nonteleologically, then "the only word that comes to mind" to describe it, de Man writes, "is that of a *material* vision" (*AI*, 82). The passage
resembles but differs decisively from romantic pairings of mind and nature: "No mind is involved in the Kantian vision of ocean and heaven. To
the extent that any mind, any judgment, intervenes, it is in error—for it
is not the case that heaven is a vault or that the horizon bounds the ocean
like the walls of a building." The eye sees only what the eye sees, as the

tautology of *Augenschein* indicates. This *Schein* is thus neither illusory nor real, and consequently Kant's architectonic figures, read aesthetically, are not figures: "Heaven and ocean as building are a priori, previous to any understanding, to any exchange or anthropomorphism. . . . Kant's vision can therefore hardly be called literal, which would imply its possible figuralization or symbolization by an act of judgment" (*AI*, 82). "It is in no way possible to think of this stony gaze as an address or an apostrophe," de Man adds in "Kant's Materialism." "The dynamics of the sublime mark the moment when the infinite is frozen into the materiality of stone, when no pathos, anxiety or sympathy is conceivable; it is indeed the moment of a-pathos or apathy, as the complete loss of the symbolic" (*AI*, 127).

Aligning this materiality with the scene's optical and architectonic thematics, de Man thereby coordinates the "material" with the category it traditionally opposes, the "formal." A nonteleological consideration of the architectonic would not imply its total disintegration: "sea and heaven, as the poets see them, are more than ever buildings." However, "it is no longer certain that they are articulated [*gegliedert*]" (*AI*, 88). What is lost is not all definition, as would be the case in a classical postulate of matter without form, matter as pure potentiality; rather, what is lost is the possibility of establishing an internal necessity for the patterns of relations that allow signs to function as signs. The concatenation of matter and form in "aesthetic vision" produces, within the context of organic structure that informs Kant's critical enterprise, a narrative of dismemberment that ceases at minimal units of form: the vault of the heavens; the limbs (*Glieder*) of the body; the letters of a word[15]:

We must, in short, consider our limbs, hands, toes, breasts, or what Montaigne so cheerfully referred to as "Monsieur ma partie," in themselves, severed from the organic unity of the body, the way the poets look at the oceans, severed from their geographical place on earth. We must, in other words, disarticulate, mutilate the body in a way that is much closer to Kleist than to Winckelmann, though close enough to the violent end that happened to befall both of them. . . . From the phenomenality of the aesthetic (which is always based on an adequacy of the mind to its physical object, based on what is referred to, in the definition of the sublime, as the concrete representation of ideas—*Darstellung der Ideen*) we have moved to the pure materiality of *Augenschein*, of aesthetic vision. . . . To the dismemberment of the body corresponds a dismemberment of language, as meaning-producing tropes are replaced by the fragmentation of sentences and propositions into discrete words, or the fragmentation of words into syllables or finally letters. (*AI*, 88–89).

One may hypothesize that a similarly fragmenting "aesthetic vision" helped produce Matthew Arnold's image of the "girl named Wragg" that we analyzed in the previous chapter, decomposing Arnold's aestheticized formalism into a play of letters. How aesthetic vision ties into, or transforms itself into, questions of gender is a problem to which we shall return. At present, we need to continue to elaborate the strange career of language within the aesthetic problematic. For to view a "letter" nonteleologically would not be to view it as part of an alphabet, or as the instrument of a sign. Kant's eye thus sees at the heart of the aesthetic "the absolute randomness of language, prior to any figuration or meaning" (*AR*, 299). If we graft on another of de Man's terms, we can say that this eye is seeing history.

not sure about this leap!

II

Earlier we had occasion to note the elliptical intensity with which de Man's writing invokes the term "history"; and at this point we are better prepared to insist that those charged figures are the by-product of a critique that, far from repressing or trivializing the notion of history, grants it the dignity of being what Fredric Jameson's vocabulary would render as "the untranscendable limit of our understanding in general and our textual interpretations in particular."[16] Our everyday post-Enlightenment discrimination between history and fiction reflects (in starkly institutionalized form) our desire to locate history in the place of truth, and de Man, after his fashion, is true to this desire. Hence, in fact, his notorious resistance to period terms and genetic historicisms: "Such a narrative can only be metaphorical, and history is not fiction" (*BI*, 163). History is precisely *not* trope, and there is a sense in which history is thus the site of truth: not of a stable, transcendent *Wahrheit*, opposable to error in a cognitive system, but of what de Man, citing Hölderlin, liked to call *das Wahre*, "what is bound to take place" (*CW*, 221). History names that which, as event, resists figuration. Aphoristic claims such as Jameson's "history is what hurts" (102) derive their rhetorical force from a superficially similar invocation of the nonfigurative—but such tropes are unable to stand up to rhetorical critique, which must at a certain point consider pathos (i.e., the constitution of a meaning or an identity out of "what hurts") as a possible product of rhetorical systems. As we have seen, neither genetic narratives nor pathetic terminologies are foreign to rhetorical critique, which must reiterate versions of the error it interrogates. However, the critique cannot be halted by such figures.

History must rather be "true" in the sense of being an *event* that leaves a mark on tropological systems of truth and falsehood. Such an event must be external to the circulation of meaning, but it must also disrupt, alter, and generate meaning. In other words, the event is historical to the extent that it is linguistic, not empirical. When de Man writes that "the bases for historical knowledge are not empirical facts but written texts, even if these texts masquerade in the guise of wars or revolutions" (*BI*, 165), he does not simply have in mind the truism that texts provide our access to the past; he is gesturing toward the inscriptive violence with which meaning—a call to interpretation—*occurs*. Wars and revolutions are historical precisely to the extent that they inscribe the necessity of a future understanding; "in themselves," whatever their pathetic rhetorical charge, death or pain or catastrophe do not possess the slightest historicity. And since the rhetorical critique has removed all illusion that natural or phenomenalizable processes generate meaning, history can only occur in the passage from a cognitive to a performative dimension of language. As the mark of a performative—of a disruptive, impossible "performance" of meaning—the historical event is an inscription, not an identity; and its force, being irreducible to meaning, must be thought of as random.[17]

The task of reading, then, is to take account of the random play of the letter that dis-figures the structure of comprehension that tropes allow. A rhetorical reading is in this sense profoundly historical in orientation, and history is also the trace of a resistance that the reading encounters within its own possibility. De Man's texts register and slide away from the historical, reinscribing, as we saw earlier, the pathos they renounce in the very asceticism with which they invoke history.[18] In remarking history, theory resists itself. History is the site of resistance: the truth of history, for theory, can only be conveyed as a stutter bearing the unspeakable gravity of a trauma. For, as Cathy Caruth has remarked, trauma may be thought as "a symptom of history," precisely insofar as the traumatic dream or flashback, recurring against the sufferer's will and without symbolic distortion, is "*true* to the event," being "absolutely literal, unassimilable to associative chains of meaning."[19] This is also to say, however, that the traumatic truth is a crisis of truth: its literalness is not that of an experience one can possess, but of an inscription that possesses, soliciting a deferred and belated, hence historical, act of understanding. "The historical power of the trauma," Caruth writes, "is not just that the experience is repeated after its forgetting, but that it is only in and through an inherent forgetting that it is first experienced at all. . . . For history to be a history of trauma means that it is referential precisely to the extent that it is not fully perceived as it occurs; or, to put it somewhat differently, that a history can be grasped only in the very inaccessibility of its occurrence" (7).[20]

If theory has no choice but to resist itself at such moments, betraying as well as remarking the historical event, the difference between critique and ideology, reading and reception, will always be potentially unreadable. And since the possibility of reading can never be taken for granted, ideology presents itself as an irreducible reserve, an insistent (though never absolute) occlusion of history as material inscription. In this sense, "ideology," for de Man as for Althusser, "has no history," which is of course not to say that ideologies escape historical deformation—quite the contrary.[21] In a moment I shall take up the effects that this reserve of error performs within the dynamic of de Man's own reception, but here I wish to insist on the theoretical and historical unfolding of resistance as aesthetic ideology, "one of the most powerful drives to act upon the reality of history" (*RR*, 264).[22] If critique necessarily erects a text into an example— Schiller, say, into a figure for the kind of recuperation that de Man calls "reception"—this in no way relieves critique of the task of technically accounting for the production of a full-scale ideology of the aesthetic, one that closes off "the road that goes from . . . *Schein* to the notion of materiality" (*AI*, 152) and that institutionalizes aesthetic judgment as "aesthetic education," "the articulation of history with formally arrived-at truth" (*RR*, 276). History, in the full unfolding of the model, will become aesthetic form rather than formal disarticulation. This is the final fallout of "the trap of an aesthetic education which inevitably confuses dismemberment of language by the power of the letter with the gracefulness of a dance" (*RR*, 290). Rewriting the Kantian sublime in his early essay "Vom Erhabenen," and subsequently elaborating the aesthetic into a full-fledged political system in *On the Aesthetic Education of Man* (1795), Schiller domesticates Kant's critique by reproducing it as idealist empiricism.[23] Or, in the terms we have been elaborating here, aesthetic ideology evades language's trauma of meaning by reinforcing the tropological structures that language provides.

I shall be examining Schiller's text in the final section of this chapter, and at this point I wish only to recall the main lines of de Man's semi-improvised critique. The paradox that de Man addresses, and accounts for, is that an allegiance to the empirical makes possible the most thoroughgoing idealism, and that "an ideology of organic form," as Cynthia Chase notes, can go hand in hand with a "commitment to sheer mechanical technical power" ("Trappings," 62). A pragmatic deflation of linguistic issues leads to ever more coercive linguistic structuration. The aesthetic renders language a property of the world, and in doing so, it gives the world over to the indifferent cruelty of tropological structures fundamentally alien to the universe of meaning they articulate. De Man's critique of Schiller's "Vom Erhabenen" makes two points: first, that Schiller grounds figural pattern in the phenomenal world by understanding chiasmic oppositions and transfers as the expression of drives (*Triebe*); and second (and here is the main thrust of the argument), that Schiller polarizes Kant's text, re-coding the troubled passage from a "mathematical" to a "dynamic" sublime as a binary opposition between a "theoretical" and a "practical" sublime. In Schiller's mature text, the *Aesthetic Education*, this opposition becomes a chiasmic exchange between a form-drive (*Formtrieb*), allied with reason, law, and other totalizing imperatives, and a sensual drive (*sinnlicher Trieb* or *Stofftrieb*), which pursues the sensuous appeal of the moment. The *Formtrieb* and the *Stofftrieb* achieve synthesis thanks to what Schiller calls *Wechselwirkung*, "reciprocal action": a chiasmus that, given its purely formal nature, has no referential necessity and is forced to derive its necessity from the empirical fact of human existence.[24] Language is thus grounded in the "human," and out of this synthesis, Schiller derives the most humanistic of drives, at once the sign, the cause, and the effect of the human, the play-drive or *Spieltrieb*, directed at the appearance, *Schein*.

In short, Schiller's text produces and polices a representational concept of language, and the force of de Man's critique lies in its insistence on the formal structure of this linguistic model. The phenomenal world of "reality" appears to direct the mimetic exchange but can only do so through binary oppositions (such as that between "language" and "reality") that are necessarily linguistic. For critical thought must at a certain point recognize mimesis as a trope: the formal patterns that permit the polarization and valorization of terms such as empirical and ideal, particular and general, are not natural—that is, self-evident and self-identical—but cognitive or tropological. A discourse that uncritically naturalizes linguistic structures will thus shuttle between opposites that imply each other. The initial privilege granted the phenomenal world can be—and is—revoked by chiasmic inversion: from a valorization of the empirical, one passes with ease to a celebration of the spiritual. Language, initially domesticated as a reflection of empirical drives or intentions, can now receive inverse valuation as a prefiguration of the ideal. Thus the aesthetic is both domesticated and granted exemplarity—in Schiller's case to the point of making aesthetic harmony the telos of individual and collective pedagogy, and a model for the State. The synecdochic power of trope guarantees the passage from individual to nation, artwork to culture, pedagogy to politics; and the logical end to the system is the aesthetic state, the *Staat des schönen Scheins*, which is for Schiller an ideal, realized only in a beautiful soul or within a circle of friends (27.12), but which is in its turn vulnerable to tropological reinforcement and empiricization. It is thus that de Man can claim that Goebbels's vulgarization of Schiller repeats, however crudely, the essential gesture of Schiller's own text:

The statesman is an artist too. For him the people is neither more nor less than what stone is for the sculptor. . . . Politics are the plastic art of the State, just as painting is the plastic art of color. This is why politics without the people, or even against the people, is sheer nonsense. To shape a People out of the masses, and a State out of the People, this has always been the deepest intention of politics in the true sense.[25]

The continuity between statesman and artist, life and art, human being and aesthetic object, so ferocious as to expunge any overt recognition of violence (there can be no politics "against the people" in a structure of such symmetry), violates every cautious, humanistic gesture to be found in the *Aesthetic Education*. But Schiller's aesthetic state is nonetheless finding its degraded realization here, and the lethal consequences of that realization are not irrelevant to (though of course also not simply the "result" of) the rhetorical predicament under examination. When, thirty years after the publication of Schiller's treatise, Clausewitz erected *Wechselwirkung* into the structural dynamic of war in *Vom Kriege* (*On War*; 1832), he was recognizing and elaborating the violent possibilities of a totalizing chiasmus that can never properly account for itself: a figure in which each turn (*Wechsel*) performs (*wirkt*) more than it can control—except through another *Wechsel*, and so on. "A reciprocal action [*Wechselwirkung*] is thus started which must lead, in theory, to extremes [zum Äußersten]."[26] The "human," as a principle of closure, names an effacement of this condition of instability, not least, as de Man remarks in closing "Kant and Schiller," when the "human" itself discovers the necessity of deriving its closure from binary valorizations: "Just as the sensory becomes without tension the metaphor for reason, in Schiller, woman becomes without oppression a metaphor for man" (*AI*, 154). The cost of such Clausewitzian spirals in real violence and actual oppression can be as enormous or as modest, as literal or as symbolic, as any particular context happens to occasion. The tropological patterns that make such distributions of meaning possible are essentially indifferent to the notion of the human they enable. It is the specter of such indifference that humanism seeks to exorcise by appropriating and naturalizing linguistic structures, a gesture that sustains itself only in the mode of violent repetition, since the principle of its success is also that of its disarticulation. A threat is being taken as a solution, and the meaning and the performance of such a constitutive act of expulsion must thus ultimately be at odds.[27]

III

The affect proper to the irruption of "historical modes of language power" is more often than not, in the de Manian corpus, terror. Confronted with the possibility of the "uncontrollable power of the letter as inscription," Saussure proceeds with a caution that "supports the assumption of a terror glimpsed" (*RT*, 37). The vision of sea and heavens is "a terrifying moment in a sense—terrifying for Kant, since the entire enterprise of philosophy is involved in it"—though de Man hastens to discredit the idea of Kant "shuddering in his mind" as he scribbled, "Any literalism there would not be called for. It is terrifying in a way we don't know" (*AI*, 134). For we are, after all, speaking not of empirical conditions of danger, but of the peculiar predicament of *reading*, staged here as the aesthetic question of the sublime. In the de Manian allegory of this predicament, (the figure of) "literal" affect derives, as we have seen, from the effacement of undecidability that produces the possibility of literal meaning, which is to say the possibility of trope. Rhetorical critique, in narrating its scrupulously reductive allegory, thematizes affect as a dimension of language's resistance to the random violence of the inscription. Rousseau's parable of primitive man, experiencing fear in the face of language's event, is indeed a paradigmatic text for the de Manian narrative. Fear is a privileged affect in a discourse about resistance—though any fear one can *experience* in reading lags behind the uncertainty that makes it possible. For, before becoming properly affective, we recall, fear was an impersonal epistemological suspension of semantic determination (*AR*, 150–51): an allegorical personification of reading per se, and thus perhaps another figure for the "true mourning" or nonempirical "terror" that history occasions.

It is thus perhaps also no accident that this figure of "fear," so crucial to the narrative of *Allegories of Reading*, should provide the axis for one of the most densely intertextual negotiations in de Man's oeuvre.[28] A few years earlier, in "The Rhetoric of Blindness," de Man had taken issue with Derrida's reading of the covert propriety of Rousseau's originary "giant" metaphor—which professes nonreferentiality but actually denotes a proper and internalized meaning, fear. "Rousseau's text has no blind spots," de Man had claimed: Rousseau's text knows the truth of radical figuration, and if the spontaneous metaphor "giant" finds its proper meaning in fear, this is simply because Rousseau has made a "mistake" in selecting fear to exemplify metaphor. "The choice of the wrong example to illustrate metaphor (fear instead of pity) is a mistake, not a blind spot" (*BI*, 139n). When *Allegories of Reading* recodes fear as the exemplary affect, structured like a trope that defaces its own figurativeness, de Man recodes the "mistake" as the undecidability between "mistake" and "error": the metaphor *must* deface itself to compose itself—though its instantiation may also be a random mistake. De Man's reading of fear as mistake, by implication, was a mistaking of error spurred by an error of mistaking. "If 'mistake' is random and contingent . . . and 'error' is systematic and compulsive . . . then I have stated, in a variety of terminologies, the impossibility of ever coming to rest on one or the other side of this distinction," de Man remarks in a late text, recalling his "rash assertion" in "The Rhetoric of Blindness" as an example of mistaking error for mistake.[29] The (allegorical) nexus is fear—a fear that arrives too late to witness its own traumatic origin. And the stakes of mistake are ethical–political as well as epistemological.

Ideology, "the confusion of linguistic with natural reality, of reference with phenomenalism" (*RT*, 11), is the mistaken error built into language: "It is true that tropes are the producers of ideologies that are no longer true" (*RR*, 242). "No degree of knowledge can ever stop this madness, for it is the madness of words" (*RR*, 122). We have no choice but to apostrophize the dead, monumentalize the text, phenomenalize the sign. And to the extent that the error is an error, its undoing is equally inevitable: an epistemological critique of trope is "in no one's power to evade" (*RT*, 69), even though the critique will discover nothing more than the possible mistakenness of its error. Since we as reading subjects are the products of this language machine, the exigent contingency of its operation is replayed on the level of ethics. We cannot, de Man tells us, halt the madness of prosopopeia; however, we do not have to delude ourselves into taking this process as a source of value. Such a belief "leads to a misreading that can and should be discarded, unlike the coercive 'forgetting' that Shelley's poem analytically thematizes." But the discardable misreading then becomes difficult or impossible to discard: the "aesthetification of texts" describes also "their use, as in this essay, for the assertion of methodological claims made all the more pious by their denial of piety" (*RR*, 122). And so it goes: a spiral of error that draws within it our ethical selves and the consciousness in which we cannot help but believe. As the "product" of language's error, we have no choice but to continue to choose. The ethical tonality of de Man's writing reiterates the mistaken truth of error.

The rigor with which de Man stages this predicament is what makes his work so difficult to read. One common response is to aestheticize it by repressing de Man's affirmation of language's referential drive, and by claiming that de Manian theory teaches political or ethical apathy by projecting "all those paralytic feelings of the literary onto the terrain of society and history" (Lentricchia, 50). A more attentive reading discovers, with J. Hillis Miller, that under the terms of de Man's thought the reader "*must* take responsibility for (the reading) and for its consequences in the personal, social, and political worlds."[30] To adapt Kafka's phrase, in the de Manian universe, there is an infinity of "paralysis"—but not for us. "Allegories are always ethical" precisely insofar as they deconstruct the illusions of pathos without being able to halt their referential drive (*AR*, 206). Their negative knowledge notwithstanding, they "speak out with the referential efficacy of a *praxis*" (*AR*, 208–9): it is impossible to dwell within undecidability. Reading must take place, and to read is to judge. Miller is correct to extend the consequences of this model to the concerns of practical reason. Such is, for that matter, the entire burden of aesthetic judgment: a burden produced, rather than negated, by the contradictory imperative of language. We must take responsibility, but responsibility is not ours to be taken. Responsibility is rather to be thought as exposure to alterity: to a past one never experienced, and to a future one will never inhabit. Responsibility is the risk of an uninsurable act of reading.[31]

The intense, bleak pathos that recurs in de Man's work is responding to the tenacity with which he pursues the impossible, ethical task of reading. In its full elaboration, the de Manian system—and in its inevitable error, it is a system, teachable and generalizable, "the universal theory of the impossibility of theory" (*RT*, 19)—rewrites its intentionality in the mode of the pathetic. The system has accounted for this apparent regression long ago: such pathos repeats the illusory hypostatization of "the deconstructive passion of a subject" (*AR*, 199). Ethics, the rejection of pathos, relapses into pathos in the knowledge that what one says can never necessarily be what one does. And the subject whose passion could animate such a knowledge would be a "giant" indeed: "as far beyond pleasure and pain as he is beyond good and evil, or, for that matter, beyond strength and weakness. His consciousness is neither happy nor unhappy, nor does he possess any power. He remains however a center of authority to the extent that the very destructiveness of his ascetic reading testifies to the validity of his interpretation" (*AR*, 173–74). He would incarnate the pathos of a-pathy, the sublime *Affektlosigkeit* of a subjectivity that recuperates phallic interiority in the mode of invulnerable impotence. He would derive castration out of disarticulation, achieving thereby the funereal grandeur of an architectonic erection.

Thus to the pathos deriving from the power of de Man's thought corresponds the monumentalization of de Man as teacher, thinker, and text. From the perspective of rhetorical critique, it makes little difference whether this monumentalization occurs in the mode of celebration or defiance, whether de Man's text is fetishized and imitated, or castigated and ritually sacrificed. From this perspective, it is also of relative indifference whether one speaks of institutional effect or libidinal investment: of the professionalization of theory, or the coercion of charisma. Both these modes of recuperation appear united with exemplary force in the funereally monumental issue of *Yale French Studies* dedicated to de Man, and an essay in that issue by Carol Jacobs provides an exemplary trope for the paradoxes that control his reception: de Man "may offer us a mirror of sorts, but his writings . . . are an aegis to which the head of the Medusa is affixed and which we contemplate at our own risk."[32] Jacobs is analyzing Percy Shelley's ekphrastic poem "On the Medusa of Leonardo da Vinci in the Florentine Gallery," and her trope for de Man and his theory is a shrewd gesture of homage. Her reading of Shelley proposes "two ways . . . of looking at the Medusa. The one allows the spectator to regard it from a safe distance, as object; the other draws the beholder into a conception of the Medusa as the performance of a radical figural transformation, of itself, of the beholder, of the language that attempts to represent it" (172). Those "two ways" of looking correspond to the double turn of figure in de Man's theoretical narrative, and by representing de Man's text as a shield with the Medusa's head affixed (and thus implicitly characterizing de Man as Athena, the shield's bearer), Jacobs implies two things: first, that the theory that accounts for such doubleness is itself doubled and self-resistant—a source of terror, but also a sheltering shield; and second, that the critic who seeks to read like de Man inevitably monumentalizes de Man (and thus "theory"). The theory, as we have seen, concurs: an allegory of reading that begins in "fear" predicts—and performs—its own reception as petrifying and petrified. Fear becomes the monumental figure of fear. In this sense, the Medusa's head, which simultaneously offers us the face of terror and the consolation of face, is a paradigmatic figure of theory's reception.

In Neil Hertz's terminology, the Medusa's head may be taken as an exemplary "lurid figure"—that is, a "disfigured specular double of the subject of pathos" of the sort that Hertz tracks throughout de Man's theoretical writing:

The attempt to dwell, speculatively, on the difference between language as meaning and language as performance cannot issue in a coolly univocal discourse: instead, the effort will trigger what I earlier called a pathos of uncertain agency, in which questions of intelligibility will be reinscribed as questions of activity or passivity, guilt or innocence and play themselves out in compulsively repeated figures. De Man has to warn himself and his readers against this pathos, for it will appear as a distraction: it will never be quite what he is talking about. But he can neither avoid falling into it, nor—and this is a stronger claim—can he or any other reader make do without it.[33]

In their most "lurid" instantiation, these "compulsively repeated figures" turn out to be hanging or dead maternal figures—figures recalling the Medusa's head as read by Freud, which draws on the horror (*Grauen*) that accompanies the (male) subject's glimpse of the mother's genitals.[34] These figures translate linguistic undecidability into the idiom of the fetish. The fetish is at once the memorial (*Denkmal*) of a trauma and a defense or shield against trauma; it erects itself as the visible sign of a "lack" that in turn must be taken or read as such before the fetish can come into being. Like Rousseau's "giant" metaphor, in other words, the fetish transforms a condition of undecidability into a drama of presence and absence: a drama charged with erotic as well as epistemological possibility. "Writing," de Man writes, "always includes the moment of dispossession in favor of the arbitrary power of the signifier and from the point of view of the subject, this can only be experienced as a dismemberment, a beheading or a castration" (*AR*, 296). In and as the lurid figure of the Medusa, the subject records its "experience" of the power of the signifier, or what de Man's late texts call the materiality of the letter. "Dissemination will always have threatened signification there," Derrida writes of the fetish, as we recalled when we dared a brief glance at Medusa's head in this book's introduction; yet the fetish nonetheless transforms the stony terror of random form into a petrification that consoles even as it frightens ("for becoming stiff [*das Starrwerden*] means an erection," Freud writes, explicating the double character of the Medusa's threat, "thus in the original situation it offers a consolation to the spectator: he is still in possession of a penis, and the stiffening reassures him of the fact").[35] In the institutional context of theory's reception, we would say that in the mirror of Medusa, the figure of a master "as far beyond pleasure and pain as he is beyond good and evil" sparks a fantasy of reification and contagion that is more wishful than scary, insofar as the Medusa's petrifying gaze betokens the performance of that identification with the affectless master which the ephebe desires. The fetish frightens and consoles, eliciting love and aggressivity. As fetish, theory becomes the master as a monstrous and beloved, invulnerable and decapitated maternal figure—a specular double for the reader, and thus the cynosure of an intersubjective drama of projection and internalization, submission and empowerment. Highly aestheticized versions of the Medusa's head of theory may be imagined, as Schiller demonstrates in the course of his revision of Kant in the *Aesthetic Education*.

IV

De Man's interpretation of Schiller, as we have seen, centers on Schiller's uncritical deployment of tropological structure as a defense against trope. Imposing rigid polarities that stabilize and naturalize differences, Schiller's text evades the perils of aesthetic *Schein* by relegating language to a mimetic role:

[Kant's *Augenschein* is] certainly not in opposition to reality, but was precisely what we see and as such more real than anything else, though it is reality which exists on the level of vision. . . . And [in the case of both Kant and Hegel] there is a road that goes from this notion of *Schein* to the notion of materiality. Such a road cannot be found in Schiller, and that is why for Schiller the concept of art, which at that moment is mentioned and is stressed, will always and without reservation be a concept of art as imitation, as *nachahmende Kunst. (AI, 152)*

That last claim, although correct, is vulnerable to the charge of not being sufficiently nuanced. Schiller's notion of *Schein* appears in the treatise's penultimate letter as the outward sign (*Phänomen*) of the psyche's aesthetic mode. As such, the object of the play-drive, aesthetic *Schein* is in one sense radically antimimetic: although Being (*Dasein, Wesen*) proceeds from nature, *Schein* proceeds from man. Any appearance that pretends to (natural) being or (referential) truth is not aesthetic *Schein*, or is not being perceived aesthetically. In this sense, *Schein* is nonreferential, though in another sense, it is the most referential of signs, because it refers to the Human. Obeying the classic maneuvers of what Derrida has called "economimesis," Schiller's text thus recuperates mimesis by way of an analogical chain leading from *Schein* to Man to what Schiller sometimes calls "Nature" and sometimes "Absolute Being" or "the Godhead." This covert imitative chain incites the return of the very language of mimesis that the text denies. The binary opposition between *Schein* and *Wesen*, appearance and reality, is maintained with such enthusiasm in Schiller's text that the opposite of the real drifts implacably into its classical role of being an image of the real, and thus with no apparent sense of contradiction, Schiller can indeed write that the *Spieltrieb* is followed by the "shaping spirit of imitation [*nachahmende Bildungstrieb*]" (26.7). De Man is not wrong, but the maneuvers of Schiller's idealist empiricism are more complex than "Kant and Schiller" allows for. If no road leads to the "material" in Schiller, what signs mark, at least, the road's closure?

One way to pursue the track of *Schein* would be to examine the origins of the drive proper to it, the *Spieltrieb*, which makes its appearance near the middle of Schiller's treatise under curious conditions. Schiller has just identified the principle of chiasmus, *Wechselwirkung*, with the principle of the human, and he is now moving from his version of transcendental critique to more empirical considerations. A pure *Wechselwirkung* between man's formal drive and his sensory drive exists only as an ideal, as "the Idea of Human Nature" (14.2); in the empirical world, we can only approach this ideal asymptotically, through time. Schiller is then faced with the question of what enables the asymptotic approach. And though at other points in the treatise originary questions are dismissed as precritical distractions, here we are offered a curiously empirical and ambiguous ontological fable. Its telling involves Schiller in his most extended recourse, in this text, to the subjunctive mood:

So long as man only feels, his Person, or his absolute existence, remains a mystery to him; and so long as he only thinks, his existence in time, or his Condition, does likewise. Should there be cases, however [*Gäbe es aber Fälle*] in which he were to have this twofold experience simultaneously . . . then he would in such cases, and in such cases only, have a complete intuition of his human nature, and the object [*Gegenstand*] which afforded him this intuition would become for him a symbol [*würde ihm zu einem Symbol*] of his accomplished destiny, and, in consequence (since this is only to be attained in the totality of time), serve him as a manifestation of the Infinite.

Assuming that cases of this sort could actually occur in experience [*Vorausgesetzt, dass Fälle dieser Art in der Erfahrung vorkommen können*], they would awaken in him a new drive, which, precisely because the other two drives cooperate within it, would be opposed to each of them considered separately and could justifiably count as a new drive. (14.2–3)

The subjunctive, I think, is taking up the strain felt by a passage that does not entirely want to be what it is—the account of a revelation. Of Schiller's several accounts of the relation between ideal and real, this version, offered at a crucial point in the treatise, is coming close to proposing a *Schein* that precedes and incites the drive proper to it. Before man can become man he must experience an intuition of man, and such an intuition can only be had in the presence of a *Schein* that by the same token does not yet properly exist. Schiller's essentially theocentric system would counter here with the claim that the "human" exists always already in potentia, as a promise or prefiguration (*Anlage*) at the "origin" of humanity (4.2); that is the sense in which the "case" postulated in Letter 14 would merely "awaken" rather than "create" the *Spieltrieb*. For though the transformation of a mere *Gegenstand* into the specular, and spectacular, promise of a *Symbol* suggests a dramatic positional act on man's part, here, as elsewhere, Schiller's Fichtean gestures are actually being controlled by a more classic model of prefiguration and fulfillment. But the subjunctive mood of the passage signals discomfort. All of a sudden the prefiguration of the human seems vulnerable, at the moment of its instantiation, to chance—to the possibility that the two drives will just happen to coincide exactly, at some luminous but fundamentally unpredictable moment—in which case *schöner Schein* would be a promise of destiny blind to its own randomness. Schiller's text has no interest in pursuing this possibility, of course; but enough de Manian—or, according to de Man, Kantian—burdens are borne by this "case" or *Fall* to require a ceremony of exorcism, which takes place in the treatise's next letter.

For if it can only be postulated that "cases of this sort" occur in experience, Schiller's text can at least offer a certainty on the level of its own engagement with the *Fall* of the aesthetic. In the wake of a long discussion of the beautiful, Schiller invokes the example of the Greeks, a people whose only error in the realm of the aesthetic was to "transfer to Olympus what was meant to be realized on earth" (15.9). In Olympus, beauty itself gains a face, and Schiller's letter closes with a vision that operates rhetorically, and to some extent thematically, as a "symbol of man's accomplished destiny":

Inspired by this spirit, the Greeks effaced from the features of their ideal physiognomy, together with inclination, every trace of volition too; or rather they made both indiscernible, for they knew how to fuse them in the most intimate union. It is not Grace, nor is it yet Dignity, which speaks to us from the superb countenance of a Juno Ludovisi; it is neither the one nor the other because it is both at once.

While the woman-god demands our veneration, the god-like woman kindles our love; but even as we abandon ourselves in ecstasy to her heavenly grace, her celestial self-sufficiency [*Selbstgenügsamkeit*] makes us recoil in terror. The whole figure reposes and dwells in itself, a creation completely self-contained, and, as if existing beyond space, neither yielding nor resisting; here is no force to contend with force, no frailty where temporality might break in. Irresistibly moved and drawn by those former qualities, kept at a distance by these latter, we find ourselves at one and the same time in a state of utter repose and supreme agitation, and there results that wondrous stirring of the heart for which the understanding has no concept nor speech any name. (15.9)

Throughout the *Aesthetic Education*, classical statuary bears a heavy figurative burden, representing the intersection of form and matter, meaning and medium, or, most generally, reason and phenomenality, the articulation of which composes the text's philosophical and political task. The fact that the nobility of the past can be preserved "in meaningful stone" (9.4), "stamped in silent stone" (9.6), means not only that atemporal Form, phenomenalized in art, can intersect the temporal world, but that the aesthetic can underwrite and direct political history. The aesthetic support (*Stütze*) which will ensure the endurance of the political world as we know it while laboring (eternally) at its transformation into the Aesthetic State (3.4), obtains a face and a name as the Juno Ludovisi (Figure 2).

Schiller's treatise has at this point strayed considerably from Kant's dry, abstract postulation of the "ideal of beauty" as a "human figure" capable of summing up "the visible expression of moral ideas": "The correctness of such an ideal of beauty," Kant continues, "is proved by its not permitting any charm of sense [*Sinnenreiz*] to be mingled with the liking for its object, while yet making us take a great interest in it" (84). The *Reiz* of Schiller's Juno, however, is similar to that of the human figure whom Freud in his turn was to conjure up as an ideal of narcissism: the woman whose "self-sufficiency [*Selbstgenügsamkeit*]" produces her "great charm [*Reiz*]," which finds its "reverse side" in her "enigmatic being."[36] Frozen into monumental stone, *schöner Schein* appears personified in the *Aesthetic Education* as an affectless, narcissistic god-woman (*gottgleiche Weib, weibliche Gott*), who substitutes her aesthetic countenance for Kant's architectonic of sea and sky, while her worshipper's fetishistic rhythms of empirical "terror" and "ecstasy" replace Kant's impossible injunction to see as the poet sees. If we follow Sarah Kofman's lead and understand Freud's narcissistic

FIGURE 2. Cast of the Juno Ludovisi. Courtesy of Freies Deutsches Hochstift–Frankfurter Goethe Museum.

FIGURE 3. Cast of the Medusa Rondanini. Courtesy of Freies Deutsches Hochstift–Frankfurter Goethe Museum.

woman as evoking the "fantasmatic omnipotence of the mother," we may take Schiller's Juno as an aestheticized double of Freud's or Carol Jacobs's Medusa.[37] Like the Medusa (Figure 3), she not only calls up the terrors and splendors of maternal omnipotence, but also serves as a prop for the castration fantasies proper to oedipal rivalry—for in coveting this forbidden, desirable maternal visage, Schiller enjoys the additional thrill and anxiety of having mimed and appropriated Goethe's desire.[38] The artwork as narcissistic god-woman thus installs the male subject within the substitutive triangulations of mimetic rivalry. Within this aesthetic primal scene, meaning circulates on the tracks of chiasmus, ordered by the binary oppositions human/divine, subject/artwork, man/woman, ecstasy/terror. Concrete and sensual as this scene is, a rhetorical structure controls its possibilities: here, gender identity lends empirical content to a rigidly formal pattern of exchange and reversal and becomes in its turn imaginable only as a binary opposition. Thus the transformation of Kant's material vision into Schiller's erotic drama registers the emergence of an aesthetic and fetishistic ideology: the elaboration of theory's resistance to itself into a systematic resistance to theory. "Woman becomes without oppression a metaphor for man" to the extent that the violence of metaphor is effaced, as the inhuman turns of an aestheticized tropological exchange substitute their charms for the uncertain terrors of reading.[39] Such scenarios reconfirm that aesthetic ideologies have empirical consequences because of, rather than despite, their reliance on figurative language. A theory that accounts for such a predicament cannot expect an easy reception, but no evasion of de Man's work will be able to prevent the recurrence of the question it asks about reading and the challenge it poses to the aesthetic tradition.

4

Lucinde's Obscenity

The subject for discussion here is Friedrich Schlegel's celebrated novel *Lucinde*, the gospel of Young Germany and the system for its *Rehabiliation des Fleisches*, which was an abomination to Hegel. But this discussion is not without its difficulties, because inasmuch as *Lucinde* is a very obscene book, as is well known, by citing some parts of it for more detailed consideration, I run the risk of making it impossible for even the purest reader to escape altogether unscathed. I shall, however, be as circumspect and careful as possible.
—Søren Kierkegaard, *The Concept of Irony*

It has been many years since anyone needed to apologize for reading or writing about *Lucinde*. Over the course of the twentieth century, Schlegel's odd, fragmentary novel has become, in Hans Eichner's words, "the most read novel of the romantic era," as well as an integral and incontestable part of the German romantic canon.[1] It has become easy to dismiss the sort of ironic sidestepping we find in the comments of Kierkegaard quoted above as a response to an obsolete system of manners and proprieties.[2] Yet the nature of *Lucinde's* scandal resists easy explanation. It is one thing for a text taken as a salacious roman à clef to shock and titillate its immediate audience, as *Lucinde* did when it was first published in 1799. But the novel retained its power to scandalize when it was reissued in 1835, six years prior to Kierkegaard's *Concept of Irony*; and as late as 1870, Wilhelm Dilthey was calling it "a small monster from an aesthetic perspective,"[3] whereas Rudolph Haym, in *Die romantische Schule*, denounced it as not just an "aesthetic outrage" but "at the same time a moral outrage."[4] With the professionalization of German studies in the twentieth-century academy, *Lucinde* ceased to occasion axiological and ethical hyperbole, but the resulting gains in scholarly understanding may have been obtained by aestheticizing the text to the point that we have become blind to its unruliness. What "obscenity" did Kierkegaard, like his then-master Hegel before him, sense to be at work in the novel? No doubt *Lucinde*'s extramarital eroticism and double entendres had something to do with it, and no doubt the chapter in praise of laziness irritated more than one generation of the nineteenth-century *Bildungsbürgertum*. But the text's ability to disturb (or delight) its readers seems out of proportion to its actual offense against public moeurs. *Lucinde* is possibly the only novel in the world that owes some of its fame to the fact that it has been attacked and defended by philosophers (Hegel and Kierkegaard on one side, Fichte and Schleiermacher on the other), and as Dilthey's and Haym's comments make clear, the novel's scandal was always also an aesthetic, which is to say to some extent a "philosophical," scandal.[5] Indeed, *Lucinde* may even be argued to have become "obscene" in the first place because of its offense against form.

These questions haunt our contemporary efforts to interpret *Lucinde* insofar as they recall the sheer difficulty of *reading* this "meistgelesene Roman der Romantik." *Lucinde*'s allegories resist interpretation not because they are forbiddingly esoteric, but because of their ironic and slightly absurdist flavor. No matter how one parses the chapter called "Allegory of Impudence," for instance, one is likely to feel unsatisfied; it will never be entirely certain whether the allegorical figures of the "true novels, four in number" are telling us something about Schlegel's aesthetic, or whether they are mainly out to pull our readerly leg (V, 16/53). Arguments for the novel's unity rarely seem to get far beyond the minimalist observation that the "Lehrjahre der Männlichkeit" ("The Apprenticeship for Manhood") comes in the middle of the text, flanked by six sections before and after (if, that is, one doesn't count the "Prologue"); though the text's narrator claims to have set out "to shape raw chance and mold it to the purpose" (9/45), it is never entirely clear that a higher purpose or *Zweck* will emerge out of the seemingly aleatory scene changes. Most studies of *Lucinde* consequently focus on the "Lehrjahre" section, in order to understand the novel as a *Bildungsroman* and ignore as much as possible the text's slippery irony.[6] For in this novel, Schlegel's irony, besides being a "clear consciousness of eternal agility, of an infinitely full chaos" (II, 263), seems to function as a "permanent parabasis" (XVIII, 85) that constantly disrupts its own illusions.[7] In order to interpret the text, one needs to take certain statements literally (or figuratively) and close off alternatives—but in this novel, the alternatives nag. Thus, every interpretation of *Lucinde* inevitably becomes in its turn the "Confessions of a Blunderer" that the novel itself, in its subtitle, confesses itself to be.

In the pages that follow, I propose to take up the question of *Lucinde*'s irony in relation to what Kierkegaard called the novel's "obscenity," on the one hand, and to some of the questions that recent critics of the novel address as issues of gender, desire, and sexuality, on the other. Thus far in this book, we have examined the intersection between questions of gender and aesthetics from angles tending to emphasize the ways in which the discourse of aesthetics, at moments of stress, invokes gender difference in an effort to stabilize its own rhetoric—by appealing to the seemingly natural binary opposition between the sexes; by naturalizing linguistic force as a figure for maternal productivity; and by fetishizing and casting out the maternal body. Fichte's personified Nation, Arnold's girl named Wragg, and Schiller's aestheticized Juno all play out versions of an apotropaic role epitomized, in the previous chapter, by the Medusa's head as a figure for the reception of "theory." Our analysis of these scenarios, however, has left relatively unexamined the status of gender as *difference*. The present chapter proposes to sharpen our sense of the volatility of gender by examining how literature, irony, and obscenity become, in Schlegel's text, insistently overlapping categories. *Lucinde*'s eroticism and double entendres, in other words, enact the aesthetic and philosophical scandal that Schlegel calls "irony," and in the process, the novel suggests what Judith Butler calls the performativity of gender—that is, the so-called constructedness of gender identity, with construction understood as "neither a subject nor its act, but a process of reiteration by which both 'subjects' and 'acts' come to appear."[8] *Lucinde* furthermore, I shall argue, suggests that we understand gender identity as "ironic" in the sense of being potentially illegible, and that we understand the materiality of the body as the pressure of an uncertainty that enables and destabilizes gender. These claims emerge out of a close reading of the section of *Lucinde* entitled "Eine Reflexion" ("A Reflection"). Before attempting that reading, however, I propose to spend a few pages recalling a long essay by Philippe Lacoue-Labarthe, "L'Imprésentable" ("The Unpresentable"), which examines Hegel's allusions to Schlegel's novel and can help situate Kierkegaard's sense of *Lucinde*'s "obscenity" within a philosophical tradition.

I

Lacoue-Labarthe's "The Unpresentable" belongs to a group of essays by this author from the mid-1970s that worry the question of "a possible literary *filiation* of philosophy." This particular piece travels paths similar to those pursued in Lacoue-Labarthe and Jean-Luc Nancy's *L'absolu littéraire* (*The Literary Absolute*, 1978) and sets itself the ambitious task of aligning the question of literature-and-philosophy with that of romanticism, on the one hand, and that of the figure of "woman" within speculative philosophy, on the other.[9] Lacoue-Labarthe's "example" is *Lucinde*, though he doesn't focus on Schlegel's text, refers to it only in passing, and, indeed, never once quotes from it. In this, he is tacitly and carefully miming Hegel, whose rare, fleeting, and seemingly inconsequent references to *Lucinde* are what Lacoue-Labarthe sets out to analyze.[10] Focusing on a moment in the *Aesthetics* in which *Lucinde*'s moral depravity (*Liederlichkeit*) is denounced, and on a marginal note (consisting of one word: "*Lucinde*") handwritten in a copy of the *Philosophy of Right* that Hegel used as a teaching copy, Lacoue-Labarthe elicits links between romanticism, irony, literature, and the feminine that make of *Lucinde* a figure of the "scandal of the aesthetic" (156). I cannot, of course, do justice here to the care—a care not at all adverse to risk, even to a certain recklessness—with which Lacoue-Labarthe performs his argument, but our sense of *Lucinde*'s performance within the critical and philosophical tradition will be sharper if we follow out the main turns of his essay and put some pressure on one or two of his claims.

Hegel's offhand denunciation of *Lucinde* in the *Aesthetics* occurs in a chapter titled "The Dissolution of the Classical Form of Art," which is to say at a point in Hegel's historical narrative in which classical art yields to romantic art and aesthetic religion to Christianity, or revealed religion. Its era over, art becomes a thing of the past. As romantic art, it survives as a form that, willingly or not, registers the fact that aesthetic representation no longer serves as the Spirit's essential manifestation. Hegel identifies good and bad varieties of aesthetic self-dissolution. The good kind tends to be exemplified by Schiller and the bad or dissolute kind by Friedrich Schlegel. Hegel contrasts Schiller's "Götter Griechenlands," which movingly portrays the disappearance of the anthropomorphic Greek pantheon, with Parny's satiric "La guerre des Dieux," which makes fun of "Christian ideas."

There is worse than Parny, though: "But these pleasantries went no further than frolicsome levity [*ausgelassene Leichtfertigkeit*], and moral depravity [*Liederlichkeit*] was not made into something sacred and of the highest excellence as it was at the time of Friedrich Schlegel's *Lucinde*."[11] In his next sentence, Hegel turns back to Parny's poem, and we hear no more of *Lucinde*, the appearance of which in this context is in any case rather peculiar: as Lacoue-Labarthe notes, Schlegel's novel has nothing to do with the gods of Greece or their disappearance; it receives mention here purely as an example of the scandalous and frivolous per se.

What goes into the making of the opposition between Schiller and Schlegel? Putting pressure at once on Hegel's historical narrative and on the Hegelian relation between poetry and philosophy, Lacoue-Labarthe suggests that Schiller's "philosophical poetry" represents for Hegel the promise or guarantee of a necessary aesthetic moment within speculative dialectics:

> Schiller did not merely take the aesthetic a decisive step forward *within* aesthetics; he was also able to relate to philosophy itself this premonitory conception of art, thus accomplishing—Hegel almost says so outright—what *had* to be accomplished in order for the speculative as such to be established, namely, the unity of sense and the sensuous without the presupposition of which, it is easy to understand, no phenomenology of the Spirit, no absolutizing of the phenomenon (and hence none of what Heidegger calls the *onto-theio-logical*) would have been conceivable. (124–25)

Art's function is thus to establish a "unity of sense and the sensuous" that speculative philosophy relies on and transcends. Such dependence on aesthetic or poetic practice carries its dangers, however. Romanticism represents the corrosion, the bad dissolution, of art, in which philosophy fails to recognize itself. This corrosive force bears many names: depravity, subjectivity, and above all and most formally, irony. Here we may simply recall that romantic irony, in Hegel's analysis, derives from an appropriation of Fichtean subjectivism and that, as Lacoue-Labarthe summarizes, "subjectivism equals immorality" because it occasions "the desubstantialization of the substantial" (128), or, more precisely, because it "does not attain to the truth of dissolution, that is, to the speculative, reconciling truth of *determined* negativity" (129). "Literature," Lacoue-Labarthe adds, emerges here as a concept closely related to that of irony—that is, to "this nondialectical or predialectical, insufficiently speculative 'aesthetics' which the *Aesthetics* itself proposes to correct and to redress, be it on the basis of a firm and salutary 'return to Schiller'" (129). And *Lucinde* haunts this return as the figure of literature itself: dissolute, ironic, and out of step with the historical progress of Spirit.

At this point, Lacoue-Labarthe turns to his second object of analysis: Hegel's marginal reference to *Lucinde* alongside the Remark to Paragraph 164 of the *Philosophy of Right*. The "substantiality" of marriage—which *Lucinde*, given its exemplary impudence (*Frechheit*), cannot grasp—consists in the sublation of natural sexual difference into a concrete unity in which the sensuous is negated and preserved.[12] This sublation of sexual difference performs "the speculative distribution itself" (133) in distributing masculine and feminine roles. Marriage, one could say, transforms sex into gender, and gender into speculative philosophical discourse, by transforming "natural" difference into the active, ethical, differential destiny of man and the passive, subjective, undifferentiated identity of woman.[13] "One recognizes here," as Lacoue-Labarthe comments dryly, "the major tenets of 'phallogocentrism'" (134). Furthermore, this passage through a "sexual symbolic" grants to knowledge a figural register in which it can represent itself to itself:

For what is at stake in this very differentiation is no less than the possibility of the philosophical as such. As we shall verify from other texts, nothing in the speculative is alien to what, for lack of a better word, we are compelled to call a "sexual" "symbolic" (in the most general sense) constitutive, in the mode of a kind of *anthropo-phenomeno-logic*, of the "figuratic" in which emerging knowledge must necessarily (re)present itself. (134)

And if, with the aesthetic and ethical scandal of *Lucinde* in mind, we refer this sexual symbolism back to the question of the artwork, we find that "woman," within the differential system of marriage, plays a role analogous to that played by art and the aesthetic within speculative philosophy. Woman figures the union of the spiritual and the sensuous, and thus she figures the aesthetic realm, "which her ethical (male) destination sublates. . . . Between woman and art, the 'symbolic' equivalence, or the analogy, is rigorous and strong" (136). Lacoue-Labarthe thus aligns the question of woman with the questions of aesthetics, literature, romanticism, and irony that Hegel summarizes and dismisses under the sign of "*Lucinde*." Noting that Hegel defends nudity in classical sculpture by affirming the ancient

Greeks' indifference to purely sensual desire, yet that, although he finds classical male nudity acceptable, Hegel requires the aesthetic female figure to be veiled, Lacoue-Labarthe concludes that "if woman alone needs to be veiled, it is because she alone expresses—and arouses?—*sensual* desire. . . . There is, properly speaking, no *pudendum* other than female *pudendum*; or, what amounts to the same thing, male homosexual desire (we should write: *hommosexual* desire) is spiritual desire: the phallus is the 'organ' of the Spirit" (141). It is precisely because woman expresses sensual desire that she becomes—when veiled—the figure of the beautiful. Since beauty is the unity of sensuousness and spirit, the male figure cannot represent the beautiful. Being indifferent to the sensual, the male figure is always already moving beyond beauty, toward the unveiling of the spiritual. Or, as Lacoue-Labarthe puts it, the male figure is "figured only in being feminized." Woman, however, becomes the figure of beauty when her sensuousness hides itself in the doubling of body and clothes—the latter serving as "a sensuous veil thrown over the sensuous" (142). Hegel, Lacoue-Labarthe suggests, is wrestling here with the problem of the necessity of manifestation itself, and in the closing pages of his essay, he names the threat represented by woman as that of aesthetics as "the theory of fiction," "the locus where fiction, the fictional in general, becomes worthy of theory" (151):

And it is in such a conflict, in such a struggle with philosophy, that woman is at stake. . . . Woman is at stake because she represents, not as Hegel through Schiller would have liked, the sensuous itself in opposition to the spiritual, or—which amounts to the same once it has been rigged with a veil—the "inner fusion of the sensuous and the spiritual," but the sensuous in *its* truth, which is the "truth" of figure and the fictional. (155)

Venus or Aphrodite—the one exception, according to Hegel, to the rule that the aesthetic woman must be veiled—is the "figure" of this figurality, which Lacoue-Labarthe names as the "*the scandal of the aesthetic*—which, like every scandal in the eyes of knowledge and the Spirit, consists in having revealed that *there is nothing to unveil.* Or at least that there might be nothing to unveil" (156).

A number of questions arise in the wake of Lacoue-Labarthe's ambitious reading. His final gesture has about it the aura of a well-planned gamble, and much depends on how, and in what context, one decides—or feels compelled—to play one's cards. Is this Aphrodite, this tutelary goddess of

aesthetics, the *necessary* figure for the scandal of the aesthetic? Does this figure perhaps repeat or mime a little too programmatically the Hegelian,
"phallogocentric" identification of woman with the sensuous, the fictional,
the narcissistic? And what do we make of the fetishistic gesture toward
antifetishism that closes off Lacoue-Labarthe's text? The staging, the bringing onto stage, of the naked body of a woman (indeed, of Venus herself);
the zooming in toward a lack ("there is nothing to unveil") that perhaps
n'en est pas un ("or at least there might be nothing to unveil")? Lacoue-
Labarthe is well aware of these questions. He would probably accept them
as the necessary fallout of any critical attempt to mime and displace Hegel's
text. And they remain questions without easy answers. "We cannot do
without the feminine," Drucilla Cornell comments; and her sense of the
feminine as "an aesthetic idea that breaks open the ground of fundamental
metaphysical concepts," and is thus "always the door to a radical future,"
accords with Lacoue-Labarthe's emphasis on the "fictional."[14] Yet the feminine in this sense—as a utopian, ethical instance, radically other to the
real—would also exceed and disrupt the dualisms of the symbolic order,
and to the extent that Lacoue-Labarthe's figure of sexual difference tends,
in "The Unpresentable," to remain a binary opposition, it risks simplify-
ing the tensions and compromises at work in philosophy's gendered self-
representations and produces unwieldy heterosexist generalities. It is
highly questionable, for instance, whether "male homosexual desire" has
ever been successfully quarantined within the parameters of "spiritual desire" in the Western tradition. It is equally uncertain, for that matter,
whether one can justify the notion of a specifically "homosexual desire,"
particularly one that would span continuously, without fracture or detour,
the entirety of Western philosophical discourse. What concerns us here,
thankfully, is a more modest issue: the radically misleading character of such
generalizations within the conceptual and rhetorical world of Schlegel's *Lucinde*. Lacoue-Labarthe's analysis of Hegel's allusions to this novel helps us
situate within the history of philosophical aesthetics Hegel's famous identification of "woman" as "the eternal irony of the community"[15]; but in order
to grasp Schlegel's difference from Hegel—from the official, philosophical
Hegel, in any case—it will not suffice simply to reverse Hegel's values while
keeping intact the equation between woman and irony. A close reading of
Lucinde demonstrates the advantage of thinking gender in terms of irony
rather than irony in terms of gender, and consequently, as we shall see, it

suggests that the "scandal of the aesthetic" is better characterized as a certain materiality of signification rather than as "the sensuous in its truth" incarnated in "woman."

II

Feminist criticism has not been slow, however, to discern in *Lucinde* the pretenses and ruses of phallocentrism, and it would certainly be difficult to deny that Schlegel's novel frequently seems to be offering us a subtler and more playful version of the Hegelian sexual symbolic. The character and sometime narrator Julius's male narcissism and androcentric allegorizing are not derailed by the fact that Lucinde herself is on to his game and only half-willing to play:

> I am not, my Julius, the sanctified person you describe, even though I might like to sing laments like the nightingale, and though I am, as I inwardly feel, consecrated to the night alone. You are that person; when the turmoil has died down and nothing common distracts your noble soul, then you see reflected in me—in me who am forever yours—the marvellous flower of your imagination [*Fantasie*]. (V, 78–79/126)

No matter: Lucinde will remain the mirror of male desire, the lamp toward which Julius strives; she is the lunar *lux* to his *veritas*, the passivity into which he voyages to find himself. As numerous critics have shown, the novel's ideal of androgyny is heterosexist and masculinist in contour and "serves in a regulatory manner to inscribe binaristic codes and to naturalize the proper unity between love and marriage."[16] The novel's highly traditional discrimination between friendship and love, for instance, excludes woman from the former: "Friendship is for you"—says Julius to Lucinde— "too many-sided and one-sided. Friendship must be completely spiritual and must have thoroughly fixed limits" (34/74). The pure spirituality of friendship exceeds the grasp of woman, whose nature it is to represent the natural as the sensuous—and, as we have seen Lacoue-Labarthe extract from Hegel, to represent the beautiful as the synthesis of sensuousness and spirit. Friendship is spirit, and furthermore, *limited* spirit. Its limit or division (*Absonderung*) marks the province of male striving: "Your womanly nature would be destroyed by this kind of division: more subtly, perhaps, but just as completely as it would in mere sensuality without love"

(34/74–75). The doubleness of the homoerotic bond—loving, but purely spiritual, and thus defined through a limit: *not* sexual—opposes itself to the singleness of women, who "in the midst of human society have remained natural creatures [*Naturmenschen*]" (55/99).

Yet these phallocentric structures also repeatedly turn fuzzy and uncertain in *Lucinde*. In the first place, as Martha Helfer has recently argued, the text's autoerotic and homoerotic registers frequently turn intensely sensual and become legible as "same-sex desire."[17] At the beginning of his "Lehrjahre," Julius pursues young men with a love that dares to speak its name rather passionately:

Women he actually didn't understand at all, though he had early been accustomed to being with them. They seemed to him wonderfully strange, often completely incomprehensible and hardly like creatures of his species. But he embraced young men who were more or less like him with hot love, and with a real rage for friendship. (36/77–78)

And a little later in his mini-*Bildungsroman*, having had some painful heterosexual experiences, Julius goes through a phase when he decides to make of "male friendship" the "true business of his life": "He sought out every man who seemed interesting to him, and didn't rest until he had won him, and had conquered the other's reserve through his youthful forwardness and confidence" (45/88). (And the narrator adds: "It is obvious that Julius, who felt that practically anything was permitted to him and was able to put himself above ridicule, had a different sort of propriety in mind than the commonly accepted one.") In one of Julius's letters to Antonio which follow the "Lehrjahre" section, he tells off his friend with more than a touch of campy bitchiness: "I'm going to Eduard. It's all arranged. We don't just plan to live together, but to act and work together in brotherly union" (76/123–24). The text warns us on the same page that friendship is possibly "something false and perverted [*etwas Falsches und Verkehrtes*]" (76/123). We should also note that as part of *Lucinde*'s destabilization of Lacoue-Labarthe's "Hegelian" identification of the homoerotic and the spiritual, the novel renders shifty the difference between friendship and love.[18] At one point, Lucinde is Julius's "most perfect friend" (10/47); at another point, love becomes a term capable of absorbing its spiritualized double: "There is everything in love: friendship, pleasant society, sensuality, and passion too" (35/76). The "rhetoric of love," we are told, should be directed at women—but "after women, of course," the text adds, in a democratic spirit, "it should be directed at young men, as well as at those men who have remained youthful" (20–21/58). It is true, as Catriona MacLeod writes, that the novel tends to depict "male homosexuality as a seductive but perilous phase in the hero's erotic *Bildung*, a phase that is domesticated in favor of the relationship with a woman, and a woman who is also, and importantly, a mother" (207–8). But it is nonetheless also true that no process or state of "erotic *Bildung*" achieves real stability in *Lucinde*. Julius's letter to Antonio about Eduard, for instance, as noted a moment ago, comes *after* the "Lehrjahre" interlude; and *Lucinde*'s narrative organization is sufficiently underdetermined, or at least sufficiently opaque to analysis, that one could imagine a second part of *Lucinde*—the part Schlegel never completed—made up of any number of erotic permutations.

The phallocentric economy thus incorporates into its workings a good deal of ambiguity and slippage, and I suggest that there is reason to take the "something false and perverted" that labors, at least potentially, at the heart of friendship, as a version of something Schlegel elsewhere calls irony. We may consider at this point a bit of dialogue from one of his fragmentary drafts for the second part of *Lucinde* entitled "Of the Essence of Friendship," in which two men, Julius and Lorenzo, discuss irony as part of a discussion of joking, pain, and friendship. "A joke [*Scherz*] can make a joke about everything; a joke is free and universal," Julius remarks. For this reason he is opposed to jokes: "There are places in my being, the most inward ones in fact, where for that reason an ordinary hurt is not to be thought of, and in these places a joke is intolerable to me." Thus, he continues, "it is irony that has often disturbed me in the music of friendship with its distinctly discordant note [*Mislaut*]" (85/132–33). Lorenzo, however, suggests that irony and friendship are inextricable, if not always entirely compatible, and the discussion takes one of those dizzying turns we associate with Schlegel on irony:

> LORENZO: And who know if that is not the irony of irony, that in the end one grows to dislike it.
>
> JULIUS: The final irony, I think, is to be found rather in that it seems to be becoming impossible for you to talk about irony without irony.
>
> LORENZO: I'm afraid it is exactly the other way around. Where's the irony, when in bitter earnest one doesn't know where one is at? And the more I think about it the more incomprehensible it becomes. (V, 85/132)

What is remarkable here is that Lorenzo goes on to specify that what is incomprehensible is that Julian should find irony incompatible with friendship: "Well, if irony isn't the real essence of friendship, then perhaps the gods know what it really is, or irony itself knows. I don't" (86/133).

Note that Lorenzo is canny enough—ironic enough—to overstate and understate his claim in the same breath: irony may not be the essence of friendship, since Lorenzo may not know what irony is, but on the other hand, it seems that if irony has anything to do with friendship, the relation will be essential. Irony, it seems, has something fundamental—if also something fundamentally uncertain—to do with social life and libidinal relations. Love itself, it turns out, is always possibly another name for irony.[19] The irony of eros binds the social order: "the finest and best part" of good society is "the playing at love and the love of playfulness [*der Scherz mit der Liebe und die Liebe zum Scherz*]" (34/75). Yet this binding is also a wounding.[20] In the present context, it is perhaps worth emphasizing not so much the incomprehensibility of irony as the aesthetic effectivity that characterizes this incomprehensibility. Irony disturbs friendship but threatens to be its essence, causing pain in the most inward places of being. The freedom and universality of the joke makes its contact with the world unpredictable, but if anything more forceful for being incalculable. Irony's "absolute power to do anything," as Kierkegaard puts it, does not result in or derive from a flight from historical actuality: irony rather inscribes itself on the world precisely *because* it is incalculable.[21] Nor is this force simply negative in its effects: friendship and love themselves possibly derive from the pains (or pleasures) of irony.

How might gender difference and sexual identity be thought in relation to this performative power of irony? The question is not as strange as it might at first sound. If Schlegel is thinking of irony as a force capable of wounding, inspiring, and perhaps even constructing a desiring self, his notion of irony would resemble aspects of what Judith Butler calls the "psychic life of power." Far from being either the rhetorical stratagem or the self-reflexive play of a self-conscious subject, irony would be a movement of incomprehensibility, *Unverständlichkeit*, that enables (and destabilizes) the acts of meaning production through which bodies and subjects come into being. Contemporary theory has various vocabularies in which to indicate these formative acts; Butler's exemplary texts draw on—and critique, and displace—speculations by Foucault and Althusser as well as Lacan and

Freud (among many other texts, of course), in order to mount arguments for the constructedness of gender identity, sexual orientation, and the body. As we saw in Chapter 2, Butler radicalizes Freud's resonant claim that "the ego is first and foremost a bodily ego [*ein Körper-Ich*]"[22] so as to suggest that both the body and the ego are constructed through fantasmatic processes of projection, incorporation, and exclusion: that gender is "performed" as a reiteration of norms and conventions that constitutes the (gendered) subject in and as this very process of reiteration; that the (sexed) body is "material" in and as a somewhat analogous process of "materialization." "To claim that discourse is formative is not to claim that it originates, causes, or exhaustively composes that which it concedes," Butler writes; "rather, it is to claim that there is no reference to a pure body which is not at the same time a further formation of that body." Both in the case of the gendered subject or the sexed body, in other words, "the constative claim is always to some degree performative": the process of reiteration *generates* the illusion of an "essential" gender, a "material" body.[23] To name Schlegel's uncanny notion of irony as the transcendental precondition of such processes of subjection is in a sense to do no more than to insist on their radical ungroundedness. But one can also follow out in a Schlegelian vein Butler's recent speculations on the melancholy character of gender identity. The argument here is that the achievement of a gendered identity, above all a heterosexual one, not only requires the subject to renounce other (above all, same-sex) love objects, but also requires the subject to disavow this very renunciation: "what ensues is a culture of gender melancholy in which masculinity and femininity emerge as the traces of an ungrieved and ungrievable love."[24] Melancholy may not be the mood one tends to associate with *Lucinde*, but like Sterne's *Tristram Shandy*, Schlegel's novel skirts the edges of pain and disaster: *Musik* can become *Mislaut* (85/133); "blundering" can turn violent.[25] And what Schlegel calls "irony" would here name something like the inevitable risk of damage and loss: an immemorial risk that leaves in its wake irreducible possibilities of melancholy as well as of mirth.

   Lucinde addresses the ironic instability of gender systematically in the chapter entitled "Eine Reflexion" ("A Reflection"). Parodying Fichtean metaphysics, this chapter proleptically deconstructs Hegel's canonical definition of romantic irony as a concept that has its "deeper ground [*tieferen Grund*], in one of its aspects, in Fichte's philosophy, insofar as the principles of this philosophy were applied to art."[26] *Pace* Hegel, "Eine Reflexion" tells a story about the uncertain formation of identity—and does so via the sort of double entendre that the male voice of the chapter entitled "Treue und Scherz" ("Fidelity and Playfulness") recommends: "Man is inherently a serious beast. But one should fight against this shameful and abominable inclination. . . . To that end, double entendres [*Zweideutigkeiten*] also can do good service, except that they are so rarely double [*zweideutig*], and when they're not, and allow of only one interpretation, they're not immoral but simply obvious and stupid" (34/75). In the process, the text destabilizes gender difference and disarticulates identity, to the point that one is forced to conclude that if *Lucinde* is a *Bildungsroman*, as the secondary literature occasionally suggests, it is so only in the ironic sense in which Schlegel understood *Bildung*:

> *Bildung* is antithetical synthesis, and completion to the point of irony.—The inner being of a person who has achieved a certain height and universality of *Bildung* is a continuing chain of the most monstrous revolutions. (XVIII, 82)

III

Lucinde, as we have seen, constantly reflects upon sexual difference, but never more vibrantly or crazily than in "Eine Reflexion." It and the "Dithyrambic Fantasy on the Loveliest Situation" were the two sections of the novel that most scandalized the educated orators (*gebildete Redner*) of the era, who, Schlegel tells us, would prefer to name sexual matters only through their namelessness, "nur durch ihre Namenlosigkeit"—a prohibition that the Reflection both respects and violates through a running double entendre:

> It has often struck me as strange how sensible and respectable people can with untiring industry and with such great seriousness repeat the little game in an eternal cycle, and always from scratch: a game which obviously has no use or goal, even though it may be the oldest of all games.
> Then my mind inquired what nature, who is always so thoughtful, and so enormously cunning, and who instead of merely speaking wittily, acts wittily, might mean by those naive allusions that educated orators [*gebildete Redner*] only name through their namelessness.
> This namelessness [*Namenlosigkeit*] itself has a double meaning. The more

shamefaced and modern one becomes, the more fashionable it becomes to interpret it as shamelessness. For the gods of antiquity on the other hand, all life had a
certain classical dignity, even the shameless heroic art of begetting life. The number of such productions and the degree of ingenuity determine their rank and nobility in the realm of mythology. (72/118–19)

Before it can even be said to be well underway, the Reflection has gathered
enough density to slow commentary to a crawl. And it has done so in that
inimitable Schlegelian tone—half sly, half enthusiastic—that for two centuries has infuriated certain readers of Schlegel: the tone of a serious joke,
an *ernsten Scherz*, which renders ludicrous, or as Schlegel would say,
ungeschickt, the interpretive activity it provokes.[27] Nor is there a graceful
way out from such blundering: if one were to stride through the difficulties
of the Reflection with, for instance, the insouciance of an aesthete, enjoying
Schlegel's joke and paying no mind to his text's difficulties, one would simply blunder more ludicrously. The entire scandal of *Lucinde* replays itself in
miniature and at triple speed in "Eine Reflexion": the text thematizes a sexual, aesthetic, and hermeneutic "obscenity" that, because of the radically
unstable character of its irony, it also *performs*. But if we are condemned to
blunder, this fate has its consolations: as the text gathers density here, it reflects upon the language of gender that structures Schlegel's novel. Blundering is a male prerogative in *Lucinde*; but what is it to be male as we approach the force field of the obscene? Is blundering gendered at such
points, or is gender itself the effect, or act, of a certain blundering?

As a first step, or stumble, toward such issues, we need to consider
the way in which the text speaks the unspokenness of "sex"—the little
game played, like that of interpretation, with such ludicrous earnestness,
over and over again. The game, a parodic double of Schillerian *Spiel*, has
no usefulness and no goal (*Ziel*); oddly enough, it doesn't even seem to be
motivated by what we ordinarily think of as desire. Elsewhere in *Lucinde*,
Schlegel writes eloquently of the pleasures of the body, but here, the
game's players seem driven by a compulsion so absurd as to make any sort
of pleasure, even aesthetic pleasure, irrelevant. In its sheer formalism the
"little game" also has nothing to do with the reproductive sexuality celebrated by *Lucinde*'s narrator in the first of the "Two Letters" that precede
"Eine Reflexion." When the narrator asks himself what Nature was thinking of when she invented this game—asks, that is, after the meaning of
the game—he pointedly avoids naturalistic or teleological language, and

instead he emphasizes "language" per se: "Then my mind inquired what nature . . . might mean by those naive allusions that educated people only name through their namelessness." As an *Andeutung*—a hint, allusion, intimation—the sexual game is a textual act, a referral of meaning elsewhere, which accords with the game's repetitive character. The sexual act refers for its meaning to other instances of its own repetition: to the sheer iterability through which the game retains its identity. Its meaning is its performance; and indeed, "Nature," in Schlegel's odd allegory, lends nothing natural to the game—neither affective content nor reproductive purpose—but rather seems to personify the performative force of language. Nature, who "instead of merely speaking wittily, acts wittily," emits *Andeutungen* that *occur* as the witticism of sex.

Sex, then, is akin to a speech act: the game is a performance, and has no constative function. Yet the narrator, keen to know Nature's thoughts, asks after the game's meaning anyway, and indeed, the performative's iterative structure translates performance into meaning as tautology, as we have already seen. The meaning of fucking is fucking; the act "means" the formality of its own occurrence as repetition. At this point, however, Schlegel's text introduces a further complication. Confronted by the denaturalized linguistic performance of the *kleinen Spiel*, cultured people, the *gebildete Redner*—that is, anyone capable of reading, let alone writing, *Lucinde*—name it through and as its namelessness, its "Namenlosigkeit." This trope, Schlegel's narrator tells us, is a perversion particular to our modern era. The ancients troped the sexual act with dignity, in the figural language of myth; we moderns react against the shame with which we are burdened by shamelessly pretending that we can name namelessness. The trope "Namenlosigkeit" is the product and the denegation of shame. *Lucinde* offers us here a compressed version of Freud's insight that sexual repression makes culture and its *gebildeten Redner* possible, yet also suggests the pertinence of Foucault's sly twist: the repression exists in order to confirm, indeed, to generate, the existence of something called "sexuality" in the first place. The prohibition is enormously productive: of witticism and double entendre; of respectability and scandal. In a Foucauldian vein, one might extrapolate the production of scientific or medical–legal discourses that would pursue the nameless truth of reality as "sexual identity." In its abstract, single-minded negativity, the trope "Namenlosigkeit" pretends to be a name rather than a figure, and the more literally one thinks one is naming the thing in question, the more deluded one is—which, of course, makes us the real bunglers when we think we have named the referent of *Lucinde*'s parody ("the sexual act"), let alone when we indulge in late twentieth-century rhetorical braggadocio ("the meaning of fucking is fucking") as I did a moment ago. "Namenlosigkeit" totalizes the endless, mechanical iteration of a performative (Nature's performative, the "little game") into meaning as the absence of meaning. Like the phallus, the sign of lack that organizes the symbolic order, "Namenlosigkeit" symbolizes a sexual prohibition that would be coextensive with language itself. Naming the impossibility of naming, it is castration as pure signifier, signifying the endless displacement of meaning. Such is Schlegel's allegory of the phallus: the idealization of repetition as lack.

Yet though in a certain sense the phallus has already arrived on the scene, sex and gender differences have been hesitating in the wings. The "little game," contentless as it is, thus far could be played by anyone and is played by everyone, and thus it presumably entails any and every possible ensemble of sexes, genders, and erotic dispensations. Sexual difference and heterosexual emplotment only emerge after the "Reflexion" has moved fully into its parody of Fichte:

> This number and this ingenuity are good, but they are not the best. Then where does the longed-for ideal lie hidden? Or does the searching heart find in the highest of all plastic arts only more mannerisms and never a perfect style?
>
> Thought has this peculiarity, that next to itself it loves to think most about something it can think about forever. Hence, the life of the cultivated and meditative man is a continual cultivation and mediation on the lovely riddle of his destiny. He continually determines it anew for himself, for that is precisely his whole destiny, to be defined and to define [*Er bestimmt sie immer neu, denn eben das ist seine ganze Bestimmung, bestimmt zu werden und zu bestimmen*]. Only in the search itself does the human mind find the secret that it seeks.
>
> But what, then, is the definer or the defined itself? In the masculine it is the anonymous [*das Namenlose*]. And what is the anonymous [*Namenlose*] in the feminine?—the indefinite [*das Unbestimmte*]. (72/119)

Classical art, empowered by its healthy language of myth, achieved a good way of naming of the nameless, but the representational arts of the era of the French Revolution, *Wilhelm Meister*, and Fichte's philosophy can perhaps aspire to an even more glorious mode of *Darstellung*—to a *vollendeten Styl*—because of the self-developing self-determination of Fichtean humanity. Schlegel's first extended double entendre had concerned the useless and directionless "little game" that sensible and respectable people repeat endlessly, "with untiring industry and with such great seriousness"; now, he transposes that activity into a Fichtean key: "Hence, the life of the cultivated and meditative man is a continual cultivation and mediation on the lovely riddle of his destiny [*Bestimmung*]." *Namenlosigkeit* becomes the riddle or secret, the *Rätsel* or *Geheimnis*, fueling the human subject's endless self-reflexive self-development. In Schlegel's hands, the Fichtean process of *Bildung* becomes as absurdly mechanical and repetitive as the little game it plays: "Er bestimmt [seine Bestimmung] immer neu, denn eben das ist seine ganze Bestimmung, bestimmt zu werden und zu bestimmen." This magnificently tautological stutter repeats the repetitive insistence of the *kleinen Spiel*, but it repeats it as the illusory activity of a subject. The *Bestimmung* is an illusion because it defines itself as self-defining, whereas in fact it repeats Nature's performance. Nature, which "is always so thoughtful," is echoed as subjective thought: "Thought has this peculiarity, that next to itself it loves to think most about something it can think about forever"—the endless object of thought being, of course (thanks to the inevitable double entendre) the "little game." And since this little game *is* Nature's thought as sheer performance or act, the Fichtean language of *Selbstbestimmung* is doubly deluded: it is a repetition that pretends to be a self-sufficiency, and it is a translation of sheer performative repetition into a *Bildungsgeschichte*—a visibly illusory *Bildungsgeschichte*, to be sure, so long as the "Bestimmung des Menschen" remains a comic tautology.

It is at this point that the Reflection reflects on sex and gender difference, in a dense paragraph that provides a hinge upon which the episode turns: "But what, then, is the definer or the defined itself? In the masculine it is the anonymous [*das Namenlose*]. And what is the anonymous [*Namenlose*] in the feminine?—the indefinite [*das Unbestimmte*]." I shall return shortly to the difficult role played by the *Namenlose* in this passage; for the moment we may register the obvious fact that, thanks to the mediation of this *Namenlose*, the difference between masculine and feminine, *Männlichkeit* and *Weiblichkeit*, becomes that between the *Bestimmende/Bestimmte*, on the one hand, and the *Unbestimmte* on the other. A difference, that is, becomes an *opposition*: a logical and ontological binary opposition capable of organizing a universe. And that is exactly what happens in the remaining paragraphs of "Eine Reflexion" as modalities of determination and indetermination, gendered masculine and feminine, divide out existence itself:

> The indefinite [*das Unbestimmte*] is more mysterious, but the definite [*das Bestimmte*] has greater magical power. The charming confusion of the indefinite [*Unbestimmte*] is more romantic, but the noble refinement of the definite [*Bestimmte*] is more like genius. . . .
>
> Who can measure and who can compare two things that are infinitely valuable, when both are joined by the real definition that is destined to fill all holes [*wirklichen Bestimmung, die bestimmt ist, alle Lücken zu ergänzen*], and be the mediator between the individual man and woman and eternal humankind?
>
> The definite and the indefinite and the whole wealth of their definite and indefinite relations [*Das Bestimmte und das Unbestimmte und die ganze Fülle ihrer bestimmten und unbestimmten Beziehungen*]: that is the one and the all. . . . The universe itself is only a plaything of the definite and the indefinite [*ein Spielwerk des Bestimmten und des Unbestimmten*]; and the real definition of the definable [*das wirkliche Bestimmung des Bestimmbaren*] is an allegorical miniature of the life and web of everflowing creation. (72–73/119–20)

Schlegel's text retains its sly irony: the play of the determined and the undetermined is a "Spiel*werk*," a term that retains a hint of the mechanical repetition of the *kleinen Spiel* with which the Reflection began. And the contrasting qualities of the *Bestimmten* and *Unbestimmten* are pseudo oppositions: their characteristics are paired contrastively ("the determined is X, but the undetermined is not-X"), but don't actually oppose each other ("more mysterious" / "greater magical power"; "more romantic" / "more like genius"; etc.). More than a hint of zaniness thus enlivens a phallocentric speculation that is submitting masculine determination and feminine indetermination to the priapic rule of a "real definition destined to fill all holes." With the invocation of this truer, higher *Bestimmung*, the Reflection sums up, in terms that mix the sparkle of double entendre into the august colors of speculative philosophy, the novel's androcentric androgyny. The masculine is the whole and the part, and the feminine is the part and the lack. And the masculine is the male and the feminine is the female, since gender difference, infused with the powers of the Fichtean dialectic, absorbs sexual difference. And the masculine, as male, and the feminine, as female, pair with each other to redefine the "little game" as a heterosexual one. Thus the repetitive, emptily mechanical little game, infused with gender content and refigured as a heterosexual dialectic, becomes *Lucinde*'s version of the striving of Fichtean man, who forever creates himself in an asymptotic approach to the total freedom of self-determination.

The Reflection's playful tone, disjointed binary oppositions, and running double entendre do not incapacitate its phallocentrism, but such a degree of textual density does suggest the wisdom of reading the section with as much care as possible, particularly at the moment in which it represents the emergence of gender difference. It is never a good idea to imagine that one knows what's going on in *Lucinde*, particularly in the nameless reaches of sexuality, as becomes clear—as clear as anything becomes in this text, anyway—if we return to reexamine the peculiar role played by "das Namenlose" in the appearance of masculine and feminine:

> But what then is the definer or the defined itself? In the masculine it is the anonymous. And what is the anonymous in the feminine?—the indefinite. [*Was ist denn aber das Bestimmende oder das Bestimmte selbst? In der Männlichkeit ist es das Namenlose. Und was ist das Namenlose in der Weiblichkeit?—das Unbestimmte.*]

Given the paragraph's rhetorical structure, we might have expected Schlegel to retain "determining or determined" as the mediating term which is being split into masculine and feminine (that is, "But what is the determining or determined itself? For the masculine it is X; for the feminine it is Y"). Instead, the question of "das Bestimmende oder das Bestimmte selbst" is left dangling, attached only to the "masculine," and a new term, the neuter abstraction "das Namenlose," enters to link, or suture, masculine to feminine, determination to indetermination. One effect of this rhetorical zigzag is to grant the terms *Männlichkeit* and *Weiblichkeit* the dignity of primary terms, since they seize upon "das Namenlose" from the outside, as it were, to determine it in their various ways (as determination, as indetermination).[28] And at the same time, as we have seen, phallocentrism installs itself as the logic of this binary opposition (for if, as we had been told in the previous paragraph, "the cultivated and meditative man [*Mensch*]" is that which determines itself, the masculine becomes the very essence and destiny of this self-determining power). But the term *Namenlose*, slightly but significantly different from the term *Namenlosigkeit* that had earlier served as the privileged trope for the *kleine Spiel*, sutures the terms of the phallocentric, heterosexual conceptual universe at a cost. *Die Namenlosigkeit* is an abstract noun with an illusory but determined relation to its referent ("welche gebildete Redner nur durch ihre Namenlosigkeit benennen"); the little game, in other words, is taken to possess a quality, *Namenlosigkeit*, that educated people use as a synecdoche to describe the game itself. "Das Namenlose," however, though it inevitably triggers the double entendre and suggests the little game, also recedes from it. "Das Namenlose" is not a quality but an entity, at once specific and indeterminate, an entity named as the nameless and only as the nameless. The formal emptiness of the little game achieves here a certain radical purity. And in the process all tropes that would seek to substitute for, and thereby interpret or grant meaning to, the *Namenlose*, including the mock-Schillerian trope of a "kleinen Spiel," become legibly arbitrary and uncertain. The double entendre may be inevitable, but here also becomes as uncertain—let us also say, as unsophisticated, as blundering—as any other meaning.

Though the terms *Männlichkeit* and *Weiblichkeit* assert themselves as fundamental terms, their contact with the *Namenlose* infects and destabilizes both them and the speculative dialectic they enable. The Reflection's parody of Fichte turns on the legibility of a difference between the nameless in the masculine and the nameless in the feminine. Only thus can there be a certain difference between the determined and the undetermined—or, for that matter, a stable difference between masculine and feminine. This difference—the difference between one *Namenlose* and another—is inherently uncertain, precisely because the *Namenlose* is *namenlos*: uncertainly singular or dual or plural, uncertainly self-identical or self-different. Masculinity and femininity become a binary opposition thanks to a passage through a neutral space in which all determination is lost—as well as all "indetermination," to the extent that indetermination is opposed to determination, and thus determined by and ultimately reducible to it. Masculinity and femininity become the violent, arbitrary *taking* of a difference. Gender imposes itself as a performance and a fiction—the fictional transformation of uncertainty into the determinations of identity.

Das Namenlose thus "names" an uncertainty at the heart of the abstract negativity of *Namenlosigkeit* and its dialectic of *Bildung*. The *Namenlose* provides for the emergence of the opposition between determination and indetermination, and, through the lens of gender, it "names" the essence of determination ("Was ist denn aber das Bestimmende oder das Bestimmte *selbst*?"), but only through the nonessence of an indeterminate indeterminacy. At the turning point of the phallo-ontological system, one cannot tell the difference between determination or indetermination, masculinity or femininity; and this hinge point is also by no means either sexless or "androgynous," for the absence or presence or copresence or synthesis of genders is just as uncertain as the genders themselves. The *Namenlose* is both inside and outside the phallo-ontological system; it is the neutral at work in the negative, the blank screen upon which the phallus, as image of lack, is projected. In the terms of the metaphor that Rodolphe Gasché has elaborated out of Derrida's work, the *Namenlose* is the "tain of the mirror": the dull, unreflecting support that enables the universe of mimesis, but remains unassimilable to it.[29] Schlegel's parody of Fichte is thus also a rigorous and radical critique of speculative philosophy. A Schlegelian reader of Fichte might, for instance, hear the neutral tones of the *Namenlose* in the third-person *Ich* of Fichte's *Wissenschaftslehre*: "The I posits originally and absolutely its own existence" ("Das Ich setzt ursprünglich schlechthin sein eignes Seyn"), where the third person registers the trace of the neutral, the otherness that resists yet enables the self-positing of the I—the uncertainty which, as Werner Hamacher argues, must characterize any genuine act of positing, yet which must also instantly be forgotten.[30] In the gender allegory of "Eine Reflexion," one could rephrase this unthinkable, random neutrality as the shadow of the German indefinite pronoun *man* within *Mann* (or *Mensch*, or *Weib*). "Now everything is clear! Hence the omnipresence of the anonymous [*namenlosen*] unknown Godhead" (73/120), the narrator tells us near the end of "Eine Reflexion," pretending to affirm a genial sort of pantheism, but actually registering the force of a neutrality that ruins all clarity and all presence. The little game's *ewigen Kreislauf* thus becomes the figure of the performative force of this neutrality: the active pressure of its unbearable passivity. And at this point, in a comic reverse parabasis, the Reflection forgets itself and disappears: "Plunging deeper into this individuality, my reflection pursued such an individualistic turn that it soon ended and forgot itself" (73/120).

To bring the present reflection on "Eine Reflexion" to a less dramatic end, we may note that *Lucinde* confirms the performativity of gender and teaches us furthermore that the "materiality" of the body is best understood as a name for the nameless uncertainty through which signification occurs, and through which bodies achieve shape and meaning. Such materiality may be thought of as "linguistic" insofar as the trope of language suggests an irreducible coimplication of materiality and difference. Sexuality in *Lucinde* can occur only as a disguised and displaced version of such radical uncertainty. The regime of heterosexuality is at once coercive and fragile, as *Lucinde* takes pleasure in showing us. Yet the text's flashily camp moments are no more and no less mobile and erratic, no more and no less representative of the sexual "truth" of the novel, than are the seemingly heterosexual idylls of "Yearning and Peace" and "Dalliance of the Imagination" with which this fragmentary novel "ends," or the polymorphous perversity of little Wilhelmine with which it more or less begins. This is not to suggest that sexuality escapes history. Rather, sex and gender are historical through and through, and this is so precisely because they are always figures, uncertainly inscribed, constantly in need of reconfirmation and reinforcement. For the inscription of figure occurs via the uncertainty of the *Namenlose*, which names the impossible condition of the production of meaning. The meanings of the body are manifold and mobile. The *materiality* of the body is the *Namenlose* as the disruptive condition, which is to say the fundamental ob-scenity, of all bodily figures and combinations. *Lucinde's* truth of sex, in other words, is a permanent ironic parabasis, and from this perspective Kierkegaard was right: it may be that even the purest readers, blundering through this novel, will not escape unscathed. In this risk lies the promise of the kind of textual event that, after Schlegel, we call literature.

5

Masks of Anarchy:
Shelley's Political Poetics

> Like every generation that preceded us, we have been endowed with a *weak* Messianic power, a power to which the past has a claim. That claim cannot be settled cheaply. Historical materialists are aware of that.
> —Walter Benjamin, "Theses on the Philosophy of History"

We began this book with a review of the dense interplay between aesthetics and politics, and it is now time to return overtly to this theme and press the relation between these two charged terms. If aesthetics intends its own ultimate transformation into a political program, its dependence on figurative language, as we have seen in several contexts now, causes it to split into a critique of itself that confronts as its own condition of possibility an exposure to dispersal, dissemination, or loss. If aesthetic play teeters over into truly free play; if the aesthetic frame cuts too deep; if reflective judgment, imitating logical or ethical judgment too slowly or too hastily, remains underway toward its own possibility as judgment, then aesthetics becomes a letter that potentially fails to arrive at its destination and will thus possibly miss its prescripted appointment with politics. Or will it? If we reduce politics to pragmatism, to the facticity of the given, do we not ignore resources within our notion of politics and the political that allow the political to be reconceived in terms of difference, unpredictability, futurity?[1] The possibility of such thinking is, I shall now suggest, one of the legacies of the troubled literary–historical event and domain we call romanticism.

To a markedly greater degree than other period terms, the concept of romanticism has inspired political passions and assertions. These assertions, however, have ranged across the modern Western political spectrum. Depending on the case, the context, and the interpretive desire, romanticism's exemplary texts and figures become alternately or simultaneously progressive and nostalgic, atheistic and pious, cosmopolitan and nationalist, revolutionary and reactionary. In Germany, as Maurice Blanchot reminds us, romanticism knew extreme vicissitudes: "at certain times the most retrogressive regimes laid claim to it (in 1840 Friedrich Wilhelm IV, and then the Nazi literary theorists), at others, it was clarified and taken as a renovating necessity."[2] Even as a term of convenience within our fin de siècle American scholarly bureaucracy—for which, to all appearances, the proto-professional attacks on romanticism by New Humanists and early New Critics during the first third of the twentieth century simply represent yet more archival material to process—even here, romanticism retains a whiff of this charged ambivalence.[3] Jerome J. McGann's *The Romantic Ideology* becomes inconceivable if one imagines it retitled and launched at a different slice of literary history. As noted in this book's introduction, British romanticism developed along lines that made it peculiarly vulnerable to self-laceration: the hand-wringing much in evidence in recent books and anthologies written or edited by professionals in this field has no real equivalent in, say, Victorian studies, where even the most politicized cultural critics seem able to go about their business without worrying that the regal name of their professional field might be a synonym for "ideology." Nor, conversely, do other scholarly fields appear capable of inspiring the kind of passionate advocacy that now and then crops up within academic romanticism.[4] Romanticism remains a fundamentally ambiguous event in which we seem fated to participate as political and ethical beings.

If romanticism "is" ideology, as McGann's peculiarly definite article suggests, this is because, as argued in the Introduction, romanticism is being understood as another name for aesthetics.[5] Romantic ideology is aesthetic ideology, which is to say ideology in its most exemplary form, as the illicit, and politically consequent, universalization of a particular. In aesthetics, the universal is the human, and the particular is the acculturated subject or the artist or the artwork. By judging subjectively but disinterestedly, the subject obtains a moment of contact with its own essential humanness, whereas the artist and the artwork speak to all peoples and ages because, transcending their particularity in and through their sensuous immediacy, they represent humanity itself. This idealizing humanism is ideology as aesthetics as romanticism. The tautologies seem airtight. Yet it seems that romanticism is inevitably also the *critique* of aesthetic ideology.

"Romantic imagination emerges with the birth of an historical sense," McGann observes (79), to which the historicizing critic is indebted for his existence: "The grand illusion of Romantic *ideology* is that one may escape such a [selfish and unreflecting] world through imagination and poetry. The great truth of Romantic *work* is that there is no escape, that there is only revelation (in a wholly secular sense)" (131, McGann's italics). Here, as elsewhere, romanticism names the source of the values to which the critic appeals, even as he sets out to critique the error from which they spring. There seems no easy exit from romanticism—particularly, it must be added, if one understands one's project, as McGann does, as that of "return[ing] poetry to a human form" (160): a more romantic–aesthetic ambition would be hard to conceive. The error generates the critique, but the critique turns out to be hard to tell apart from the error.

Shelley is an interesting figure to examine in this context, not just because his reception has known exemplary extremes—from the varieties of "red Shelley" championed by Spencean socialists, Chartists, and subsequent working-class and socialist movements, to the hyperaestheticized, otherworldly naif of late nineteenth- and early twentieth-century literary scholarship and criticism—but also because his work so consistently links aesthetic practice to political struggle and thematizes the complexity as well as the necessity of genuine renovation. His sustained attention to these questions presses us toward the difficulty that composes one of romanticism's major legacies: how to think of the political force of literary texts. The political content of Shelley's writing has proved capable of inspiring wildly different assessments,[6] and this volatility is partly a consequence of the rigor with which his most openly political texts engage the politics of aesthetics as the problem of ideology. Pursuing with unflinching determination the paradox that a critique of aesthetics must risk repeating the error it critiques, Shelley discovers in radical uncertainty the condition of possibility for genuine political engagement. In the previous chapter, we elicited from Friedrich Schlegel's novel *Lucinde* an (ironic) affirmation of the fundamental irony, or undecidability, of gender difference. In a somewhat similar fashion, we are now proposing to read in Shelley's work an emphasis, and by no means simply a negative emphasis, on the rhetorical precondition of aesthetic politics. Precisely to the extent that he *fails* to "return poetry to a human form," he opens a space for affirmative action and thought. "The critical redemption value of Shelley's poetry," Forest Pyle proposes, "resides not in its reference to the present or the empirical but in its blank opening onto futurity."⁷ That orientation toward futurity represents the temporal dimension of uninsurable risk, and in that risk, Shelley, I suggest, locates poetry's political force and what we may with some caution term aesthetic ideology's political unconscious. My main display texts will be *The Mask of Anarchy* and *The Cenci*; and as is perhaps obvious, I shall be working my way toward a somewhat counterintuitive defense of Shelley's famous, and to some infamous, claim that poets are the world's unacknowledged legislators.

I

"The greatest poem of political protest ever written in English," according to one enthusiastic and knowledgeable reader, Shelley's *The Mask of Anarchy: Written on the Occasion of the Massacre at Manchester* belongs to a group of poems from the 1819–20 period that the author hoped would have immediate political effect, and that at one point he proposed to collect and publish as "a little volume of popular songs *wholly political*, & destined to awaken & direct the imagination of the reformers," as he wrote to Leigh Hunt.⁸ Unlike *Prometheus Unbound*, which was intended to "familiarize the highly refined imagination of the more select class of poetical readers with beautiful idealisms of moral excellence," *The Mask* was aimed at a wide readership; furthermore, insofar as it responded to a specific event, the Peterloo atrocity, it assumed some of the excitements and burdens of moving and persuading a specific audience.⁹ It did not reach its intended readers. Leigh Hunt was unable to publish the poem in 1819 for fear of prosecution, but thirteen years later, when both Peterloo and Shelley had receded into history and the political climate had thawed sufficiently, Hunt published a slightly bowdlerized version, at which point the poem became a Chartist and socialist classic. Shelley thus in fact did reach a wide audience, but not the one implied by the poem's rhetorical occasion. His text knew a certain political impact, though not one he could have predicted.

These facts provide an initial springboard for Susan Wolfson's severe and intelligent scrutiny of *The Mask of Anarchy* in her *Formal Charges* (1997), a study that will help speed us on our way toward the problem of aesthetic critique, if only because its argument is at times almost diametrically opposable to mine. Wolfson writes as the latest representative of a politically diverse line of Shelley interpreters, from Raymond Williams on the left to Donald Reiman on the right, who are united by degrees of sympathetic skepticism about their poet's political pretensions. Her skepticism goes hand in hand with the traditional contrast she draws between visionary poetry, dreaminess, wishfulness, and aestheticism on the one hand, and practical politics on the other. Typically in such scenarios, the latter is deemed good and the former bad—indeed, because Wolfson understands political poetry as a species of oratory, she finds the text's very boldness a liability: "the bolder aspects of this performance are exactly what rendered it unpublishable—and unable to affect the struggle it addresses" (195). Thus *The Mask* turns out to be "weirdly kin to the elitist visionary poem of the same period with which it is sometimes contrasted, *Prometheus Unbound*" (196). In this account *The Mask of Anarchy* rapidly becomes "an aesthetic processing of politics," an ideological gesture that Wolfson associates with "poetic self-absorption" (195).

These judgments are enriched by Wolfson's sustained attention to formal elements. The poem's unpublishability, she argues, "is troped by the poem itself: the news 'from over the Sea' reaches its poet in a dream state from which he is never seen to awaken" (196). She refers here to the fact that *The Mask* begins with a frame narrative to which it never returns:

> As I lay asleep in Italy
> There came a voice from over the Sea,
> And with great power it forth led me
> To walk in the visions of Poesy.
>
> I met Murder on the way—
> He had a mask like Castlereagh— (1–6)

This narrator flags his own presence in the scene once more, as a reader, when Anarchy appears ("On his brow this mark I saw" [36]); otherwise he is merely an implied spectator, relaying a drama in which he has no real part. That drama—we may take a moment here for plot summary—begins as the grisly antimasque of Murder, Fraud, Hypocrisy (as Castlereagh, Eldon, Sidmouth), and other minions of Anarchy, who pass over "English land" trampling the "adoring multitude" to "a mire of blood" (40–41). This triumph is crossed by "a manic maid" whose "name was Hope, she said: /

But she looked more like Despair" (86–88). The maid claiming to be Hope lies down before the horses' feet, expecting to be trampled, when "between her and her foes / A mist, a light, an image rose" (101–2). This phenomenon becomes "a Shape arrayed in mail / Brighter than the Viper's scale" (110–11), and its motion contrasts with and undoes Anarchy's masque:

> With step as soft as wind it past
> O'er the heads of men—so fast
> That they knew the presence there,
> And looked,—but all was empty air. (118–21)

"Thoughts" spring up "where'er that step did fall," and the oppressor falls—or, more precisely, is discovered to be already fallen:

> And the prostrate multitude
> Looked—and ankle-deep in blood,
> Hope that maiden most serene
> Was walking with a quite mien:
>
> And Anarchy, the ghastly birth
> Lay dead earth upon the earth
> The Horse of Death tameless as wind
> Fled, and with his hoofs did grind
> To dust, the murderers thronged behind.
>
> A rushing light of clouds and splendour,
> A sense awakening and yet tender
> Was heard and felt—and at its close
> These words of joy and fear arose
>
> As if their Own indignant Earth
> Which gave the sons of England birth
> Had felt their blood upon her brow,
> And shuddering with a mother's throe
>
> Had turned every drop of blood
> By which her face had been bedewed
> To an accent unwithstood,—
> As if her heart had cried aloud: (126–46)

And there follows, encased in quotation marks, an address to "Men of England," spoken by this internal orator. One and a half times longer than

the drama that preceded it, this address offers an analysis of political repression and a program of political action that in subsequent months
Shelley was to elaborate as *A Philosophical View of Reform*. Like that text,
the "Men of England" speech has seemed to many twentieth-century
readers a blend of revolutionary, reformist, and even at times agrarian-
reactionary advice: the speech's most famous stanza, the twice-repeated refrain "Rise like lions after slumber . . . / Ye are many—they are few,"
seems a call to revolutionary action, yet the Men of England are also told
to "let the Laws of your own land, / Good or ill, between ye stand. . . .
The old laws of England—they / Whose reverend heads with age are
grey" (327–28, 331–32), and to avoid retaliatory violence at all costs:

> "And if then the tyrants dare
> Let them ride among you there,
> Slash, and stab, and maim, and hew,—
> What they like, that let them do." (340–43)

The theory being that the tyrants' rage will die away and become shame:
"Every woman in the land" will mock them; "the bold true warriors / Who
have hugged Danger in wars" will desert them, and the orator's words will
then obtain volcanic national force:

> "And that slaughter to the Nation
> Shall steam up like inspiration,
> Eloquent, oracular;
> A volcano heard afar.
>
> "And these words shall then become
> Like oppression's thundered doom
> Ringing through each heart and brain,
> Heard again—again—again—
>
> "Rise like lions after slumber
> In unvanquishable number—
> Shake your chains to earth like dew
> Which in sleep had fallen on you—
> Ye are many—they are few." (360–72)

Thus the poem ends, far distant from the sleeper in Italy. As Wolfson notes,
one draft of the poem even lacks closing quotation marks—as though the
internal orator's speech had burst its frame to become the poem itself.[10]

The question is what to make of this and other formal complexities or oddities. Wolfson, as we have seen, understands "the suppression of the poem's opening frame" as the mark of a wishful "aesthetic ideology": "If the frame were to return, it would cast the oration as an unreal event—a wish and a dream, a fantasy wrought by visions of Poesy—at the very moment that Shelley wants to insist on its political potency" (Wolfson, 204). Aesthetic ideology, here, functions as a synonym for personal and vocational narcissism ("poetic self-absorption"; "aesthetic self-satisfaction" [Wolfson, 195, 196]), a narcissism that Wolfson associates with Shelley's substitution of "visionary poetry" for "an analysis of how material change might be realized in the historical moment of 1819" (202). She also suggests that Shelley's program of nonviolent resistance replays the political ambivalence that can be read into his poem's blend of activism and dreaminess, since "passivity . . . can serve the interests of tyranny." The poem's ambiguities thus ultimately compose a nervous reaction to the threat of popular revolution: "What the poem's contradictions contain, in both senses, is a specter of anarchy—not in the Crown, but in the Men of England" (202). When the Chartist and post-Chartist socialists took up this poem, Wolfson implies, they seized on its activist language ("Rise like lions") and filtered out its poetic and political complications. The poem's literary density, according to this account, *is* its ideological vacillation—its bourgeois timidity, its escapism, its Shelleyan dreaminess, narcissism, and impracticality.

Those are not quite Wolfson's terms; but such are the implications of her impressively alert and knowledgeable reading: Shelley, as so often before, is being called to account, this time by a reader ambitious enough to target the politics of literariness itself. And though one would have difficulty quarreling with many of her observations—who can doubt that Shelley indulged himself a little, imagining this address to the Nation?—Wolfson's large claims push one toward large questions: what, for instance, is being taken for granted (politically and otherwise) by a pragmatism that can assimilate a poem's very radicalism (and thus, under the circumstances, its unpublishability) to aestheticism and self-indulgence? Why, for that matter, should self-indulgence weigh so heavily in the ethical–political balance? And why should the political test of Shelley's poem be its viability as a public utterance in 1819, rather than, say, 1832? Wolfson answers that last question more or less directly. Political poetry, in her view, is oratory: it is poetry that does what it intends, realizing within an immediate social field the presence-to-self of an intention. Voice, not writing, composes its essence. Wolfson elaborates this claim by way of a subtle reading of a brace of stanzas from *The Mask*'s "Men of England" speech:

"Let a vast assembly be,
And with great solemnity
Declare with measured words that ye
Are, as God has made ye, free—

"Be your strong and simple words
Keen to wound as sharpened swords,
And wide as targes let them be
With their shade to cover ye." (295–302)

"Measured words," as Wolfson comments, suggests not just a speech act but a poetic act: here "Shelley asserts the authority of poetry in this fantasy of political performance"; yet she goes on to observe that his text undermines the fantasy:

words are not just likened to and rhymed with *swords*, but are literally infused into them: *swords*. This semantic wit, however, is also the event that exposes the poetic self-service of Shelley's fantasy. For both the rhyme and the graphemic pun of *words/swords* are forms that register only in writing and reading rather than in speech and listening, where the rhyme is off at best, or inaudible. The poetic forms that make Shelley's political point do not translate into oration, and other aspects of his verse even contribute to the obstruction: the rhymes that really chime are the ones initiated by *assembly be*—the icon of political action as static aesthetic spectacle. (200)

Wolfson's dissatisfaction with the text resolves again and again into the same register. As political poetry, *The Mask* is a "posthumous voice" (195); its poetic politics are "inaudible" effects of "writing and reading" (200). This posthumous, inaudible dimension of writing is then aligned with self-enclosure, with the "poetic self-absorption" (195) of a "self-addressed" poem (196) that, as in the quotation above, exposes "the poetic self-service of Shelley's fantasy."

Yet surely the posthumous reach of a text and the inaudible effects of writing and reading point less toward self-enclosure or self-mirroring than toward a certain loss or scattering of the self—what Wolfson herself calls "the dispersal of authority when writing becomes reading" (194). A narcissistic poetics would need to ward off such effects of writing and the signifier—and one way of doing that is by aestheticizing these effects, by seeking, that is, to transform nonphenomenal differences into sensuous and spectacular tokens of selfhood. My thesis here is that Shelley's texts consistently associate such aestheticization with political violence and that they accept a certain complicity with that violence even as they labor to unmask it. *The Mask of Anarchy* unquestionably stages an aesthetic fantasy—indeed, it stages what is arguably *the* primal fantasy of aesthetic nationalism: a vision of the nation as an assembled body, gathered into the presence and presence-to-self of an orator.[11] Yet Wolfson's fine close reading of the *words/swords* stanza suggests not the aestheticism of Shelley's poem but its resistance to aesthetic ideology. Or rather, it suggests—as the history of Shelley's reception amply demonstrates—that a critique of aesthetic ideology will always have to risk a certain "aestheticism." Self-indulgence is no doubt legible at such moments, to the extent that the poet indulges the fantasy he critiques. But it is precisely because the critique outstrips the category of selfhood that it is a *political* critique.

Wolfson has by no means overstated *The Mask of Anarchy's* formal complexities. Indeed, if anything she has understated them: the text is far more slippery than any reader, so far as I am aware, has yet acknowledged. It complicates its aesthetic–rhetorical occasion beyond all expectation, first and foremost by radically destabilizing the status of the self. Who speaks in this poem? The sleeper in Italy dreams, and never awakes; within the dream, a voice emerges to address the nation's citizenry. The more closely one attends to the poem, the more difficult it becomes to say who or what this voice is. Critics often name the internal orator Liberty or Britannia— thus, as it were, extending the masque through the entirety of *The Mask*— but all Shelley actually gives us is the twice-repeated qualifier "as if": it is *as if* the indignant Earth had felt the blood of the sons of England on her brow and, in an act of reverse transubstantiation, had turned that blood into language ("an accent unwithstood"); it is *as if* her heart had cried aloud.[12] Wolfson notes the insistence of the "as if" and hears in it an echo of the poem's opening "As I lay asleep"; the effect, she suggests, is to "restrain the political agency of the oratory to a dream" (198). Perhaps; but what then is dreaming and who is doing it? What is the provenance of "these words of joy and fear" that arise from a subject unnamable except through analogy or simile? Why does the poem tease us toward allegory, making it easy for generations of critics to write of "Liberty"'s oration in *The Mask*, and yet refuse, strictly speaking, to allow us to say that a "speaker" speaks, or even that a "voice" gives voice? For though at the beginning of the poem "a voice from over the Sea" calls the sleeping I into Poesy, at the point where the poem turns into internal oration, "words" simply "arise." When we personify these words as an orator, we both repeat and efface the poem's "as if." We give voice to a text that, as "these words," is, reflexively and a little blankly, the poem itself. We thereby produce more allegory—allegory that the poem has already provided under the aegis of dream, a dream in which an "I" wanders to the point of losing itself on allegory's road.

Not only does the oration have no certain orator, it also closes with peculiarly excessive self-reflexivity, such that the poem itself threatens to become a machine, even a broken record:

> "And these words shall then become
> Like oppression's thundered doom
> Ringing through each heart and brain,
> Heard again—again—again—" (364–67)

The tyrants slash and stab, fall into shame, are mocked on the street and deserted by the militias; the slaughter "steam[s] up like inspiration" to the Nation, "eloquent, oracular"—and the result is not utopia, or even the reforming of Parliament, but rather the production of "these words." Eloquent, oracular words, perhaps, but, as Wolfson would rightly point out, just words and more words, "heard again—again—again." Precisely where the rhetoric is most stirring, the text hollows itself out most thoroughly and insists most oddly on its resemblance to what Steven Goldsmith calls the "stifling repetition" of Anarchy's self-promotion ("I AM GOD, AND KING, AND LAW!") in the poem's opening section.[13] Its political theater culminates in a dramatization of the production of the poem—again and again: the refrain "rise like lions" closes the poem as a figure for the text's endless repetition of itself.

If, therefore, we cast our eyes back over the poem and try to summarize its narrative self-representations, we discover a reiterated, excessive self-reflexivity. On the one hand, the masque—the allegorical triumph and fall of Anarchy of the first thirty-six stanzas—reveals itself to be mere theater; after Anarchy's death, we obtain not utopia but an oration. Anarchy's fall is a fiction, a dream, a shadow of futurity. The real political work, as described by the clarion-toned but indeterminate voice that speaks the second part of the poem, lies ahead, beyond and outside the poem, in the extratextual futurity of political struggle. On the other hand, the oration that springs out of the masque and confirms the masque's fictionality is an oration grounded not in voice but in a figure of voice ("as if") that repeatedly effaces its spokenness as the repetition of "these words" ("again—again—again"). The referent of "these words" being undecidably and equally the ringing refrain, the stanza that announces the refrain's repetition, the internal oration, the masque dreamed by the dreamer, and finally the entire poem, the text returns us to the mystery of its production as text. If the masque produced nothing but an oration, the oration produces nothing but itself—and the poem as a whole, which is to say the masque, which is to say the oration. *The Mask* is a dream that generates and destroys its dreamer both as a character and as a source of authority; it collapses into the stutter of "these words"—these words on the page that, as professional academics, we read again, again, again.

Though always misreadable as aestheticism, this hyperreflexivity in fact destroys the self, both as a thematic element within the text and as a metaphor for the text itself. Offering us nothing more than the blank fact of its own material occurrence, the text collapses reflexivity into the mechanical iteration of an inscription. At the same time, it draws attention to the inevitability with which we project meanings onto inscriptions, give voice to written signs. Voice, therefore, becomes inseparable from rhetorical personification. *The Mask* stages a drama of personification. As we have seen, critics inevitably ascribe a voice, and thus an identity and a gender, to "these words," and the poem renders that gesture simultaneously necessary and fictional. In this poem, personification is exemplified as allegory. A commentator notes that in *The Mask*, "the irony is that the reality is abstract evil; its appearance merely takes the form of persons"[14]: Murder wears Castlereagh as a mask. Once again, however, the poem inscribes a difference it encourages us to efface. Murder's mask is *like* Castlereagh; Fraud has on, *like* Eldon, an ermined gown; Hypocrisy is "clothed with the Bible" *like* Sidmouth.[15] There is never any doubt about the political bite of these "as ifs": the poem's topical satire is not in the least tempered by them. They efface themselves before the proper names of the entities they invoke. The masque thus performs felicitously by masking itself. When we imagine

Murder to be incarnate or grounded in Castlereagh, we make a mask into a person and fall into the naiveté of taking a mask for a face, literalizing a prosopopoeia. Thinking that we have reached a political or historical referent, we in fact fall into ideology. The error—the effacement of the "as if"—is necessary, and so is the consequent instability of all acts of personification, a lesson Shelley emphasizes by passing from historical masks (Castlereagh) to allegorical masks (Anarchy, Hope) as the masque develops. The progression underscores what personification forgets, which is allegory itself: the figural mode in which sign and meaning remain visibly different. Like Giotto's Charity in *Du côté de chez Swann*, whose "energetic and vulgar face" shows no trace of the virtue she signifies and who depends upon the inscription "Caritas" for her legibility, allegorical figures in *The Mask of Anarchy* are arbitrary signs, the meanings of which cannot be intuited; they require supplemental labels.[16] Hope has to gloss her own meaning ("And her name was Hope, *she said*"), because she looks like Despair. The potential for error and deceit in this signifying structure is realized in the figure of Anarchy, the epicenter of the masque:

> He was pale, even to the lips,
> Like Death in the Apocalypse.
>
> And he wore a kingly crown,
> And in his grasp a sceptre shone;
> On his brow this mark I saw—
> "I AM GOD, AND KING, AND LAW!" (32–37)

Anarchy's is a double mask: he mimes allegorical representations of Death (and once again a difference composes this identity: he is pale *like* Death), and he supplements that mask with a "mark" that distills into a list of Shelley's favored targets the lie of ideology itself. To claim to be God, King, and Law is to claim to ground signification in an absolute personification. Anarchy, personified, styles himself the Arche, though only thanks to a label that enacts the difference it denies. Anarchy, capitalized, masks anarchy—masks, that is, the materiality of an uninsurable inscription. Such is the main thrust of Shelley's poem—and the reason it takes the form of a masque in the first place.[17]

The aestheticization of signs thus, within the poem, composes the possibility both of Anarchy's reign and of the poem that dethrones Anarchy.

Furthermore, this aestheticization enables the satire—the identification of Murder and Castlereagh, Anarchy and King George—that made the poem unpublishable in 1819, and politically effective in the 1830s. An essential, inescapable ambiguity thus marks the critique. *The Mask* registers this ambiguity in its narrative. Anarchy's horse first tramples the adoring multitude "to a mire of blood" (40–41) and then, riderless, grinds the murderers to dust (133–34); the two acts of trampling have wetter or drier results, but are deliberately symmetrical. After Anarchy's overthrow, Hope walks ankle deep in blood (127)—presumably the blood left over from the first trampling; yet can we be sure that the second didn't spill any? The Shape, it is true, bears only defensive war gear, a helm and coat of mail, yet light rains through the helm's plumes like "crimson dew" (117). Besides being blood colored, this dew recalls the "dew / Which in sleep had fallen on you" of the reveille—the objective correlative of oppression's sleep, a sleep that in turn recalls the slumber of the poet-narrator in Italy. Political poetry here holds out the possibility that it repeats what it condemns: tyrants flee "like a dream's dim imagery" (212) within a dream that to some extent recycles tyrannical imagery. If the poem's endlessly repeated "words" ring "like oppression's thundered doom," the ambiguously objective and subjective genitive (the words ring like the death knell of oppression; the words ring like the sort of doom that oppression is in the habit of thundering) forms no accidental pun: throughout the poem, oppression's overthrow teasingly reiterates oppression's terms and figures. Shelley's attitude toward revolutionary violence can be and often has been read as ambivalent, but his wavering between revolutionary and reform politics, or between an ideal of passive resistance and a pragmatic acceptance of violence, arguably responds to a fundamental ambiguity scripted in the text's figurative language.[18] The poem itself is a mask as well as an unmasking of anarchy. Yet in this ambiguity resides its political force. We may call this ambiguity the text's "political unconscious," so long as we understand that unconscious not as Fredric Jameson's "uninterrupted narrative" or "single great collective story," but rather as something more like interruption itself—an endless interruption, figured in *The Mask of Anarchy* as the mechanical, iterative ringing of the dream-text's words.[19] Making legible this pulse of death and dispersal within its political–aesthetic dream, the poem comments on, and offers itself to, the risk that makes politics possible.[20]

II

Shelley's recorded responses to the massacre in Manchester include, besides *The Mask of Anarchy*, two letters to close male friends in which he was inspired to self-quotation. "The torrent of indignation has not yet done boiling in my veins," he wrote to Ollier, shortly after receiving word of Peterloo. "I wait anxiously [to] hear how the Country will express its sense of this bloody murderous oppression of its destroyers. 'Something must be done. . . . What yet I know not.'"[21] He was, of course, appropriating the voice of his recently created Beatrice Cenci. Two weeks later, writing to Peacock (who was the friend who had sent him news of the massacre), he allowed Beatrice's *mot* a freer rendering: "What an infernal business this is of Manchester! What is to be done? Something assuredly."[22] The Chernyshevskyan echo may be taken, perhaps, as a shadow of futurity caught by the poetic mirror; in a more worldly spirit, thinking along Wolfsonian lines, one might want to pick up on the staginess of these moments—their blend of outrage, self-indulgence and uneasiness, as a poet in exile, highly conscious both of his cultural patrimony and his political impotence, negotiates his relationship to "the Country." But an additional peculiarity bears thinking about here: Shelley's nervous self-reflection occurs as a moment of identification with a traumatized heroine on her way toward the act of vengeance that will destroy her. His ventriloquized Beatrice may be read as a wishful, and to some extent erotically playful, moment of identification with a violated national body; it must also be read as yet another politically ambiguous sign, an appropriate origin for a poem like *The Mask*. Something must be done in advance of, in the absence of, knowledge. The imperative begins in blindness, facing the blankness of futurity. Yet it also quotes; it recalls a scripted, tragic past. What is to be done may turn out, when done, to repeat the violence it sets out to destroy.

I have suggested that *The Mask of Anarchy* forces this ambiguity on us as the condition of all political or historical action. Shelley's quotation compresses the lesson of that text into a fractured, polyvalent phrase. The blindness of the future-oriented imperative is also a blindness to its own past, to its own status as citation: to quote Beatrice here is also to forget that one is quoting Beatrice. The imperative's knowledge of its own citationality or iterability haunts it as its condition of possibility without ever catching up with it. Life itself, Nietzsche tells us, depends upon our ability to forget. Yet in the forgetting, the repressed returns: the poet, identifying with a fictional character of his own creation, repeats that character's blindness. For Beatrice, like Shelley in his letters to Ollier and Peacock, and like many real and fictional characters before and since, is dreaming of an absolute act—a "tremendous deed," as Shelley's preface to *The Cenci* puts it (*SPP*, 238)—that would heal the past by rupturing time and causality with the force of divine redemption, annihilating trauma through a gesture unindebted to and in no way repetitive of that trauma, and thus capable of utterly forgetting it.[23] How else might history be redeemed? Shelley's poems thematize again and again the irreducible double bind of an ethical-political act that must forget the past it must remember, and must repeat a version of the violence it dreams of effacing.[24] Sometimes his texts mine the self-reflexivity of allegorical personification (as when "Conquest is dragged Captive through the Deep" in Demogorgon's visionary speech at the end of *Prometheus Unbound* [IV, 556]); occasionally, as at one memorable point in the "Ode to Liberty," he turns to the figure of a violent, ambiguously redemptive inscription:

> O that the free would stamp the impious name
> Of KING into the dust! or write it there,
> So that this blot upon the page of fame
> Were as a serpent's path, which the light air
> Erases, and the flat sands close behind!
>   Ye the oracle have heard:
>   Lift the victory-flashing sword,
> And cut the snaky knots of this foul gordian word (211–18)

The stanza may be read as a compulsive effort to refigure the initial paradox, according to which the act of stamping repeats what it annihilates: because *stamp* means writing as well as erasing, the ode's narrator first tries to absorb the word's doubleness by reimagining writing as a wind- and sand-obliterated trace, then constructs a more aggressive scenario in which the reader is interpellated not so much as Hercules as Perseus, cutting the "snaky knots" of a Gorgon word with a "sword" that, as Wolfson reminds us, contains the word it cuts within it.[25]

These double binds do not add up to nihilism, because the imperative remains absolute ("Something must be done") and the future remains

open. But they translate with delusive ease into the terms of despair, the
last temptation, as in the Fury's final torment of Prometheus:

> The good want power, but to weep barren tears.
> The powerful goodness want: worse need for them.
> The wise want love, and those who love want wisdom;
> And all best things are thus confused to ill.
> Many are strong and rich,—and would be just,—
> But live among their suffering fellow men
> As if none felt: they know not what they do. (I, 625–31)

Despair here may be understood as a name for the illusion that one can
know the incompatibility between knowledge and performance (from this
point of view, cynicism is merely a defensive and inauthentic form of despair). Prometheus feels the force of the temptation but trumps the Fury:
"Thy words are like a cloud of winged snakes / And yet, I pity those they
torture not" (I, 632–33). In the end, and despite his endless complicity with
Jupiter, he is futurity. Shelley keeps faith with the Promethean affirmation,
but his mature work understands affirmation as bound up with the
strange, intertwining noncoincidence of performance and knowledge: the
incompatibility of "good and the means of good," as the narrator of *The
Triumph of Life* puts it (231).[26] Furthermore, Shelley suggestively complicates the Promethean appeal to affect. Stating that he pities those who fail
to feel pity and fear at the spectacle of life's tragedy, Prometheus wards off
the Fury by transforming despair into sympathy. His pity comprehends the
split between knowledge and performance by aestheticizing this split as a
tragic spectacle. Thus, his pity repeats the totalizing structure of the despair
that pity overcomes. In *The Cenci*, Shelley explores the provenance and
structure of tragic affect in ways that allow us to understand Promethean
affirmation in relation to the radical fictionality of the affect it affirms. "In
writing the *Cenci*," he told Trelawny, "my object was to see how well I
could succeed in describing passions I have never felt, and to tell the most
dreadful story in pure and refined language."[27] If Shelley's goal in reimagining this Renaissance tragedy is to "clothe it to the apprehensions of my
countrymen in such language and action as would bring it home to their
hearts" (*SPP*, 239), his retelling involves him in acts of fictional identification that receive thematic and figurative elaboration in the text as the pressure, within aesthetics, of a certain anaesthesia.

III

We may first rapidly review the well-known spiral of complicity and pain that *The Cenci* sets in motion. Beatrice's tremendous deed—parricide—is, of course, reactive to another deed: the unspeakable crime she has suffered at the hands of her father, the Count, who embodies in Gothic fashion the full weight of patriarchal oppression. The Count appears to have an understanding with God, "whose image upon earth a father is," according to Beatrice (II, i, 16–17), and who answers the Count's prayers for the death of his sons. The Pope's sympathy for the Count derives in part from financial self-interest but also from the fact that he stands between God and the Count in the patriarchal chain of being, "the paternal power, / Being, as 'twere, a shadow of his own" (II, ii, 55–56). Earl Wasserman's influential reading of the play discerns in Cenci a personification of the mystery of evil itself: "Like God, he is the fatherless father, the uncaused cause, the point beyond which evil cannot be traced."[28] It must be added, however, that in *The Cenci* paternal power is also bound up with self-destruction. The Count's crimes damage his patrimony, since for each evil deed discovered he pays compensation to the Pope; and though from a God's-eye view this self-destructive activity simply feeds resources back up the patriarchal food chain, from the Count's perspective, it represents a modest step toward the dream of self-annihilation that fuels his villainy. When all is done, he says, he will pile up his remaining riches "And make a bonfire in my joy, and leave / Of my possessions nothing but my name; / Which shall be an inheritance to strip / Its wearer bare as infamy" (IV, i, 59–62). That autoaesthetic spectacle would for the Count be the ultimate act, the most tremendous deed. It would preserve patriarchy as the reflexivity—the fascist dream—of autoproduction in and as pure autodestruction.

As a surrogate for this absolute deed, the Count rapes his daughter Beatrice. It is very much part of the texture of this play, as well as being historically characteristic of this particular sort of violence, that the Count's crime is at once unspeakable and overpublicized: we inevitably know the name of this deed, but Beatrice also insists with authority that we do not:

What are the words which you would have me speak?
I who can feign no image in my mind

Of that which has transformed me. I, whose thought
Is like a ghost shrouded and folded up
In its own formless horror. Of all words
That minister to mortal intercourse,
What wouldst thou hear? For there is none to tell
My misery; if another ever knew
Aught like to it, she died as I will die,
And left it, as I must, without a name. (III, i, 107–15)

Or again: "there are deeds / Which have no form, sufferings which have no tongue" (III, i, 141–42). The violence of the Count's deed is linguistic in a thoroughly nontrivial sense: it is traumatic; it strips language from its victim, and in doing so, it acquires the character of a verbal act even before the literal rape occurs (to her mother Lucretia's anxious question, "What did your father do or say to you?" [II, i, 59], Beatrice answers: "It was one word, Mother, one little word" [II, i, 63]). The real violence of the Count's deed lies in the destruction of the victim's full comprehension of the deed: trauma destroys the knowledge of its source. "Her spirit," Lucretia concludes, "apprehends the sense of pain, / But not its cause; suffering has dried away / The source from which it sprung" (III, i, 34–36). With the loss of language or knowledge in trauma comes the victim's debilitating identification with the torturer. Beatrice answers the maternal question, "What has thy father done," by asking, "What have I done?" (III, i, 69). The Count exults precisely in this more than literal force of rape: "She shall become (for what she most abhors / Shall have a fascination to entrap / Her loathing will) to her own conscious self / All she appears to others" (IV, i, 83–88). He imagines her having his child, suggesting as the epitome of his "tremendous deed" the transformation of female generativity into the ghastly specularity of patriarchal autodestruction: "May [the child] be / A hideous likeness of herself, that as / From a distorting mirror, she may see / Her image mixed with what she most abhors, / Smiling upon her from her nursing breast" (IV, i, 145–49).

Beatrice's own tremendous deed responds to this unspeakable, self-destroying injury and in certain ways repeats its violence, as nearly every critic of the play has observed.[29] Early on in the text, she calls pain's traumatic effacement of the source of pain "parricide," as though the effect were indistinguishable from the cause. Responding to Lucretia's comment that "suffering has dried away the source from which it sprang," she comments,

"Like Parricide . . . / Misery has killed its father" (III, i, 37–38). The self-destructive destructiveness of patriarchy makes its crime paradoxically congruent with parricide. Cenci, appropriately enough, is the first to utter the word in the play (in a curious phrase, to which we shall return) and the first to propose ways of doing it, including the way Beatrice eventually chooses ("How just it were to hire assassins, or / . . . smother me when overcome with wine" [II, i, 141, 143]). Thus, in killing her father, Beatrice slips back into the father's self-immolative logic of torture. She becomes, in her turn, a torturer as, at the end of the play, she wrings a negation of parricide from the hired assassin Marzio. After suffering the papal rack, Marzio has confessed all and named Beatrice as his employer. Yet after suffering Beatrice's eloquence, he retracts his confession: "A keener pain has wrung a higher truth / From my last breath" (V, ii, 164–65). The play suggests that Beatrice has evaded the full trauma of victimage—the ghastly self-alienation imaged by the mother imaged in the child of incest—only by "becoming the thing she hates" without knowing it. The initial trauma, which consists in the inability to say what one knows, becomes the inability to know what one says. The radical, tremendous deed of parricide in a sense obliterates the self even more thoroughly than the Count's original crime was able to do.[30]

It is still not clear, however, why patriarchy's dream of plenitude takes negative—that is, self-immolatively sadistic—form, which suggests that we should look a little more closely at the sadist's account of sadism. "All men delight in sensual luxury," the Count generalizes.

> All men enjoy revenge; and most exult
> Over the tortures they can never feel—
> Flattering their secret peace with others' pain. (I, i, 78–80)

This is a significant statement, in part because it is a reflection upon tragic affect or catharsis. Pain is the foundation of the sadistic economy, but pain belongs only to the victim, whereas the sadist experiences a pleasure that has no existence in itself, but resides entirely in the spectacle of the other's pain. Hence the curious insistence, even the bizarre, glancing pathos, of the Count's description of men exulting "over the tortures they can never feel." It is as though this inability to feel pain, or at least *those* pains, is a loss—indeed, an absolute loss: the sadist *can never* feel the effect of his own sadistic action. The voluptuous pleasures of sadism cover an underlying numbness or impotence. In a sense, this numb foundation creates the voluptuous pleasure which covers it, since the sadist's pleasure (his "secret peace") resides precisely in the irreversibility of the torturer–tortured relation. Yet this irreversibility also shows up as the flickering plangency of a loss.[31]

The sadist's pleasure in pain both politicizes and, willy-nilly, demystifies tragic catharsis. The pleasure we derive from aestheticized suffering is laced with anaesthesia because it is grounded in our inability to identify, except fictionally, with the tragic other of fiction. What we call fiction, in other words, is a name for the absolute otherness of the other. Tragedy, or we may say more generally, poetry, attends to the absolute and infinite loss of the other, even as it betrays this loss by shunting it into the specular illusions of mourning and tragic identification, through powerful and unstable acts of personification. The sadist, trapped in this predicament, seeks to transform loss itself into a ground for self, to exploit the other's otherness, and he succeeds only at the price of destroying others endlessly as part of a self-consuming spiral that can never close. Put another way, God, in this sadistic, patriarchal economy, can do everything except be his own victim. His sacrifice of himself to himself is a lie. He can never know the pain of the other, even the other who is himself. Such is the infinite pain of his existence, which his sadism forecloses and repeats.

The Cenci allows us another way to characterize the sadistic paradox: the sadist seeks to aestheticize his an-aesthesia as the formalism of a total self. As the play comes to an end, the master trope of patriarchy becomes the machine, the aestheticized figure of form divorced from meaning:

> The Pope is stern; not to be moved or bent.
> He looked as calm and keen as is the engine
> Which tortures and which kills, exempt itself
> From aught that it inflicts: a marble form
> A rite, a law, a custom: not a man. (V, iv, 1–5)

To personify a rite or custom—and this personification here defines patriarchy—is to replay the sadistic economy in which the sadist affirms his inability to feel the victim's pain (the machine being "exempt itself / From aught that it inflicts"), and thereby disavows this inability. To personify a formal pattern is to deny, by pretending to celebrate, the word's inability to know its own deed. (Hence Beatrice's apostrophe: "Cruel, cold, formal man; righteous in words, / In deeds a Cain" [V, iv, 107–8].) The sadistic economy derives its possibility from a radical incompatibility within itself that it translates either into the sublime indifference of the machine, or the sublime spectacle of its own ruin. "Its self-alienation," as Walter Benjamin wrote of mankind under fascism, "has reached such a degree that it can experience its own destruction as an aesthetic pleasure of the first order."[32] Composing yet disarticulating that spectacle is a different, less spectacular parricide, of a sort suggested by the first use of the word in the play, when Cenci characterizes one of his sons as having been "taught by rote / Parricide with his alphabet" (II, i, 131–32). The truth of patriarchy's self-immolative aesthetic is allegory, and "Parricide" appears in *The Cenci* as the exemplary allegorical figure, destroying its own knowledge of its linguistic provenance ("Like Parricide . . . Misery has killed its father"). It is in making legible the irreducibility of linguistic play to aestheticization that poetry's words are swords—politically cutting, if always also double edged.

IV

Readers have often observed that Count Cenci is a dark parody of the artist. He tells stories, manipulates the action, and fathers Beatrice's parricidal plot, to the point of appearing "an evil counterpart of the poet who embodies imagination in language," according to one critic.[33] But "counterpart" suggests a binary opposition more stable than the play of resemblances one finds again and again in Shelley's texts. Consider briefly, in conclusion, the famous final sentences of the *Defence of Poetry*, particularly the penultimate sentence, with its cascade of predicates and uncertain pronouns:

Poets are the hierophants of an unapprehended inspiration, the mirrors of the gigantic shadows which futurity casts upon the present, the words which express what they understand not; the trumpets which sing to battle and feel not what they inspire: the influence which is moved not, but moves. Poets are the unacknowledged legislators of the World. (*SPP*, 508)

The cadences are so familiar that we sometimes, I think, have difficulty perceiving how strange Shelley's writing is here. It seems relatively comprehensible that poets should be hierophants or mirrors. But what is it for them to be "words which express what they understand not"—and who is the "they" here: the poets or the words? But of course the poets *are* the words—words that enact meanings blindly. And if at this late hour that trope has a familiar deconstructive ring to it, what do we make of the follow-up clause, that poets are "the trumpets which sing to battle and feel not what they inspire"? Is Cenci's anaesthesia lacing this hyperaesthetic performance? In some sense, yes, for, as legislators, poets seem at once blind and numb, "unacknowledged" both because the world ignores them and because they themselves lose their self-awareness—including their aesthetic sense—as they leave their mark upon the world.

Our reading of *The Cenci* indeed suggests that the closest cousin to this poetic anaesthesia is a machinal affectlessness that Shelley associates with the worst kinds of political violence. About a year before writing *The Defence of Poetry*, he had written about soldiers in *A Philosophical View of Reform* in terms thematically opposed but rhetorically oddly similar to those he would use to describe poets:

From the moment that a man is a soldier, he becomes a slave. He is taught obedience; his will is no longer, which is the most sacred prerogative of man, guided by his own judgment. He is taught to despise human life and human suffering; this is the universal distinction of slaves. He is more degraded than a murderer; he is like the bloody knife which has stabbed and feels not; a murderer we may abhor and despise, a soldier is by profession beyond abhorrence and below contempt.[34]

The poet is everything the soldier-slave is not—apart from that teasing echo. The former is a trumpet that sings to battle and feels not what it inspires; the latter is a bloody knife that stabs and feels not what *it* inspires. In addition to the rhetorical heightening of a favored Shelleyan inversion ("feels not"), the two figures share an appeal to the particular kind of affectlessness that can be associated with a tool—a technical prosthesis of, in this case, voice (the trumpet) or hand (the knife). That the poetic trumpets "sing to battle" tightens this counterintuitive accord between poet and soldier. Not only are they both tools, blind to the sensation they elicit or the meaning they perform, but they both also seem caught up in political forms of violence. They veer inevitably if sacrilegiously toward each other, such that, at their meeting point, the poet as trumpet unfeelingly inspires the unfeeling soldier to his knife work.[35]

Perverse though it undoubtedly is to hear such echoes and draw such comparisons, which obviously run counter to Shelley's most prominent themes, in doing so we respond to a vibrant ambiguity in Shelley's work that shows up both on his texts' thematic and figural levels. Poets are not soldiers any more than the Shape is Anarchy or freedom is tyranny or Beatrice (or Shelley) is Count Cenci. Yet these all-important differences come into existence only at the price of their potential displacement and repetition. Poetry is risky, given over to the drift of inaudible inscription and posthumous effect. Its tropes are uninsurable and thus radically ambiguous in their political effects. Tyranny takes its root in the effort to transform this anarchy into the Arche: a gesture that poetry cannot avoid repeating, but one that poetry also endlessly deconstructs, dethroning power by stamping the name of king into the dust and teaching parricide by rote with its alphabet. By making legible the fact that poetic words do not understand what they express, or feel what they inspire, poetry functions as the political unconscious of aesthetics precisely to the extent that poetry opens aesthetics to the contingency of history, and the constitutive uncertainty of futurity. Poetry is the unacknowledged disease of politics, but also its only hope, since poetry ensures that the possibility of revolution will always remain absolute. Romanticism remains, for us, another name for this paradox.

Coda: Aesthetics, Romanticism, Politics

> If one ceased publishing books in favor of communication by voice, image, or machine, this would in no way change the reality of what is called "the book"; on the contrary, language, like speech, would thereby affirm all the more its predominance and its certitude of a possible truth. In other words, the Book always indicates an order that submits to *unity*, a system of notions in which are affirmed the primacy of speech over writing, of thought over language, and the promise of a communication that would one day be immediate and transparent.
> —Maurice Blanchot, *The Infinite Conversation*

A study that develops through close readings generates an imposing amount of textual detail, and perhaps it will not be judged overrepetitive if I cast the previous chapters into a recapitulatory narrative. We began with a brief survey of issues to which I shall in a moment want to return: the insistent but convoluted, and at times self-occluding, intimacy between the discursive fields of aesthetics and politics; the peculiar visibility of literary theory in Western high-cultural and elite-pedagogical contexts during the last third of the twentieth century; the sense shared by a variety of commentators that modernity constitutes an aesthetic as well as a technological or economic crisis—that the crisis, in fact, has something to do with the increasingly dense symbiosis among these various spheres. We then examined the overlap or commerce among the complex semantic nodes aesthetics, technics, theory, literature, and romanticism, all of which may be said to resist themselves in de Man's sense, or, in a Heideggerian idiom, to be different from themselves, to the extent that they all engage, displace, repress, and render legible a self-difference that, following de Man, we called language. "Language" is of course the grandest of master tropes, as well as the most absurdly fictional of personifications; but I believe it is also our most insistent name—our most pressing catachresis—for the radical singularity, materiality, and nonidentity of inscription as an event irreducible to the comprehension it enables. "Literariness" is a historically appropriate aesthetic term for this nonaesthetic difference within aesthetics and technics—for the error and exposure of a general writing. Aesthetics is the resistance to literariness, and theory is the story of this resistance, as told within the professionalized, technologized institutions of literary study and aesthetic education in the (post)modern university. Romanticism, within this academic context, then becomes the symbolic locus of aesthetics and theory. It also names the event of revolution and reaction, apocalypse and apostasy—the promise and duplicity of a politics of and for modernity.

The theme of nationalism and the figure of the body dominate this book's first movement and play a subtler organizing role in its second. A reading of Benedict Anderson's work elicited our definition of aesthetic nationalism as a hallucinated limit to iterability. The imagining of the national body, in other words, occurs through the aestheticization of communicational technology—the rhetorical personification of technical mediation and reproduction as the "unisonance" of a voice. The imagined community that results from this imaginative and rhetorical act is at once irreducible to the state and endlessly tangled up in state institutions, for, despite its putative spontaneity, the national imagination always needs training and must be produced through aesthetic pedagogy and the various apparatuses of acculturation. This imagined community is also always given over to mourning and the denial of mourning. Originating in unacknowledgeable loss, it cherishes its tombs and memorials, and it finds its most striking symbol in the abstract death of the Unknown Soldier, from whose tomb all traces of literal death—death in the form of an *identifiable* corpse—has been expunged. With the theme of mourning, gender difference comes into prominence as an aesthetic concern and rhetorical resource. This book's first and second chapters hew different paths toward broadly similar scenarios: a woman mourns, if excessively (Fichte's personified Age), or by omission and proxy (Arnold's Wragg) over a body that is in one case the Age or Nation itself and in the other a body that the woman has created and killed, and that stands in uneasy specular relationship to the narrating critical consciousness. Arnold's text suggests that the act of imagining the nation not only elicits scenes of mourning (for without Wragg and the national decrepitude she represents, aesthetic culture would have

no purpose), but also encourages the abjection of maternal figures—
symbolic scapegoats who pay the price for the nation's rhetorical instability. If the nation responds to and partly wards off the shock of modernity,
the mother (of the nation, of criticism as acculturation) serves here as a
supplemental shock absorber, an extra figure in and through which the
anonymous dissemination and difference of technical or linguistic mediation can be given face, defaced, and ritualistically expelled.[1]

In Chapter 2, we mapped the nation's rhetorical instability onto that
of the body as an aesthetic figure. Arguably the most invested and uncertain
of all of aesthetic discourse's master tropes, the body figures both the possibility and the ruin of form. It promises to incorporate referentiality per se
and to stabilize difference as the seemingly visible difference between the
sexes. Yet it exceeds this task and falls short of it, to the point that the fatality of the body—its vulnerability and permeability, its sexuality, its con-
signment to death—becomes inextricable from the linguistic predicament
that allows meaningful bodies to come into being. The problematic of the
body as the aesthetic tradition's figure for the limits of figuration develops
in an arc from Chapters 1 to 4. As we saw in Chapter 3, Paul de Man's reading of Kant stages a fragmentation of the body under the impact of formal
materialism: "We must, in short," de Man tells us, ventriloquizing the
predicament of reflective aesthetic judgment, "consider our limbs, hands,
toes, breasts, or what Montaigne so cheerfully referred to as 'Monsieur ma
partie,' in themselves, severed from the organic unity of the body. . . .
We must, in other words, disarticulate, mutilate the body. . . . To the dismemberment of the body corresponds a dismemberment of language, as
meaning-producing tropes are replaced by the fragmentation of sentences
and propositions into discrete words, or the fragmentation of words into
syllables or finally letters."[2] Formal materialism provides a theoretical narrative for the kind of linguistic defacement to which Arnold's Wragg gives
face. This theoretical narrative inevitably replays versions of the error it critiques. Like the "giant" produced and eventually dissipated within what
looks like (but is perhaps not quite, or not quite yet) a same-sex encounter,
as Rousseau's primitive man meets his other, gender and sexual differences
emerge as the transformation of uncertainty into fear into normalization.
Analogously, the materiality of the letter manifests itself in de Man's texts
as "a terror glimpsed," a lurid figure enabling a fetishistic play of identifications.[3] Yet if theory to some extent reiterates the hysterical and fetishistic

personifications it critiques, this repetition makes a difference: the theoretical critique underscores the arbitrariness of the mother's abjection and encourages us to treat with a grain of skepticism personifying scenarios of all sorts—even, as we noted in Chapter 4, when the personification serves progressive themes, as in the case of Philippe Lacoue-Labarthe's nomination of Aphrodite as the tutelary goddess of the "scandal of the aesthetic," the figure of figurativeness and fictionality.

Anderson's and Fichte's mourning women; Arnold's Wragg; Schiller's Juno; Lacoue-Labarthe's Aphrodite; the Medusa who appears in Carol Jacobs's account of de Man, or in my own account of theory in this book's Introduction—this insistent sequence of maternal, divine, or monstrous female figures suggests the degree to which the promise and threat of the feminine has laced aesthetic discourse. And indeed, it may be that any critique of aesthetics—or of technics, or the body—will need to preserve a certain loyalty to the idea of the feminine.[4] In Chapter 4, I noted in passing Drucilla Cornell's argument that "we cannot do without the feminine" as "an aesthetic idea that breaks open the ground of fundamental metaphysical concepts."[5] The reading of *Lucinde* that my chapter went on to offer could conceivably be understood as an oblique gloss on the feminine in this sense: the *Namenlose*, the anonymous condition "prior" to determination or indetermination that we discovered at the heart of Schlegel's allegory of gender difference, could be aligned with the feminine as the difference that opens, exceeds, and ruins the opposition between male and female, *Männlichkeit* and *Weiblichkeit*. I have preferred here, however, partly for reasons having to do with the idiom of Schlegel's text, to insist simply on the rhetoricity of such moments and to propose that gender and sexual difference be thought from the point of view of irony rather than thinking irony from the point of view of gender. Irony is no more authoritative a metalinguistic term than any other; but a reading attentive to irony in Schlegel's sense will at least be predisposed to affirm the ludic as well as the tragic vicissitudes of sexual difference and gender identity. *Lucinde* could certainly be interpreted in ways that would cause us to add its eponymous heroine to our list of fetishized female givers of face to the aesthetic. But the novel also tells a refreshingly affirmative story of gender as radically queer, of sexual identity as fundamentally unstable, and of the body as formally material. Such a story retains a place for the work of mourning, and the possibility of damage or loss—irony for Schlegel is a name for that possibility—but it shakes off some of the melancholy and melodrama attendant upon the fetishistic cycle of gendered representations that we tracked throughout much of this book.

Finally, in Chapter 5, we returned explicitly to the politics of aesthetics and offered a reading of Shelley that sought to provide for the political sphere a commentary analogous in many respects to that on sexuality and gender difference provided by our reading of Schlegel. Once again, we found ourselves confronting the ur-scene of aesthetic nationalism: the Nation as assembled body, gathered into the presence of an orator. Yet this time, we were reading a text thoroughly alive to the fictionality of that primal scene and interested in exploring its fantasies, anxieties, and conditions of possibility. Despite its rough-hewn appearance, Shelley's *Mask of Anarchy*, as we saw, constitutes a rigorous deconstruction of a politics grounded in identity and voice. Over the course of my reading of Fichte's *Addresses to the German Nation*, I offered the half-humorous comment that, given their reliance on print technology and their determination to sublate this technology into the metaphor of voice, Fichte's *Addresses* can be said to imagine Germany precisely to the extent that they imagine the possibility of radio.[6] *The Mask of Anarchy* translates this technical extension and displacement of voice into the turns of a self-effacing rhetoric. Aesthetic nationalism is unmasked, and politics is reimagined as action irreducible to the subject and its calculations—as the incalculable residue of an intentional act. This revision of the political proceeds in a slightly different key in Shelley's *Cenci*, where the modern and romantic dream of political apocalypse—of a Revolution, a "tremendous deed," that would annihilate and heal the trauma of history—finds itself dramatically exposed to the risk that constitutes it: the more tremendous the deed, the more acute the danger of repeating the violence to be expunged. Shelley pursues this paradox with unflinching rigor. His texts present political action as necessary ("something must be done": the imperative remains absolute), *and* as radically exposed to dissemination, error, and the vicissitudes of mechanical reproduction (minimally imaged, in the *Defence of Poetry*'s famous closing paragraph, as the technical prosthesis of the trumpet which "feels not what it inspires"). Such are the anaesthetic conditions of possibility of aesthetic politics and the genuine predicament of a romantic political unconscious.

"Romantic," however, is a teasing adjective here, a knot of questions rather than a stable period metaphor. Throughout this book, reflections bounce between late twentieth-century and late eighteenth- to mid-nineteenth-century texts and contexts—between Benedict Anderson and J. G. Fichte; Terry Eagleton and Matthew Arnold; de Man and Schiller; Lacoue-Labarthe and Schlegel; McGann and Shelley. The point has not been to collapse quite different historical moments but to open paths toward an understanding of aesthetics as a genuinely historical rather than safely distant and objectifiable phenomenon. Mapping aesthetics onto romanticism, I have allowed the former term to inflate and deform the latter, to the point that, of the various authors discussed in this book, only two, Schlegel and Shelley, are indisputably romantic. But as noted in the Introduction, romanticism has never been a stable term, and my abuse of it pays homage to historical precedent. Schiller, never identified as a romantic in the German tradition, is rarely considered anything else in French scholarship; Arnold and the Victorians have often been assimilated to an expanded romanticism; and so have the literary movements of the twentieth century. The specialists in British romanticism who reduce "romanticism" to aesthetics as "ideology" save their unkindest cuts for precursors in their own twentieth-century institution—as though romanticism were above all a product of scholarship's professional era, a twentieth-century dream projected backward onto literary history. Nor do such observations always limit themselves to the relatively petty affair of professional romantic studies. "Romantic imagination is the source code (by way of Edgar Allan Poe, the Beats, Thomas Pynchon, and others) of [Willam Gibson's] *Neuromancer*, the novel that marked the emergence of the 'cyberpunk' or 'mirrorshades' movement in postmodern science fiction," Alan Liu asserts; and he goes on to characterize as "neuromantic" much recent writing of the cultural criticism sort: "cultural anthropology, new cultural history, New Historicism, New Pragmatism, new and/or post-Marxism, and finally that side of French theory—overlapping with post-Marxism—that may be labeled French pragmatism (i.e., the 'practice' philosophy and/or semiotic 'pragmatics' of the later Michel Foucault, Pierre Bourdieu, Michel de Certeau, Jean-François Lyotard)."[7] Standing on its head the McGannite claim to have identified and chastised a "romantic ideology," Liu proposes that "romanticism is the most common ancestor of the various cultural criticisms" (87). He has in mind their interest in narratives of "self-fashioning," their invocations of "ordinary language," and above all their investment in

a "romanticism of detail." The "local threatens to go transcendental" insofar as the accretion of detail, which provides this sort of criticism with its
stamp of referential and historical authenticity and triggers the rhetoric of
the sublime: "Postmodernism . . . is continuous with [modernism] and its
romantic predecessor: the moment of sublimity is there at the root" (91,
92). For the details are nothing unless they can be totalized as sublime fragments: "By this trope, the least detail points to total understanding. . . .
Culture, that is, can be understood in its totality only if we believe that our
inability to understand totality *is* the total truth" (93).

Liu is documenting here some concrete consequences of the fact,
noted at several points in the previous chapters, that, partly because of the
slice of European history it designates, but mainly because it functions as a
trope for aesthetics, romanticism is a period metaphor that names the invention of period metaphors, historicism, and the other major aesthetic
categories of modernity. Various aspects of contemporary criticism's effort
to comprehend past cultures or the present historical moment could be
cited in support of Liu's analysis: one thinks of J. F. Lyotard's or Fredric
Jameson's well-known attempts to explain postmodernism via eighteenth-
century theories of the sublime, or the New Historicism's prejudice (as Liu
himself puts it) "for synchronic structure—for the paradigmatic moment-
in-time in which the whole pattern of historical context may be gazed at in
rapt stasis."[8] But to characterize such phenomena as "romantic" is to run
on a wheel: we project into the past an ideology that we then discover to be
our own, not least at the very moment when we perform such recogni-
tions. The potential narcissism of that encounter, furthermore, is complicated by the fact that the texts we style romantic often provide a more rigorous critique of aesthetic–romantic ideology than texts from subsequent
literary–historical periods, including our own. It is for this reason that romanticism remains, as we noted in the Introduction, a locus of extravagant
political hopes and anxieties. Our historical moment is of course far removed from those of Wordsworth or Novalis, Keats or Baudelaire. If we
still look to those variously romantic texts and contexts for an understanding of our own predicament, this is because we remain entangled within
aesthetic institutions and discourses in an era that has witnessed a massive
proliferation of technically produced aesthetic effects in the spheres of
commerce, information, and entertainment. As Liu and others have noted,
a localist aesthetic is precisely what one might expect to flourish in an era

of globalization. The putatively antiaesthetic localism of American-style cultural studies folds back into the generality and transparency of "culture" as the sign of the human, technically inflated to girdle the globe. Tilottama Rajan suggests, in fact, that the recent cultural studies phenomenon in North American universities responds to the homogenizing imperatives of globalization. As "the organizational structure for the transparent society," she argues, cultural studies "interpellat[es] minority identities and localisms into a disciplinary complex" and then "reprojects the affect of identity politics onto a jubilant specular identification with technology and economics."[9] Rajan's analysis complements those of other astute observers. Bill Readings suggests that cultural studies promotes culture's "dereferentializ[ation]" within what he calls the university of excellence (anything can be culture, just as anything can be excellent: "Excellence is clearly a purely internal unit of value that effectively brackets all questions of reference or function, thus creating an internal market").[10] And Wlad Godzich, with composition programs rather than cultural studies in mind, writes of what he calls "the new literacy" or "the new vocationalism" in contemporary educational systems: literacy as "the mastery of specific codes of linguistic usage defined by the career objectives of the student."[11] Like Rajan, and to some extent Readings, Godzich suggests a congruence between the aims of such technoliteracy and "Hegel's grand design," according to which the end of history occurs when "the Spirit is coextensive with all there is to be known, and the only problems that remain are problems of local management" (14). Cultural studies and the new vocationalism are two faces or facets of a posthistorical, global economy, in which local or individual differences are supposed to occur precisely as the homogeneity of culture, self-expression, and careerism. That the "end of history" is itself a myth—arguably *the* myth of the West, and one that flies in the face of the new world order's barbaric political and economic realities—does not in the least detract from its ideological and thus to some extent referential force.[12]

All of the critics I have just mentioned are in fact writing about aesthetics and about the dense intimacy between aesthetics and technics, whether or not these themes surface explicitly. The nonreferential, formalist–bureaucratic idea of "excellence" that, according to Readings, sums up the crisis of the postmodern (and, in his view, posthistorical and postnational) university, may be taken as one symptom among many of the symbiosis between technological and aesthetic rhetorics of formalization in late-capitalist Western culture. And Godzich's intuition—shared by so many other critics, from any number of perspectives—that a technoculture of image and information flow is supplanting an older "culture of literacy," leads him to emphasize a congruence between the image's sensuous, aesthetic promise and its technical, communicational efficiency ("As the designers of the Macintosh and Windows interfaces have discovered, images have a greater efficiency in imparting information than language does" [11]). The technological gimmicks of a fin de siècle aesthete such as des Esseintes—absurd enough even back in the 1880s—have long since become utterly otiose. Synesthetic simulacra are now effortlessly and involuntarily consumed by the masses, as part of the global penetration of capital and its technical wizardry, its powers of standardization and replication, its endless reproductions of auratic effects that conceal both the grim realities of capitalist production and the disseminating movement within modern technics.[13] One such effect, we have suggested here, is nationalism. And despite its palpably anachronistic character, the nation remains today a fundamental structuring device within the academic study of the humanities—and a potent force in the world at large.[14] I write these pages in the immediate aftermath of the destruction of the World Trade Center towers: a horror that has also been, as the terrorists certainly intended, an overwhelming media event, beamed instantly around the world. The towers were targeted not just as material extensions of their name—as, that is, the symbolic center of world trade—but as icons of the America that is inseparable from globalization. As a form of economic, semiotic, and military domination, globalization is a profoundly hybrid phenomenon in which the political unit of the nation-state—even the nation-state turned superpower—plays only a partial and erratic role. But globalization is inevitably imagined as a nation, "America," and both acts of terror and state responses to terror mobilize the rhetoric and anxieties of nationalism insofar as they involve their own media representation. In the United States, the coverage has been "coverage" in all senses: on the one hand, a recording of material damage and human death and suffering (and resilience, and courage); on the other hand, an ongoing, paradoxical covering over, a simultaneous exposure and denial of a phantasmatic wound suffered by a national body—a body that required the wound to remember its unity. Everything and nothing has changed, we are told, with the repetitiveness of which only mass media systems are capable: America, reassembled in and through its unprecedented act of mourning, is more unified than ever. Patriotic sentiments, Benedict Anderson reminds us, can rank among the most deeply felt emotions available to human beings in our era. But that does not change the fact that nationalism relies for its existence upon media representation, print and image technology—the communicational networks that also, paradoxically, exceed the nation and inscribe it within a global context that is itself a delusively totalizing aesthetic metaphor for the radical uncircumscribability of communication. The nation-state is no longer, and perhaps never was, the genuine subject of historical action, but nationalism is no simple vestige or archaism in the world's new order. Nationalism partakes of the generalized production of aesthetic and political effects within a globalizing (if never truly global) capitalist technoculture, the figure for which, mass-produced and inescapable, is America.

Returning to the less momentous matter of the humanities and their vicissitudes in the late twentieth- and early twenty-first-century university, we may note finally that the "jubilant specular identification with technology and economics" that critics discern in cultural studies, or vocational pedagogy, or the postmodern university per se, never occurs without signs of strain. Postmodern localism frays into less controllable sorts of fragmentation. Despite its best efforts, cultural studies remains tangled up in the literary theory it ambivalently abjures and will always be misreadable by anxious or angry readers as "deconstruction," just as deconstruction or rhetorical reading will always be misreadable as aestheticism or professional–bureaucratic technologism. Both aesthetics and the critique of aesthetics inhabit this ambivalence. Picking up on the themes of intoxication and substance abuse that shadow aesthetics generally and romanticism in particular, we could say that we are hooked on aesthetics and its theory, so long as we keep in mind that the compulsions of habit respond to our exposure to contingency.[15] And when, in the wake of romanticism, we imagine a politics open to contingency—to the risk of the other—we begin to think our way out of aesthetic politics by way of the aesthetic. "Art is loyal to humanity," Adorno writes, "only through inhumanity toward it."[16] This book has proposed that affirmation as a romantic one, and as the irreducible, utopian possibility—what Benjamin calls the weak messianic claim—of the politics of aesthetics.

Notes

INTRODUCTION

1. Matthew Arnold, "The Function of Criticism at the Present Time," in *"Culture and Anarchy" and Other Writings*, ed. Stefan Collini (Cambridge: Cambridge University Press, 1993), 42.

2. Harold Bloom, *How to Read and Why* (New York: Scribner, 2000), 22.

3. "Remember: You never know where culture is gonna come from; you never know what culture is gonna look like; you never know when or where you're gonna need culture; you never know what culture is gonna do, and you never know what culture is for." Conrad Atkinson, letter to the editor, *New York Times* (Tuesday, August 16, 1994, A14). J. Hillis Miller quotes these sentences in his *Black Holes* (Stanford: Stanford University Press, 1999) in the context of a discussion of recent attempts to reconceive comparative literature as cultural studies, and he rightly comments that "culture becomes a term progressively emptied of meaning by coming more and more to include everything in human life . . . a magic elixir, an omnipotent cure-all" (509, n. 43). He might have added: culture, in formulations like Atkinson's, expands its Arnoldian, aesthetic purview ("you never know when or where you're gonna need culture") to cover the entirety of "culture" in its anthropological sense. For a powerful analysis of the tensions built into our notion of culture, see Werner Hamacher, "One 2 Many Multiculturalisms," in *Violence, Identity, and Self-Determination*, ed. Hent de Vries and Samuel Weber (Stanford, Calif.: Stanford University Press, 1997), 284–325.

4. As John Guillory puts it, "The primacy of the social identity of the author in the pluralist critique of the canon means that the revaluation of works on this basis will inevitably seek its ground in the author's experience, conceived as the experience of a marginalized race, class, or gender identity. The author returns in the critique of the canon not as the genius, but as the representative of a social identity. . . . Hence the critique of the canon remains quite vulnerable to certain elementary theoretical objections, but this fact is itself symptomatic of a political dilemma generated by the very logic of liberal pluralism. It suggests that the category of social identity is too important politically to yield any ground to theoretical arguments

which might complicate the status of representation in literary texts, for the simple reason that the latter mode of representation is *standing in for* representation in the political sphere." John Guillory, *Cultural Capital: The Problem of Literary Canon Formation* (Chicago: University of Chicago Press, 1993), 10–11. Guillory's overall point is that such a politics of the image effaces the material role of the school as institution: "those members of social minorities who enter the university do not 'represent' the social groups to which they belong in the same way in which minority legislators can be said to represent their constituencies" (7).

5. Fredric Jameson, *Postmodernism, or, the Cultural Logic of Late Capitalism* (Durham, N.C.: Duke University Press, 1991), 4. The fundamental insight here returns to the notion of the "culture industry" elaborated in Max Horkheimer and Theodor W. Adorno, *Dialektik der Aufklärung* (1944) (*Dialectic of Enlightenment*; New York: Continuum, 1982).

6. Thus, principally with writers such as Jean Baudrillard in mind, Christopher Norris, in *What's Wrong With Postmodernism: Critical Theory and the Ends of Philosophy* (Baltimore, Md.: Johns Hopkins University Press, 1990), characterizes much writing about postmodernism as driven by "aesthetic ideology" and defines aesthetic ideology as a "refusal to acknowledge any limits to the realm of imaginary representation" (24). My brief cento here alludes to Guy Debord, *La société du spectacle* (1967) (*The Society of the Spectacle*; New York: Zone Books, 1994 [1967]); Martin Heidegger, "Die Zeit des Weltbildes" ("The Age of the World Picture") in *"The Question Concerning Technology" and Other Essays* (New York: Harper and Row, 1977), 115–54 (Heidegger's essay was originally given as a lecture in 1938 and was published in 1950; for the German text, see *Holzwege*, in *Gesamtausgabe* [Frankfurt am Main: Klostermann, 1977 (1950)], 5:75–113) ; Jameson, *Postmodernism*, on the "waning of affect" in postmodern texts and cultural performances; and Walter Benjamin's writings on the waning of the aura and the shock experience, above all in "Das Kunstwerk im Zeitalter seiner technischen Reproduzierbarkeit" ("The Work of Art in the Age of Mechanical Reproduction," 1936) and "Über einige Motive bei Baudelaire" ("Some Motifs in Baudelaire," 1939), in *Illuminations: Essays and Reflections*, ed. Hannah Arendt, trans. Harry Zohn (New York: Schocken Books, 1969), 217–51 and 155–200; *Gesammelte Schriften*, ed. Rolf Tiedemann and Hermann Schweppenhäuser (Frankfurt am Main: Suhrkamp, 1980), 1.2:431–508 and 605–64.

7. Marc Redfield, *Phantom Formations: Aesthetic Ideology and the Bildungsroman* (Ithaca: Cornell University Press, 1996).

8. Jonathan Culler, *Literary Theory: A Very Short Introduction* (New York: Oxford University Press, 1997), 15.

9. See, for a recent example of scholarly interest in de Man, the fine collection of essays edited by Tom Cohen, Barbara Cohen, J. Hillis Miller, and Andrzej Warminski, *Material Events: Paul de Man and the Afterlife of Theory* (Minneapolis: University of Minnesota Press, 2001). Guillory discusses the phenomenon of

de Manian "discipleship" keenly if unsympathetically in *Cultural Capital*, 182–87; and I provide my own analysis of the peculiarities of de Man's reception in Chapter 3. For a recent example of an irritable response to de Man, see n. 11 below.

10. David Simpson, *Romanticism, Nationalism, and the Revolt Against Theory* (Chicago: University of Chicago Press, 1993), 1. As intelligent observers of various critical orientations have noted (including Guillory in the comment quoted above, and Simpson, more tangentially, in remarks footnoted below), the furor over de Man's wartime journalism was always really about de Man as the representative of theory. In themselves, these 180-odd newspaper articles would be of interest only to a highly specialized historian. Since memories fade as the decades pass, and since the resistance to theory often resorts to caricature, it is perhaps worth recalling that most of these pieces, which de Man wrote in occupied Belgium in 1940–42 for the national newspaper *Le Soir* and the small Antwerp daily *Het Vlaamsche Land*, are relatively unremarkable literary reviews: aestheticist and organic–historicist in orientation; at times naively idealistic about the possibility of cultural renewal in German-dominated Europe; at times visibly engaged in making compromises in the hope of preserving a degree of autonomy—unadmirable material, certainly, but hardly the stuff of scandal. The "de Man affair" of 1988 mostly concerned a single article, "The Jews in Contemporary Literature," which was commissioned by *Le Soir* for a special issue titled "The Jews and Us" on March 4, 1941. Compared with the other contributions to the special issue, it is not a particularly virulent text—indeed, its author probably intended it as a clever compromise with political reality: it condemns "vulgar anti-Semitism" and offers instead the supposedly more cultured assurance that European literature, developing "according to its own grand evolutionary laws," has not been harmed by Jewish writers, and would not be harmed by "the creation of a Jewish colony isolated from Europe." (De Man alludes here to the so-called Madagascar solution, a topic of public discussion in German-dominated Europe during this period; Hitler's clandestine adoption of the Final Solution did not occur until some nine months later, at the Wannsee Conference of January 20, 1942; in Belgium, deportations would begin in August 1942.) Jacques Derrida elicited furious responses when he noted ambiguities in this article, but its young author does seem to have been playing, to some extent, a devious game and seeing what he could get away with (he lists "Kafka," for instance, as an example of great European literature). That doesn't mean we shouldn't judge the article harshly: although I think a careful reading of this and the rest of the journalism makes it clear that the young de Man had no allegiance to ("vulgar") Nazi racism, he was callous and opportunistic enough to juggle such rhetoric as part of the price he was paying for the opportunity—a heady one, surely, for a twenty-two-year-old—to dispense sage judgments about European literature in a national forum. Responsible readers can come to different conclusions about aspects of de Man's collaboration; what concerns us here is the way this article was used, half a century after its publication, to construct a

timelessly abject "Paul de Man" who could embody the sins of theory in the last decade of the twentieth century. One is not in the least excusing de Man by pointing out the bizarre disproportions that characterize the wartime journalism scandal. All sorts of complications, of interest to those who cared about de Man as a person or about the moral complexities of life under the Occupation, did in fact turn up when Belgian contemporaries of de Man's were interviewed (he was under the influence of his famous uncle, the politician and political theorist Hendrik de Man, who for a time advocated and practiced collaboration; he seems to have more than once sheltered Jewish friends at great personal risk; he never appears to have displayed any trace of anti-Semitism in his personal life, during the war or afterward; and so on). The point, however, is not that de Man's article is excusable— we may agree that it is not—but simply that the attempts to use it as an *ad hominem* grenade with which to explode de Manian literary theory have necessarily relied on ahistorical and wildly tendentious argumentation. (The case of de Man is hardly comparable, for instance, with that of Heidegger, whose collaboration, if never uncomplicated, was for a brief period quite serious, and was furthermore the act of a mature philosopher, rather than that of a recent college graduate whose serious intellectual work lay many years in the future.) For the texts, see Paul de Man, *Wartime Journalism, 1939–1943*, ed. Werner Hamacher, Neil Hertz, and Thomas Keenan (Lincoln: University of Nebraska Press, 1988); my quote above is from the March 4, 1941, article, reproduced on p. 45. For a large collection of responses, see *Responses: On Paul de Man's Wartime Journalism*, ed. Werner Hamacher, Neil Hertz, and Thomas Keenan (Lincoln: University of Nebraska Press, 1989). For Jacques Derrida's "Like the Sound of the Sea Deep Within a Shell: Paul de Man's War" and the debate it inspired, see *Critical Inquiry* 14, no. 3 (1988): 530–652 and 15, no. 4 (1989): 765–873.

11. Though I don't wish to minimize in any way the ongoing resistance that Jacques Derrida's work inspires both within and outside of the academy, it is nonetheless the case that when accommodations have been made for "deconstruction" over the last thirty years, de Man has repeatedly represented a negative element to be chastised and discarded. It is de Man, according to this slender but clearly defined genre of criticism, who domesticates, Americanizes, and aestheticizes the revolutionary Derridean insight: for a relatively recent and well-circulated version of this story, see Jeffrey T. Nealon, "The Discipline of Deconstruction," *PMLA* 107, no. 5 (1992): 1266–79. If de Man really were simply a tame Derrida— a New Critic with a deconstructive hat on—one imagines that he would have inspired less homage and hatred over the last thirty-odd years. Certainly the animus unleashed against de Man and de Manian criticism both before and after the discovery of the wartime journalism has often been pathological in its intensity. Let me offer here one example, taken from an otherwise sedate and competent book that I footnote approvingly in the next chapter: David Aram Kaiser, *Romanticism, Aesthetics, and Nationalism* (Cambridge: Cambridge University Press, 1999).

Kaiser invokes and disposes of de Man in a paragraph that, on the strength of a two-sentence summary, labels de Man's reading of Schiller's *Aesthetic Education* a "misreading," declares this misreading "inaccurate" and "intellectually dishonest," and without further argument, a sentence or so later, winds things up with an unpleasant *praeteritio*: "Without wishing to engage in *ad hominem* arguments, I will simply point out the back-handed way in which de Man is insinuating an equivalence between Schiller and Goebbels, and leave it to individual readers to draw whatever irony they might find in the fact that it is Paul de Man making such a charge" (40). (Kaiser in turn back-handedly insinuates here, of course, an equivalence between de Man and Goebbels.) There are no other moments of comparable rhetorical intensity elsewhere in Kaiser's book—no other hills and valleys where a charge of misreading could so rapidly snowball into one of "intellectual dishonesty"—and no obvious clues that would help one understand why the author needs to summon up and cast out de Man here. The passage, in other words, is a symptom: it relays a disturbance that has to be interpreted. David Simpson, well aware of the symbolic link between de Man and theory, suggests we relate this abjection of de Man to a persistent nationalistic discomfort with cosmopolitanism: "It is hard not to conclude that much of the animus directed against Paul de Man, even before the notorious revelations of his wartime career, was a function of his internationalism and his commitment to a seriously comparative literature. In the Enlightenment tradition, de Man threatened any literary criticism founded in the 'screen of received ideas' that passes for 'humanistic knowledge,' delivered in the rhetoric of moral indignation and religiosity" (*Romanticism*, 181). Simpson is surely right that de Man's cosmopolitanism allowed him to personify theory's irreducibility to nationalism's inside/outside tropes: theory's is an uncertain foreignness that spurs nationalistic hyperbole (theory is always too "French," too "American"). But the intensity of a response like Kaiser's—an intensity that characterizes so much writing about de Man—requires for its understanding that we situate aesthetic nationalism within the broader context of aesthetic discourse—a principal task of the present book, and one that will in fact involve us in an extended consideration of de Man's reading of Schiller (see Chapter 3).

   12. Paul de Man, "The Resistance to Theory," in *The Resistance to Theory* (Minneapolis: University of Minnesota Press, 1986), 8.

   13. René Wellek and Austin Warren, *Theory of Literature* (New York: Harcourt, Brace, Jovanovich, 1948); René Wellek, "Destroying Literary Studies," *New Criterion* 2, no. 4 (1983): 1–8. Wellek notes ironically, near the close of his article: "I sometimes feel guilty of having helped to propagate the theory of literature. Since my book, theory has triumphed in this country and has, possibly, triumphed with a vengeance" (8).

   14. Guillory's ambitious narrative in *Cultural Capital* arguably needs nuancing in various ways. That recent decades have witnessed both financial and cultural capital flight from the humanities is undeniable; but the picture is complicated.

Elite universities continue to offer a humanities curriculum that increasingly marks these pedagogical sites *as* elite; furthermore, where the humanities have been most savagely downsized—in the state schools and the polytechnics—a very real contempt for literary education coexists with a rhetoric of value—value for the money—that systematically translates into the demand that literary instruction furnish aesthetic–humanistic platitudes as copiously and efficiently as possible. Literary instruction on the preuniversity level, meanwhile, remains overwhelmingly aesthetic in its presuppositions and practices. My comments here also take a bit of distance from the influential argument of Bill Readings, in *The University in Ruins* (Cambridge, Mass.: Harvard University Press, 1996), that the university's aesthetic task of forming national subjects has been superseded in a globalized economy. That observation is largely true; but like Guillory, Readings slightly overstates his case, in part because he underestimates the persistence of aesthetic nationalism as an ideological force—one paradoxically bound up with globalism, as I suggest in Chapter 1.

15. For a somewhat differently pitched short critique of some of Guillory's major claims, see *Phantom Formations*, 35–36, 211–13. Guillory's chapter on de Man is by far the longest and most passionate chapter in *Cultural Capital* and is thus itself yet another example of the obsessive intensity with which critics so often engage (de Manian) theory. If de Man haunts this text more persistently than its author is prepared to acknowledge, this is at least partly because Guillory remains deeply invested in the utopian potential of aesthetic politics, as witnessed by his book's closing call for an "aestheticism unbound": "If there is no way out of the game of culture, then, even when cultural capital is the only kind of capital, there may be another kind of game with less consequences for the losers, an *aesthetic* game. Socializing the means of production and consumption would be the condition of an aestheticism unbound, not its overcoming" (340). I briefly discuss this passage, which is squarely within the Schillerian aesthetic tradition, in *Phantom Formations*, 212–13.

16. Friedrich Schlegel, *Critical (Lyceum) Fragments*, no. 40, *Kritische Friedrich-Schlegel-Ausgabe*, ed. Ernst Behler with Jean-Jacques Anstett and Hans Eichner (Paderborn: Schöningh, 1958), 2:151. Unless otherwise noted, all translations in this and subsequent chapters are mine.

17. Geoffrey Galt Harpham, "Aesthetics and the Fundamentals of Modernity," in *Aesthetics and Ideology*, ed. George Levine (New Brunswick: Rutgers University Press, 1994), 124.

18. On the emergence and changing significance of these words, see Raymond Williams' classic study, *Keywords: A Vocabulary of Culture and Society*, rev. ed. (New York: Oxford University Press, 1985); see also n. 24 below.

19. For a classic account of the ancient intimacy between literature and pedagogy, see Ernst Robert Curtius, *European Literature and the Latin Middle Ages*, trans. Willard R. Trask (Princeton: Princeton University Press, 1973 [1948]): "Literature

forms part of 'education.' Why and since when? Because the Greeks found their past, their essential nature and their world of deities ideally reflected in a poet. They had no priestly books and no priestly caste. Homer, for them, was the 'tradition.' From the sixth century onwards he was a schoolbook. Since that time literature has been a school subject, and the continuity of European literature is bound up with the schools. Education becomes the medium of the literary tradition: a fact which is characteristic of Europe, but which is not necessarily so in the nature of things" (36).

20. I should note that I have designed this section of the introduction to be independent of, yet also to complement, my survey of aesthetics (and my discussion of the intimacy between aesthetics and theory) in chap. 1 of *Phantom Formations*; there will be a few points of inevitable overlap, of course, and one or two places where I shall refer readers to my previous book for fuller discussion of certain aspects of aesthetic discourse or theory.

21. Terry Eagleton, *The Ideology of the Aesthetic* (Oxford: Blackwell, 1990), 13.

22. Edmund Burke, *A Philosophical Enquiry into the Origin of Our Ideas of the Sublime and the Beautiful*, ed. James T. Boulton (Notre Dame: University of Notre Dame Press, 1986 [1958]), 13.

23. Howard Caygill, *Art of Judgment* (Oxford: Blackwell, 1989), 38.

24. Raymond Williams tells us that *culture* is "one of the two or three most complicated words in the English language" (*Keywords*, 87); his commentary provides a definitive brief summary of the history and some of the complexities of our notion of culture, though one may now also consult Terry Eagleton, *The Idea of Culture* (Oxford: Blackwell, 2000), and, for a sustained critical analysis, Hamacher's article "One 2 Many." In its early uses, the term *culture* was "a noun of process: the tending of something, basically crops or animals" (*Keywords*, 87); subsequently, by metaphorical extension, it came to mean the tending of the mind; and over the course of the eighteenth century, it began to acquire its three principal modern meanings: (1) humanity's general "intellectual, spiritual, and aesthetic development" (here, *culture* serves as a close synonym for another Enlightenment keyword, *civilization*); (2) the specificity of a local or folk or traditional culture (often in contrast to the globalizing rationalism and technologism of *civilization*); and (3) intellectual and artistic activity. These meanings form a chord, as it were, in aesthetic discourse: the artwork (#3) represents its specific culture (#2) and in doing so also represents essential humanity (#1). In this fully aesthetic sense, the word *culture* took slow root in Britain (Matthew Arnold felt compelled to defend his use of it in the 1860s). It has been convincingly argued, however, that an aesthetic notion of what we now call *culture* developed during the late eighteenth century; see David Lloyd and Paul Thomas, *Culture and the State* (New York: Routledge, 1998).

25. An important aspect of aesthetic pedagogy that, for reasons of economy, I pass over here is its dependence on example. The example is the formalized sensuous

particular that teaches the subject of an aesthetic education to identify with humanity: such is the function of the "canon" within aesthetic discourse. For a sustained discussion of aesthetic exemplarity in Kant, Schiller, and the tradition of *Bildung*, see *Phantom Formations*, esp. 17–27 and 49–55.

26. Friedrich Schiller, *On the Aesthetic Education of Man, in a Series of Letters*, bilingual edition, ed. Elizabeth M. Wilkinson and L. A. Willoughby (Oxford: Clarendon Press, 1967), 8/9 (Second Letter) and 17/18 (Fourth Letter), translation modified in the interest of literal accuracy, though Wilkinson and Willoughby's added phrase, which I italicize here, is certainly Schillerian in spirit: "an ideal man, *the archetype of a human being*, and it is his life's task." For a discussion of Schiller's text, see Chapter 3.

27. Matthew Arnold, *Culture and Anarchy*, in *"Culture and Anarchy" and Other Writings*, 83, Arnold's italics. Subsequent citations are from this edition.

28. Lloyd and Thomas trace "a considerable shift from direct domination to hegemony" in Britain over the course of the nineteenth century (140). They discover in radical and working-class writings of the 1820s and 1830s a "systematic refusal" to imagine culture apart from the economic and political sphere and a deep suspicion of the abstracting processes of representative democracy, but they conclude that by the 1860s, working-class journals had become heavily marked by a rhetoric of self-discipline and acculturation. Thus, they argue, a middle-class rhetoric of acculturation had come to dominate the social field by the time of the Second Reform Bill.

29. The institutional history of literary study, for instance, has been attempted by many critics in recent years: see, e.g., Chris Baldick, *The Social Mission of English Criticism, 1848–1942* (Oxford: Oxford University Press, 1983), or, for German developments, Peter Uwe Hohendahl, *Building a National Literature: The Case of Germany, 1830–1870*, trans. Renate Baron (Ithaca: Cornell University Press, 1989). The most fundamental texts on aesthetics and material history are arguably those of Walter Benjamin; see esp. "The Work of Art in the Age of Mechanical Reproduction" and related texts in *Illuminations*. Historical studies of the development of such fundamental institutions of modernity as the national schools, the press, and museums are of course legion; on education, a helpful survey is provided by Fritz Ringer, *Education and Society in Modern Europe* (Bloomington: Indiana University Press, 1979). The development of the modern museum has inspired particularly sophisticated historical and theoretical work in recent years; see Tony Bennett, *The Birth of the Museum* (London: Routledge, 1995); Eilean Hooper-Greenhill, *Museums and the Shaping of Knowledge* (London: Routledge, 1992); and esp. Didier Maleuvre, *Museum Memories: History, Technology, Art* (Stanford: Stanford University Press, 1999).

30. Ernest Gellner, *Conditions of Liberty: Civil Society and Its Rivals* (New York: Penguin, 1994), 102, 104. I first encountered mention of Gellner's text in Tilottama Rajan, "The University in Crisis: Cultural Studies, Civil Society, and the Place of

Theory," *Literary Research / Recherche littéraire*, 18, no. 35 (2001): 8–25; she quotes some of the sentences I am citing here (see Rajan, 13–14). I sketched an early version of the point I am making here in my response to Rajan, "Crisis and Culture: Theory, Cultural Studies, and the University," in the same issue of *Literary Research / Recherche littéraire*, 31–35.

31. Gellner is well within the Shaftesbury-to-Kant tradition here, though his text may certainly be judged to be inattentive to the laborious difficulties that Kant's close examination of aesthetic judgment encounters. The possibility of taste, as Kant makes clear, is that of the *sensus communis*: "We must [here] take *sensus communis* to mean the idea of a sense shared [by all of us], i.e., a power to judge that in reflecting takes account (a priori) in our thought, of everyone else's way of presenting [something], in order as it were to compare our own judgment with human reason in general and thus escape the illusion that arises from the ease of mistaking subjective and private conditions for objective ones, an illusion that would have a prejudicial influence on the judgment. Now we do this as follows: we compare our judgment not so much with the actual as rather with the merely possible judgments of others, and [thus] put ourselves in the position of everyone else, merely by abstracting from the limitations that [may] happen to attach to our own judging; and this in turn we accomplish by leaving out as much as possible whatever is matter, i.e., sensation, in the presentational state, and by paying attention solely to the formal features of our presentation or of our presentational state. . . . I maintain that taste may be called a *sensus communis* more legitimately than can sound understanding, and that the aesthetic power of judgment deserves to be called a shared sense more than does the intellectual one, if indeed we wish to use the word *sense* to stand for an effect that mere reflection has on the mind, even though we then mean by sense the feeling of pleasure. We could even define taste as the ability to judge something that makes our feeling in a given presentation *universally communicable* without mediation by a concept." Immanuel Kant, *Critique of Judgment*, trans. Werner S. Pluhar (Indianapolis: Hackett, 1987); *Kritik der Urteilskraft*, ed. Wilhelm Weischedel (Frankfurt: Suhrkamp, 1974), par. 40.

32. Jacques Derrida, "Parergon," in *The Truth in Painting*, trans. Geoffrey Bennington and Ian McLeod (Chicago: University of Chicago Press, 1987), 17–147.

33. Samuel Weber, *Mass Mediauras: Form, Technics, Media* (Stanford: Stanford University Press, 1996), 19. I am much indebted to the remarkable study of the interplay between aesthetics and technics that Weber develops in this book.

34. Weber points out that Kant characterizes aesthetic ideas not as "ineffable," as translations often have it (see, e.g., Pluhar's edition of *Critique of Judgment*, 185), but as "unnameable," *unnennbar* (par. 49). "Far from being that which cannot be uttered, it is in the nature of aesthetical ideas to be uttered all the time, as Kant's numerous examples drawn from poetry make clear"; the point is rather that "such ideas will never be able to be named *properly*" (Weber, 29). In conceiving of aesthetic form in terms of catachresis and projection, we touch on Paul de Man's

192   *Notes to Page 19*

difficult notion of formal materialism, which will be discussed in Chapter 3 via an examination of de Man's reading of Kant. I should perhaps also take this occasion to note that a fuller study of the problem of form in Kantian aesthetic judgment than I am able to offer here may be found in *Phantom Formations*, 12–17.

35. Sophocles, *Antigone*, line 365 (the line forms part of the famous "Ode to Man"). In Sophocles, *Fabulae*, ed. H. Lloyd-Jones and N. G. Wilson (Oxford: Clarendon Press, 1990), 198. A helpful contextualization of the "Ode to Man" may be had in Simon Goldhill, *Reading Greek Tragedy* (Cambridge: Cambridge University Press, 1986), 201–5; for an extended and powerful reading of the Ode that teases out its ambiguities in the context of the play as a whole, see Charles Segal, *Tragedy and Civilization: An Interpretation of Sophocles* (Cambridge, Mass.: Harvard University Press, 1981), 152–206. I thank Molly Ierulli for directing me to Goldhill's and Segal's texts and for helping me with the Greek.

36. Philippe Lacoue-Labarthe, *Heidegger, Art, and Politics*, trans. Chris Turner (Oxford: Blackwell, 1990): I cite the relevant passage in full near the beginning of the next chapter, but perhaps it will be useful to have part of it here: "The political (the City) belongs to a form of plastic art, formation and information, *fiction* in the strict sense. . . . The fact that the political is a form of plastic art in no way means that the *polis* is an artificial or conventional formation, but that the political belongs to the sphere of *techne* in the highest sense of the term, that is to say in the sense in which *techne* is conceived as the accomplishment and revelation of *physis* itself. This is why the *polis* is also 'natural': it is the 'beautiful formation' that has spontaneously sprung from the 'genius of a people'" (66). Lacoue-Labarthe suggests here an ancient filiation for the complicity between organicism and technophilism in highly aestheticized political ideologies such as early twentieth-century fascism; for a relevant study, see Jeffrey Herf, *Reactionary Modernism: Technology, Culture, and Politics in Weimar and the Third Reich* (Cambridge: Cambridge University Press, 1984).

37. The key text here is of course Jacques Derrida, "Plato's Pharmacy," in *Dissemination*, trans. Barbara Johnson (Chicago: University of Chicago Press, 1981), 61–172; on writing and the "dangerous supplement," see *Of Grammatology*, trans. Gayatri Spivak (Baltimore, Md.: Johns Hopkins University Press, 1976). A sustained meditation on technics from Aristotle through Heidegger may be found in Bernard Stiegler, *Technics and Time, 1: The Fault of Epimetheus*, trans. Richard Beardsworth and George Collins (Stanford: Stanford University Press, 1998). Post-Heideggerian reflections on technics have been extraordinarily rich and diverse, and I am indebted to a wide range of authors and texts—above all, the work of Jacques Derrida, which has opened up many opportunities for thought in this area, but also various writings of Friedrich Kittler, Philippe Lacoue-Labarthe, Jean-Luc Nancy, Avital Ronell, and Samuel Weber, to name only the most inevitable of the many names one could catalogue here.

38. Weber, 63. Weber plays here on Heidegger's comment that *Wesen* (the noun

normally translated as "essence") derives from the verb *wesen*, which can mean "to hold sway," to "stay in place," and "to go on." Weber offers several imaginative translations of key Heideggerian terms over the course of his reading of "The Question Concerning Technology": they push the sense of the text, but they may be said to remain faithful both to Heidegger's own practice and to his claim that technics, which is "essentially" different from itself, forces us to abandon an understanding of *Wesen* as *essentia*.

39. For a compact discussion of the iterability of the mark, see Jacques Derrida, "Signature Event Context," in *Limited Inc.*, ed. Gerald Graff (Evanston, Ill.: Northwestern University Press, 1988).

40. Derrida pressures here one of the Third *Critique*'s peculiar discriminations, in this case between the pure and the ideal: a pure judgment of taste, Kant tells us, cannot provide an aesthetic ideal, since an ideal is an idea of reason. Pure judgments of taste must concern objects that do not presuppose their concept and are capable of what Kant calls "free beauty"; man, who contains his own purpose, cannot occasion a pure judgment of taste, but can and does provide an aesthetic ideal. Man thus provides aesthetics with an ideal at the cost of instituting a fundamental impurity (sections 16–17).

41. Martin Heidegger, "Die Frage nach der Technik," *Vorträge und Aufsätze* (Pfullingen: Günther Neske, 1954), 13–44, here 40; "The Question Concerning Technology," in *"The Question Concerning Technology" and Other Essays*, 32.

42. Schiller to C. G. Körner, February 23, 1793; cited in Wilkinson and Willoughby's edition of the *Aesthetic Education*, 300, and also cited (from Wilkinson and Willoughby) in Paul de Man, "Aesthetic Formalization in Kleist," in *The Rhetoric of Romanticism* (New York: Columbia University Press, 1984), 263. De Man's alterations of Wilkinson and Willoughby's translation hew a little more closely to the literal sense (though *caveat lector*: this is certainly not always the goal of de Manian translations); and I have used de Man's as a base for my translation here, which is taken from the *Nationalausgabe* of *Schillers Werke*, vol. 26: *Briefwechsel: Schillers Briefe, 1.3.1790–17.5.1794*, ed. Edith Nahler and Horst Nahler (Weimar: Hermann Böhlaus Nachfolger, 1992), 216–17. The entire letter (199–217 in the *Nationalausgabe*) is of interest in the present context and would repay careful exegesis: it details Schiller's understanding of the relation between technique (*Technik*) and beauty. "Technique and freedom do not have the same relation to the beautiful. Freedom alone is the ground [*Grund*] of the beautiful, technique is merely the ground of our representation of the beautiful" (209). I have analyzed the interplay of aesthetics, technics, and politics in relation to the Schillerian dream of an Aesthetic State in my chapter on Goethe's novel *Wilhelm Meisters Wanderjahre* in *Phantom Formations*, 95–124.

43. Schiller remains a figure capable of surprising resurrections, even in twentieth- and twenty-first-century America ("resurrection" is meant metaphorically here; for a reading of Schiller's much-buried literal corpse, see my *Phantom Formations*,

125–33). Every now and then, a cultural warrior of the right will pay homage to him: see, e.g., Roger Kimball, "Schiller's 'Aesthetic Education,'" *New Criterion* 19, no. 7 (2001): 12–19. Ian Balfour has brought to my attention the Schiller Institute (the motto of which is "The most beautiful of all works of art is the construction of true political freedom"), founded by Helga Zepp LaRouche, wife of Lyndon LaRouche. According to its Web site, it was "named after the great eighteenth-century German playwright and 'Poet of Freedom,' whose works have inspired republican opposition to oligarchic tyranny worldwide. . . . As you navigate through the following pages, you will meet the intellectual giants of our civilization, whose ideas and work brought humanity out of the Dark Ages of the past, and you will get to know some of the ideas, peronalities [sic], and policy battles that are shaping current history at this very moment." Indeed: "Were Friedrich Schiller alive today, he would be happy to see that such a beautiful soul as he described in his letters, exists in the person of Lyndon LaRouche." For further intriguing details, see www.schillerinstitute.org

44. Daniel Heller-Roazen, "Language, or No Language," *Diacritics* 29, no. 3 (1999): 22. The essay reviews work by Werner Hamacher that makes essential reading in this context: see esp. Hamacher's *Premises: Essays on Philosophy and Literature from Kant to Celan*, trans. Peter Fenves (Cambridge, Mass.: Harvard University Press, 1996). Heller-Roazan's phrase "those things of which it speaks" is elicited from a reading of Aristotle's *De interpretatione*.

45. The difficulty of delimiting an aesthetic "discourse" is touched on by Peter de Bolla in *The Discourse of the Sublime: History, Aesthetics, and the Subject* (Oxford: Blackwell, 1989): the discourse of the sublime appears "not only . . . in discussions of reading and speaking, of education in general, but also in political speeches and imaginative literature"; indeed, the discourse of the sublime "has no boundary," capable as it is of producing its own object (sublimity) (12). I have reflected further on the unstable but necessary formulation "aesthetic ideology" in *Phantom Formations*, 33–35, passim.

46. The split or doubled nature of aesthetics appears vividly in Robert Kaufman's fine recent summary of the importance of aesthetics in the Marxist tradition, "Red Kant, or the Persistence of the Third *Critique* in Adorno and Jameson," *Critical Inquiry* 26, no. 4 (2000): 682–724. Kaufman rightly stresses both the significant role accorded to Kantian aesthetic judgment in writings of Marx, Benjamin, Adorno, and others, and the critical force of aesthetic judgment: "a seemingly aestheticist or positivist Kantianism turns out to practice, by dint of aesthetic quasi conceptuality's vocation to resist external determination by extant concepts, a sustained negation of ruling concepts" (723). This claim requires Kaufman, however, to distinguish between "*the aesthetic* and the different (though certainly related) phenomenon of aesthet*icization*" (683, Kaufman's italics): the former is a critical and the latter, of course, a mystified discourse.

47. The association of deconstruction with aestheticism is one of the common-

places of antitheoretical discourse; for a reductively exemplary study, see Juliet Sychrava, *Schiller to Derrida: Idealism in Aesthetics* (Cambridge: Cambridge University Press, 1989); for a more nuanced and scholarly example, see Steven Goldsmith, *Unbuilding Jerusalem: Apocalypse and Romantic Representation* (Ithaca: Cornell University Press, 1993), a study largely fueled by its conception (and rejection) of deconstruction as a version of "Schiller's aesthetic" (15).

48. I am indebted here to Jacques Derrida's perceptive remarks on literature in his interview with Derek Attridge, "'This Strange Institution Called Literature': An Interview with Jacques Derrida." Derrida reflects here on the historical as well as the conceptual peculiarity and specificity of "this institution of fiction which gives *in principle* the power to say everything, to break free of the rules, to displace them. . . . The institution of literature in the West, in its relatively modern form, is linked to an authorization to say everything, and doubtless too to the coming about of the modern idea of democracy." Jacques Derrida, *Acts of Literature*, ed. Derek Attridge (New York: Routledge, 1992), 37. From the perspective of a critique of aesthetics, we may say that the more or less modern institution of literature offers itself to the self-violating impossibility of pure form, i.e., the inscription; this self-violation is then of course aestheticized as the determined referentiality of aesthetic education.

49. Studies of the development of modern notions and institutions of literature in eighteenth-century Britain include, among others, Franklin E. Court, *Institutionalizing English Literature: The Culture and Politics of Literary Study, 1750–1900* (Stanford: Stanford University Press, 1992); and, quite recently, Trevor Ross, "'Pure Poetry': Cultural Capital and the Rejection of Classicism," *Modern Language Quarterly*, 58 (1997): 435–56. Working with the terminology of Pierre Bourdieu, and taking off from J. G. A. Pocock's identification of a conflict between civic and commercial humanism in eighteenth-century European society, Ross argues that the newly dominant role of economic over symbolic capital produced a need for greater autonomy in the field of aesthetic production and traces the development of notions of "pure poetry" in midcentury writers such as Joseph Warton and Edward Young. For a classic discussion of the rise of aesthetics in commercial society, see Raymond Williams, *Culture and Society: 1780–1950* (New York: Columbia University Press, 1983 [1958]), especially the chapter "The Romantic Artist," 30–48.

50. Here, too, I must refer the reader to *Phantom Formations*, esp. 38–62, for a more sustained discussion of literature from the perspective of aesthetic education or *Bildung*, and a critique of Philippe Lacoue-Labarthe and Jean-Luc Nancy's identification of a notion of a "literary absolute" in the writings of the Jena romantics that "aggravates and radicalizes the thinking of totality and the Subject." Philippe Lacoue-Labarthe and Jean-Luc Nancy, *The Literary Absolute: The Theory of Literature in German Romanticism*, trans. Philip Barnard and Cheryl Lester (Albany: State University of New York Press, 1988), 15. I argue that Lacoue-

Labarthe and Nancy's rich formulations, though fundamental to an understanding of literature, *Bildung*, romanticism, etc., tend to slip away from Walter Benjamin's radical insight, which is that German romantic criticism identifies literature's self-reflexivity as nonsubjective: as an "I-less reflection [*Ich-freie Reflexion*]." See Walter Benjamin, *Der Begriff der Kunstkritik in der deutschen Romantik*, in *Gesammelte Schriften*, 1.1:40.

51. Oscar Wilde, "The Critic as Artist," in *Intentions* (London: Methuen, 1913 [1891]), 146, 145. What goes for fin de siècle aestheticism goes above all for academic movements such as the New Criticism, which was never a "formalism" except insofar as it proposed close attention to form as a device for obtaining ethical, humanist, religious, or historicist meaning.

52. The most focused work on literature's essential anonymity and self-difference is that of Maurice Blanchot; see in particular *L'espace littéraire* (1955) (*The Space of Literature*), trans. Ann Smock (Lincoln: University of Nebraska Press, 1982).

53. David Simpson makes this claim in *The Academic Postmodern and the Rule of Literature: A Report on Half-Knowledge* (Chicago: University of Chicago Press, 1995); he has in mind not the mass media but such academic phenomena as the New Historicism's extension of literary approaches to historical material; the return of autobiographical and historical storytelling; and the celebration of anecdote and Geertzian "thick description." Simpson tries to keep his argument from becoming a head-on disagreement with the work of critics such as Fredric Jameson and John Guillory, who perceive a flight of cultural capital from literature, but as Jonathan Culler notes, Simpson's claims in fact diverge interestingly. Summarizing and appropriating Simpson's argument, Culler suggests that "literature may have lost its centrality as a specific object of study but its modes have conquered: in the humanities and social sciences, everything is literary." Jonathan Culler, "The Literary in Theory," in *What's Left of Theory? New Work on the Politics of Literary Theory*, ed. Judith Butler, John Guillory, and Kendall Thomas (New York: Routledge, 2000), 289.

54. See David Perkins, "The Construction of 'The Romantic Movement' as a Literary Classification," *Nineteenth-Century Literature*, 45 (1990): 129–43; on the specific (though, it can be argued, exemplary) case of Shelley, see Mark Kipperman, "Absorbing a Revolution: Shelley Becomes a Romantic, 1889–1903," *Nineteenth-Century Literature* 47, no. 2 (1992): 187–211. Friedrich von Hardenberg's transformation into an aestheticized "Novalis" (a somewhat more complicated process insofar as it was begun upon his death by Tieck and the Schlegels, and thus represents not simply a twentieth-century act of misprision, but also what we shall be calling romanticism's resistance to itself) is analyzed by Wm. Arctander O'Brien in *Novalis: Signs of Revolution* (Durham, N.C.: Duke University Press, 1995). For authoritative essays on the history of the word *romantic* in several national and linguistic contexts, see Hans Eichner, ed., *"Romantic" and Its Cognates: The European History of a Word* (Toronto: University of Toronto Press, 1972).

55. René Wellek, "The Concept of 'Romanticism' in Literary History," *Comparative Literature* 1, no. 1 (1949): 147. We may in the present context take Wellek's invocation of "nature" both as a recollection of the thematic importance of nature in aesthetic discourse (almost all of Kant's attention in the Third *Critique*, for instance, is fixed on the aesthetic judgment of natural objects rather than of works of art) and as a vigorous repression of the technicity or rhetoricity of aesthetics. Wellek is responding, twenty-five years after its publication, to A. O. Lovejoy's article, "On the Discrimination of Romanticisms," *PMLA* 29 (1924): 229–53; reprinted in Lovejoy, *Essays in the History of Ideas* (Baltimore, Md.: Johns Hopkins University Press, 1948), 228–53, which is the source for my quotations from Lovejoy below.

56. Jerome J. McGann, *The Romantic Ideology: A Critical Investigation* (Chicago: University of Chicago Press, 1983), 1.

57. Several shrewd readers have commented on the return of "romantic ideology" in and as McGann's critique of it: see, e.g., Frances Ferguson, *Solitude and the Sublime: Romanticism and the Aesthetics of Individuation* (New York: Routledge, 1992), 147–48; and Paul H. Fry, *A Defense of Poetry: Reflections on the Occasion of Writing* (Stanford, Calif.: Stanford University Press, 1995), 112–16. As Cynthia Chase notes in the course of a critique of McGann similar to the one being offered here, "The problem may well be the tendency, marked in New Historicist criticism such as McGann's, as well as in earlier scholarship, to repeat the themes and ostensible statements of certain Romantic texts without submitting them to analytical interpretation or rhetorical analysis." "Introduction," *Romanticism*, ed. Cynthia Chase (Harlow, United Kingdom: Longman, 1993), 4.

58. This bifurcation returns to romanticism "itself," insofar as Friedrich and A. W. Schlegel used the word *romantic* in both a typological and historical sense: to designate evolutions of the romance form (an evolution that they saw as leading to a mélange of genres), and to signify modern as opposed to classical literature (modern here meaning in the first instance Dante, Shakespeare, and Calderón, rather than the historical moment of the Schlegels themselves). See Eichner's introduction to *"Romantic" and Its Cognates*, 3–16, for a helpful summary of this word's historical career.

59. The contrast between symbol and allegory—a romantic leitmotiv, particularly prominent in Goethe and Coleridge—forms, of course, a major conceptual articulation in de Man's "The Rhetoric of Temporality," in *Blindness and Insight: Essays in the Rhetoric of Contemporary Criticism*, rev. ed. (Minneapolis: University of Minnesota Press, 1983), 187–228. Interest in the Gothic as high romanticism's subversive and demotic secret sharer has been keen in British romantic studies and has found expression in a fine book by Michael Gamer, *Romanticism and the Gothic: Genre, Reception, and Canon Formation* (Cambridge: Cambridge University Press, 2000).

60. The fact that theory's phantasmatic personification, Paul de Man, was a

professional romanticist obviously played a leading role in the construction of romanticism as theory's privileged site in the last decades of the twentieth century; but the associations between theory and romanticism far outstrip the contingencies of a critic's career. For a helpful meditation on the interplay between theory and philosophical movements associable with romanticism, see Tilottama Rajan and David L. Clark, "Introduction: Idealism and its Rem(a)inders," in Rajan and Clark, eds., *Intersections: Nineteenth Century Philosophy and Contemporary Theory* (Albany: State University of New York Press, 1995), 1–35.

61. Maurice Blanchot, "The Athenaeum," in *The Infinite Conversation*, trans. Susan Hanson (Minneapolis: University of Minnesota Press, 1993 [1969]), 357.

62. John Rieder, "Wordsworth and Romanticism in the Academy," in *At the Limits of Romanticism: Essays in Cultural, Feminist, and Materialist Criticism*, ed. Mary A. Favret and Nicola J. Watson (Bloomington: Indiana University Press, 1994), 21–39, here 29. Rieder is pursuing here David Perkins's claim that McGann "wrongly conflates the aesthetic ideology of the end of the [nineteenth] century with the opinions and practices of the Romantics themselves" (Perkins, 143), and drawing attention to the fact that the academic study of the vernacular literatures was consolidating itself at the end of the nineteenth century: "what Perkins calls the 'aesthetic ideology' which produced the late Victorian version of romanticism might at the same time also be an emerging academic ideology. This ideology is based on the necessity of elevating and unifying the literature of this slice of literary history; that is, of rendering it a worthy and practical object of pedagogy as well as of serious scholarly inquiry" (Rieder, 29).

63. Paul de Man, "The Contemporary Criticism of Romanticism," in *Romanticism and Contemporary Criticism: The Gauss Seminar and Other Papers*, ed. E. S. Burt, Kevin Newmark, and Andrzej Warminski (Baltimore, Md.: Johns Hopkins University Press, 1993), 3. This is the first of de Man's six Gauss Seminar lectures of 1967.

64. For instance: "One returns to Romanticism—or, one undertakes to redeem the hopes of the past—because the pre-Enlightenment imagination students of the period are now finding in that body of writing gives a concretely sensuous and in some ways more advanced form to the post-Enlightenment stirrings and strivings that characterize the present scene." Marjorie Levinson, "Pre- and Post-Dialectical Materialisms: Modeling Praxis Without Subjects and Objects," *Cultural Critique* 31 (1995): 118. Levinson is partly engaged in this piece in a critique of a book that offers a good example of recent ecocriticism: Jonathan Bate, *Romantic Ecology: Wordsworth and the Environmental Tradition* (London: Routledge, 1991).

65. René Girard, *Mensonge romantique et vérité romanesque* (Paris: Grasset, 1961); Girard's book, which, rather unhelpfully for our purposes, was translated into English as *Deceit, Desire and the Novel: Self and Other in Literary Structure*, trans. Yvonne Freccero (Baltimore, Md.: Johns Hopkins University Press, 1965), is one of de Man's targets in his initial Gauss lecture.

66. Current discomfort with the period-trope "romanticism" has resulted in its effacement altogether from the title of an influential recent anthology: "Recognizing that the term 'Romanticism' has become the subject of interrogation by recent new historical, cultural, and feminist critics," the editors explain, "we have set it aside as a principle of selection." Anne K. Mellor and Richard E. Matlak, "General Introduction," *British Literature 1780–1830* (New York: Harcourt Brace, 1996), 3. Mellor and Matlak, it should be added, do not really end up chucking the term *romanticism*: they preserve it as a name for "expressive/subjective" aesthetics, which they oppose both to its traditional foe, "mimetic/objective (Neoclassical) aesthetics," and a middle ground they call "Probabilism" ascribed to women writers of the period (128). "Romanticism," of course, signifies "an ideological poetics of whose self-interest or class bias we should be aware" (128). For informative grapplings with romanticism as an ideological formation and semiarbitrary set of dates, see two articles by Susan Wolfson: "50–50? Phone a Friend? Ask the Audience? Speculating on a Romantic Century, 1750–1850," *European Romantic Review* 11, no. 1 (2000): 1–11, and "Our Puny Boundaries: Why the Craving for Carving Up the Nineteenth Century?" *PMLA* 116, no. 5 (2001): 1432–41.

67. Lacoue-Labarthe and Nancy remark that "a veritable romantic *unconscious* is discernible today, in the most central motifs of our modernity" (*Literary Absolute*, 15); Chandler, in his impressive study *England in 1819: The Politics of Literary Culture and the Case of Romantic Historicism* (Chicago: University of Chicago Press, 1998), notes that the "recent return to history [in scholarship in the humanities] involves, precisely, a return to Romantic historicism of a certain sort" (165–66). The claim that modernity is a fundamentally romantic condition was advanced strongly by romanticists of the so-called Yale School, from the late 1950s onward. This aesthetic inflation of romanticism is a sore point in McGann's *Romantic Ideology* for reasons we can appreciate: wanting a point external to ideology on which to ground his critique, McGann wards off the preposterous idea "that Romanticism comprises all significant literature produced between Blake and the present—some would say between Gray, or even Milton, and the present" by echoing the famous phrase of one of British romanticism's totemic opponents, Francis Jeffrey (and thus symbolically abjecting romanticism itself): "This will never do" (20).

68. Carol Jacobs, *Uncontainable Romanticism: Shelley, Brontë, Kleist* (Baltimore, Md.: Johns Hopkins University Press, 1989), ix, passim. I am indebted here to de Man's observation in one of his midcareer essays that "we carry [romanticism] within ourselves as the experience of an *act* in which, up to a certain point, we ourselves have participated" (*Rhetoric of Romanticism*, 50). The obsession with dates (beginning and ending dates, significant years, etc.) that seems part of the culture of professional romanticism these days is arguably a displaced response to romanticism's disqualification of a positivist understanding of history and the historical event. The complex relation between romanticism and postmodernism is suggestively explored in Orrin N. C. Wang, *Fantastic Modernity: Dialectical*

Readings in Romanticism and Theory (Baltimore, Md.: Johns Hopkins University Press, 1996): e.g., "Romanticism's modernity is as paradoxical as postmodernism's, for if we associate Romanticism with a certain originary historical moment, we also associate it with a discourse that exposes and demystifies the hypostatisization of that moment. . . . In other words, both Romanticism and postmodernism participate in what I call a 'fantastic modernity,' in which it is precisely the phantom nature of modernity which at once blocks and enables our access to historical identity and difference" (15).

69. On racism and aesthetic discourse, see David Lloyd, "Race Under Representation," *Oxford Literary Review* 13, no. 1–2 (1991): 62–94; Philippe Lacoue-Labarthe and Jean-Luc Nancy, "The Nazi Myth," trans. Brian Holmes, *Critical Inquiry* 16, no. 2 (1990): 291–312; and for some brief comments inspired by this latter text, my *Phantom Formations*, 24–25. Lacoue-Labarthe and Nancy emphasize that a race is the identity "of a formative power, of a singular type"—an extreme version of the story of a subject's self-determination in history (306); worthy of note in the present context is the fact that this formative power or "type" comes into political reality by way of the *stereotype* as mechanical, mass-produced iteration. Nineteenth- and twentieth-century racism partakes of the technical production and dissemination of aesthetic discourse.

70. Thomas Laqueur, *Making Sex: Body and Gender from the Greeks to Freud* (Cambridge, Mass.: Harvard University Press, 1990): "Thus, the old model, in which men and women were arrayed according to their degree of metaphysical perfection, their vital heat, along an axis whose telos was male, gave way by the late eighteenth century to a new model of radical dimorphism, of biological divergence. An anatomy and physiology of incommensurability replaced a metaphysics of hierarchy in the representations of men and women" (5–6).

71. Mary Poovey, *Uneven Developments: The Ideological Work of Gender in Mid-Victorian England* (Chicago: University of Chicago Press, 1988), 80.

72. Mary Poovey, "Aesthetics and Political Economy in the Eighteenth Century: The Place of Gender in the Social Construction of Knowledge," in Levine, ed., *Aesthetics and Ideology*, 90; Kathy Alexis Psomiades, *Beauty's Body: Femininity and Representation in British Aestheticism* (Stanford: Stanford University Press, 1997), 14. Noting that "the difference of sex, as it appears in Burke's distinction between a feminized beauty and the masculine sublime, becomes the basis for distinctions within aesthetics as well as between aesthetic contemplation and acquisitive desire" (89), Poovey suggests that the figure of (hetero)sexual difference played a fundamental role in the gradual discrimination of aesthetics from political economy, as these discourses developed out of moral philosophy. Psomiades suggests that the feminine body mediates aesthetic contradiction: "In the feminine figure, a creature of inaccessible psychological depth and tangible material surface, the central contradictions of autonomous art may be held in suspension" (3).

73. Thus, the fully commodified aesthetic of the twentieth-century culture

industry has also proved readable as rhetorically bound up with gendered oppositions. The analysis here frequently diagnoses an alignment of femininity with commodity consumption; see Rita Felski, *The Gender of Modernity* (Cambridge, Mass.: Harvard University Press, 1995). On the modernist association of the difference between high art and mass culture with that between masculine and feminine, see Andreas Huyssen, "Mass Culture as Woman," in *After the Great Divide: Modernism, Mass Culture, Postmodernism* (Indianapolis: Indiana University Press, 1986). A helpful reacquaintance with the diction and ideology of much earlier twentieth-century writing on aesthetics and gender may be had by looking through John Crowe Ransom, "The Poet as Woman," in *The World's Body* (New York: Scribner, 1938), 76–110.

74. I discuss further the link between the feminine and philosophical discourse on the beautiful in Chapter 4 as part of a reflection on texts by Philippe Lacoue-Labarthe and Friedrich Schlegel. For an ambitious account of the "feminization" of British culture in the eighteenth century, see Nancy Armstrong, *Desire and Domestic Fiction: A Political History of the Novel* (New York: Oxford University Press, 1987), 3–27.

75. Particularly fine texts to consult in this context, since they parse the subtleties of gender identification by way of an exploration of the sharply but unsteadily gendered difference between "high" and popular culture in the romantic era, are Karen Swann's two essays on Coleridge's "Christabel": "'Christabel': The Wandering Mother and the Enigma of Form," *Studies in Romanticism* 23, no. 4 (1984): 533–53, and "Literary Gentlemen and Lovely Ladies: The Debate on the Character of Christabel," *ELH* 52, no. 2 (1985): 394–418. The essays explore ways in which a possessed female body functions, both within the poem and in the context of the poem's reception, as a trope that evokes and wards off the anxious possibility that bodies and selves might be determined by cultural forms: "Female bodies 'naturally' seem to figure an ungraspable truth: that form, habitually viewed as the arbitrary, contingent vessel of more enduring meanings, is yet the source and determinant of all meanings, whether the subject's or the world's" ("Christabel," 544). Furthermore, it turns out that "it is ladies' literature—the derogated genres of romantic fiction—which conventionally represents this threat in the discourse of literary gentlemen" ("Literary Gentlemen," 396).

76. The seminal text in this tradition is of course Mario Praz, *La carne, la morte, et il diavolo nella letteratura romantica* (1930), translated as *The Romantic Agony*; see the second edition, trans. Angus Davidson (New York: Oxford University Press, 1970). A fine reading of Wordsworth's texts attentive to their erotic and semiotic complexities is David Collings, *Wordsworthian Errancies: The Poetics of Cultural Dismemberment* (Baltimore, Md.: Johns Hopkins University Press, 1994). For an important collection of recent work on gender and sexuality in Goethe and the *Goethezeit*, see Alice Kuzniar, ed., *Outing Goethe and His Age* (Stanford: Stanford University Press, 1996).

77. Fundamental texts in the feminist revision of British romanticism include Anne K. Mellor, ed., *Romanticism and Feminism* (Bloomington: Indiana University Press, 1988), and Marlon B. Ross, *The Contours of Masculine Desire: Romanticism and the Rise of Women's Poetry* (New York: Oxford University Press, 1989). For an influential study of the "romantic" ideology that associates woman, motherhood, literality, nature, and death, see Margaret Homans, *Bearing the Word: Language and Female Experience in Nineteenth-Century Women's Writing* (Chicago: University of Chicago Press, 1986). See also Mary Jacobus, *Romanticism, Writing, and Sexual Difference: Essays on "The Prelude"* (Oxford: Clarendon Press, 1989), for a theoretically sophisticated characterization of romantic "natural supernaturalism" as the "metaphoric consummation or spousal union of masculine mind and feminine nature" (206).

78. I discuss Kristeva's notion of abjection briefly in Chapter 2. This is a good place to acknowledge the work of Cynthia Chase and Neil Hertz: Chase's imaginative linking of Kristevan metapsychology with rhetorical reading began as a review of Kristeva's work in *Criticism* 26 (1984): 193–201, and was developed in several essays: see esp. "The Witty Butcher's Wife: Freud, Lacan, and the Conversion of Resistance to Theory," *MLN* 102, no. 5 (1987): 989–1013, and "Primary Narcissism and the Giving of Figure," in John Fletcher and Andrew Benjamin, eds., *Abjection, Melancholy, and Love: The Work of Julia Kristeva* (London: Routledge, 1990). Neil Hertz offers a lucid presentation of some of Kristeva's speculations in the afterword to his *The End of the Line: Essays on Psychoanalysis and the Sublime* (New York: Columbia University Press, 1985): I owe an ongoing debt to Hertz's subtle readings, many of which examine ways in which anxieties about gender shade into anxieties about language. Mary Jacobus's searching essays on the "maternal imaginary" also make necessary reading: see *First Things: The Maternal Imaginary in Literature, Art, and Psychoanalysis* (New York: Routledge, 1995). The romantic era witnessed a surge of interest in the mother as tutelary figure, linked symbolically and practically (as in, e.g., Pestalozzian educational theory) to the acquisition of language and reading skills: see n. 24 to Chapter 1 for a brief look at relevant literary–historical work in this area.

79. Or a story of hysteria: "To see it once is to know all there is to know, provided the right conditions are fulfilled, namely, that the bodies show their differences. The postures of the bodies in the alcove [of a primal scene] and the patient's subjective positioning in relation to them determine the whole sequence that constitutes the patient's history." Evelyne Ender, *Sexing the Mind: Nineteenth-Century Fictions of Hysteria* (Ithaca: Cornell University Press, 1995), 280. The scholarship on hysteria is extensive, and has formed an important part of the interdisciplinary work in psychoanalysis and literature—particularly nineteenth-century narrative fiction—over the last three decades. For a broad theoretical study, see Monique David-Ménard, *Hysteria from Freud to Lacan: Body and Language in Psychoanalysis*, trans. Catherine Porter (Ithaca: Cornell University Press, 1989); for some exemplary

reflections on psychoanalysis and literature, see Shoshana Felman, *What Does a Woman Want? Reading and Sexual Difference* (Baltimore, Md.: Johns Hopkins University Press, 1993). For studies specifically focused on nineteenth-century literary texts, see, in addition to Ender, Janet Beizer, *Ventriloquized Bodies: The Narrative Uses of Hysteria in France, 1850–1900* (Ithaca: Cornell University Press, 1995); and, in a more comparative and narratologically oriented vein, Peter Brooks, *Reading for the Plot: Design and Intention in Narrative* (New York: Vintage, 1984).

80. Lee Edelman, *Homographesis: Essays in Gay Literary and Cultural Theory* (New York: Routledge, 1994), xiv. For a summary and influential critique of Lacanian and French feminist investments in figures of the phallus, the woman, the feminine, or the lesbian, see Judith Butler, *Gender Trouble: Feminism and the Subversion of Identity* (New York: Routledge, 1990).

81. Jacques Lacan, *The Seminar of Jacques Lacan, Book 2: The Ego in Freud's Theory and in the Technique of Psychoanalysis, 1954–1955*, trans. Sylvana Tomaselli (New York: Norton, 1991), 166.

82. Judith Butler, "The Lesbian Phallus," in *Bodies That Matter: On the Discursive Limits of "Sex"* (New York: Routledge, 1993), 82.

83. Sigmund Freud, "Das Medusenhaupt," in *Gesammelte Werke*, ed. Anna Freud et al. (Frankfurt am Main: S. Fischer Verlag, 1967 [1941]), 17:47; "Medusa's Head," in *Collected Papers*, ed. James Strachey (London: Hogarth Press, 1950), 5:105.

84. Jacques Derrida, *Glas*, trans. John P. Leavey Jr. and Richard Rand (Lincoln: University of Nebraska Press, 1986), 47.

85. Barbara Johnson, *A World of Difference* (Baltimore, Md.: Johns Hopkins University Press, 1987), 7. Johnson's remarkable final chapter, "Apostrophe, Animation, and Abortion," 184–99, explores the intimacy between questions of figurative language and the figure of the mother in ways that complement my remarks above and the work of critics such as Chase, Edelman, Jacobus, and Kristeva cited earlier. Suggesting that "there may be a deeper link between motherhood and apostrophe than we have hitherto suspected," Johnson proposes that the animating rhetorical force of apostrophe shades into the primal demand addressed to the mother—the mother as personification of presence or absence: "If demand is the original vocative, which assures life even as it inaugurates alienation, then it is not surprising that questions of animation inhere in the rhetorical figure of apostrophe" (198).

CHAPTER I

1. Here and in what follows, the acronym *IC* flags a reference to the second, revised edition of Anderson's *Imagined Communities: Reflections on the Origin and Spread of Nationalism* (New York: Verso, 1991 [1983]); *S* refers to Anderson's *The Spectre of Comparisons: Nationalism, Southeast Asia, and the World* (New York: Verso, 1998). I thank Jonathan Culler and Pheng Cheah for directing me to this

latter text, and more generally for their very helpful comments on an early version of this chapter.

2. David Lloyd, "Nationalisms Against the State," in Lisa Lowe and David Lloyd, eds., *The Politics of Culture in the Shadow of Capital* (Durham, N.C.: Duke University Press, 1997), 178.

3. Wall Street is of course a synecdoche here for the dispersed centers of international capital. It is also perhaps worth underscoring that, as has often been pointed out, global capitalism's homogenizing forces coexist with its systematic exploitation of unevenly developed markets. "Globalization" is thus never simply a description of an actual state of affairs, but is always *also* the ideological narrative of a permanently deferred utopia (or dystopia).

4. *Cosmopolitanism*, however, is a term possessed of much greater range than my commentary here can indicate. See, e.g., Pheng Cheah and Bruce Robbins, eds., *Cosmopolitics: Thinking and Feeling Beyond the Nation* (Minneapolis: University of Minnesota Press, 1998), for a collection of interesting attempts to imagine nonuniversalist, local, or finite forms of cosmopolitanism.

5. Matthew Arnold, *Culture and Anarchy*, in *"Culture and Anarchy" and Other Writings*, ed. Stefan Collini (Cambridge: Cambridge University Press, 1993), 99, passim; Friedrich Schiller, *On the Aesthetic Education of Man, in a Series of Letters*, ed. and trans. Elizabeth M. Wilkinson and L. A. Willoughby (Oxford: Clarendon Press, 1967), 17. For helpful summaries and discussions of Coleridge, Ruskin, and Arnold on aesthetics and the state, see David Aram Kaiser, *Romanticism, Aesthetics, and Nationalism* (Cambridge: Cambridge University Press, 1999).

6. See the Introduction for a summary account of the development of aesthetics and aesthetic culture in nineteenth-century Europe. For a model of aesthetic politics more up to date than those of Schiller or Arnold, see F. R. Ankersmit, whose *Aesthetic Politics: Political Philosophy Beyond Fact and Value* (Stanford: Stanford University Press, 1996) is rather surprisingly featured in Stanford's postcolonial-theory "Mestizo Spaces / Espaces Métissés" series. Ankersmit claims to be proposing a non-Schillerian model of the aesthetic state because "aesthetics is invoked here not in order to argue for the *unity* but precisely for the *brokenness* of the political domain" (18). Predictably, however, "brokenness" turns out to mean aesthetic play, which permits the reintroduction of unity as aesthetic harmony; e.g.: "(Aesthetic) political representation is required since each (civil) society needs an image of itself in order to function properly; without such a mirror image of itself it will stumble around erratically and aimlessly like a blind man. Apart from its better-known and more obvious functions, the state, as the representation of civil society, is such an image of society to itself. And it follows that the clearer and more vigorous the contours of the state are, the better it may be expected to fulfill its function of being a representation or an image of civil society. . . . On the assumptions of an aesthetic political philosophy, the best political world is therefore the one in which a strong state and a strong civil society coexist in a fruitful

symbiosis" (191, Ankersmit's parentheses, my ellipsis). The tropes of mutilation and errancy that pop up here ("stumble around erratically and aimlessly like a blind man") are typical of the aesthetic tradition and function as signs of the violence with which this tradition is prepared to repress its own instability, as the present book will be documenting at some length and in various contexts; see also my *Phantom Formations: Aesthetic Ideology and the Bildungsroman* (Ithaca: Cornell University Press, 1996), esp. 1–37.

7. These comments target recent work in cultural studies rather than in history or political science, but it is rare for a scholar in any field to put real critical pressure on the figure of "imagination" in Anderson's text. Historians have argued that Anderson's account of the nation's origins in print-capitalism fails to explain why the imagined communities enabled by the circulation of newspapers, novels, etc., would take the specific form of nationalism (see, e.g., John Breuilly, *Nationalism and the State*, 2nd ed. [Chicago: University of Chicago Press, 1994], 406–7); and many postcolonialist critics have echoed Partha Chatterjee's question, "Whose imagined community?" (*The Nation and Its Fragments: Colonial and Postcolonial Histories* [Princeton: Princeton University Press, 1993], 5), but usually without questioning what it means to "imagine" a "community." Within cultural studies, one of the few texts I have encountered that scrutinizes Anderson's arguments is Homi Bhabha's rich essay "DissemiNation: Time, Narrative, and the Margins of the Modern Nation" (in Bhabha, ed., *Nation and Narration*, esp. 308–11). Bhabha's main object is to complicate Anderson's notion of the "homogenous empty time" of nationalism rather than that of an imagined community per se, but as we shall see, the complication of the one complicates the other, and I take Bhabha's account of the tensions within nationalism and national identity to be compatible with the arguments I shall be elaborating here.

8. Forest Pyle, *The Ideology of the Imagination: Subject and Society in the Discourse of Romanticism* (Stanford: Stanford University Press, 1995), vii. From a history-of-ideas perspective, the idea of the imagination as a synthetic or articulative faculty capable of transforming sensory impressions into mental images returns to classical roots. For a helpful account, see J. M. Cocking, *Imagination: A Study in the History of Ideas*, ed. Penelope Murray (London: Routledge, 1991). For a historical study focused on the eighteenth-century "creation" of "the idea of the imagination as we still understand it today," see James Engell, *The Creative Imagination: Enlightenment to Romanticism* (Cambridge, Mass.: Harvard University Press, 1981), vii.

9. Philippe Lacoue-Labarthe, *Heidegger, Art, and Politics: The Fiction of the Political*, trans. Chris Turner (Oxford: Blackwell, 1990), 66.

10. Franco Moretti, *Atlas of the European Novel, 1800–1900* (London: Verso, 1998), 17.

11. Paul de Man, "Sign and Symbol in Hegel's Aesthetics," in *Aesthetic Ideology*, ed. Andrzej Warminski (Minneapolis: University of Minnesota Press, 1996), 96. Hegel goes on to link the arbitrariness of the sign with pedagogy because such

signs must be learned. "The sign [*Das Zeichen*] must be declared to be something great. When the intelligence has signified [*bezeichnet*] something, it has finished with the content of the perception and has given the sensuous material a new meaning [*Bedeutung*] *foreign* to it as its soul. Thus a cockade or a *flag* or a *gravestone* means [*bedeutet*] something quite different from that which they immediately indicate [*unmittelbar anzeigen*]. The arbitrariness, here made evident, of the link between the sensuous material and the general representation has as necessary consequence the fact that one must first learn the meaning of signs. This holds notably for linguistic signs." *Enzyklopädie der philosophischen Wissenschaften, III*, vol. 10 of *Werke*, ed. Eva Moldenhauer and Karl Markus Michel (Frankfurt am Main: Suhrkamp, 1986), 269, Hegel's italics. Unless otherwise indicated, all translations in this chapter are mine.

12. On the sublimity of the nation, see Ian Balfour, "The Sublime of the Nation," forthcoming as part of his *The Language of the Sublime* (Stanford: Stanford University Press). Though not exactly sublime, the U.S. Pledge of Allegiance registers the nation's peculiar reliance on the power of signs: the oath-taker pledges "allegiance to the Flag," and only secondarily "to the Republic for which it stands." I thank Molly Ierulli for pointing this out to me.

13. "Reading a newspaper is like reading a novel whose author has abandoned any thought of a coherent plot," Anderson comments in a footnote (*IC*, 33, n. 54)—which is why the newspaper serves his argument better than the novel does. As soon as questions of emplotment and narrative voice arise, the temporality of narrative becomes irreducible to "a complex gloss upon the word 'meanwhile'" (*IC*, 25). An entire subfield in literary criticism, narratology, thrives on explaining how texts construct and manage temporality through such rhetorical devices as prefiguration, repetition, prolepses, and analepses. Franco Moretti's *Atlas of the European Novel* seeks in part to elaborate on Anderson's intuition of a link between novels and national consciousness. He argues, for instance, that Jane Austen's heroines, who typically have to travel to different counties to meet compatible partners, are participating in a "national" marriage market and that the novels thereby convey a sense of a middle-sized world, "the typical *intermediate* space of the nation-state" (22). Many of his readings are intriguing and helpful; they are also plagued by factual errors, ranging from Moretti's mixing up the names of the Dickens characters Little Dorrit and Fanny (122; Fanny is the unadmirable older sister of Dickens's eponymous heroine) to his misrepresentation of Goethe's *Wilhelm Meister* as a city-oriented narrative (65)—this last in large part, I think, because Moretti's notion of the genre of the *Bildungsroman* is heavily distorted by his preference for Balzac, and, more generally, for the French and English novelistic traditions over the German.

14. From Derrida's perspective, Anderson may be seen as remaining faithful to a fundamental Marxist insight: "Marx is one of the rare thinkers of the past to have taken seriously, at least in principle, the originary indissociability of technics

and language, and thus of tele-technics (for every language is a tele-technics)." *Specters of Marx: The State of the Debt, the Work of Mourning, and the New International,* trans. Peggy Kamuf (New York: Routledge, 1994), 53.

15. It should also be noted here that although print-capitalism is the fundamental precondition of nationalism in Anderson's argument, nationalism actually comes into existence by propping itself up, so to speak, on existing administrative and market units, particularly in the case of the New World "creole nationalisms" that, Anderson emphasizes, animated the first successful nationalist movements. In similar fashion, the absolutist state provides a kind of scaffold or skeleton for national imagining in Europe. Anderson also points to the importance of capitalism's transportation technologies: "The essential nexus of long-distance transportation and print-capitalist communications prepared the grounds on which, by the end of the eighteenth century, the first nationalist movements flowered. It is striking that this flowering took place first in North America and later in the Catholic, Iberian colonies to the south, the economies of which were all *pre*-industrial" (*S*, 62). Anderson thus suggests "the untenability of Ernest Gellner's argument that industrialism was the historical source of nationalism's emergence" (*S*, 63 n. 10). (For that argument, see Ernest Gellner, *Nations and Nationalism* [Ithaca: Cornell University Press, 1983].) The emphasis would rather need to fall on a certain *displacement* effected by developments in transport and communicational technologies, rather than on industrialism per se.

16. Walter Benjamin, "Über einige Motive bei Baudelaire," in *Gesammelte Schriften,* ed. Rolf Tiedemann and Hermann Schweppenhäuser (Frankfurt am Main: Suhrkamp, 1980), 1.2:615; "On Some Motifs in Baudelaire," in *Illuminations: Essays and Reflections,* ed. Hannah Arendt, trans. Harry Zohn (New York: Schocken Books, 1969 [1955]), 163. David Clark has suggested to me, as an interesting precursor to Freud's notion of consciousness as a defense against stimuli, Kant's characterization of abstraction as the mind's active power to negate representations. "Kant's insistence on the importance and needfulness of consciousness's capacity to withdraw attention is remarkably consistent, and goes back as early as the *Attempt to Introduce the Concept of Negative Magnitudes into Philosophy* (1763)" (personal communication). For discussion of this notion of negative attentiveness [*negative Aufmerksamkeit*] in Kant, see David Clark, "Kant's Aliens: The *Anthropology* and Its Others," *New Centennial Review* 1, no. 2 (2001): 201–89.

17. For a fine reading of *Madame Bovary* that stresses Emma's inability to live in time, see Elissa Marder, "Trauma, Addiction, and Temporal Bulimia in Madame Bovary," *Diacritics* 27, no. 3 (1997): 49–64; an extended version of her argument may be found in her *Dead Time: Temporal Disorders in the Wake of Modernity* (Stanford, Calif.: Stanford University Press, 2001).

18. "Our Daily Shock—the only paper many of us read," as a narrator riffs in Pynchon's *Gravity's Rainbow* (New York: Viking, 1973), 452). Of Derrida's several classic texts on writing and iterability, see esp. "Signature Event Context" and as-

208 Notes to Pages 54–59

sociated texts in *Limited Inc.*, ed. Gerald Graff (Evanston, Ill.: Northwestern University Press, 1988). My comments here converge with Geoffrey Bennington's assessment that the nation is "always open to its others, or rather, it is constituted only in that opening, which is, in principle, violent." Stories of the nation, in contrast, seek "interminably to constitute identity against difference, inside against outside." Geoffrey Bennington, "Postal Politics and the Institution of the Nation," in Bhabha, ed., *Nation and Narration*, 131, 132.

19. Leaving aside the broader genealogy of the political as fictional or fashioned that Lacoue-Labarthe sketches, we may note that the link between the nation and the power of will appears everywhere in modern nationalist discourse, playing a central role in traditions as separate in time and spirit as Ernest Renan's nineteenth-century liberal humanism and Alfred Rosenberg's twentieth-century fascist mythologizing. See, e.g., Renan: "There is something in man which is superior to language, namely, the will"; "A nation is a soul, a spiritual principle. Two things, which in truth are but one, constitute this soul or spiritual principle. One is the possession in common of a rich legacy of memories; the other is present-day consent, the desire to live together, the will to perpetuate the value of the heritage that one has received in an undivided form." Ernest Renan, "Qu'est-ce qu'une nation?" (1882), in *Oeuvres complètes* (Paris: Calmann-Lévy, 1947), 1:887–906; "What Is a Nation?", trans. Martin Thom, in Homi Bhabha, ed., *Nation and Narration* (New York: Routledge, 1990), 16, 19. I pursue the topic of will and imagination further in my discussion of Fichte.

20. In his chapter "Replica, Aura, and Late National Imaginings" in *Spectre of Comparisons*, Anderson comments further on the Tomb of the Unknown Soldier and provides some intriguing historical detail: "The British government, which seems to have pioneered these memorials in the immediate aftermath of World War I, was seriously worried, from the start, about the possibility that the Unknown Soldier might escape or be body-snatched . . . if his identity could be tracked down. . . . The search for the right remains was thus limited to those who had been killed in the first months of the war, so that, maximally decayed, they would be as much like dust and as little like bodies as possible. Four such remains were picked out by military officials, and one was chosen, by lot" (55).

21. I therefore agree with Gopal Balakrishnan's claim that Anderson tends to underplay the importance of "the language and imagery of war" in the constitution of "the pathos of national membership." Balakrishnan, "Mapping the Nation," in Balakrishnan, ed., *Mapping the Nation* (London: Verso, 1996), 208.

22. The association of mourning with maternity has a long and complex filiation in Western culture. For a reading of the mother's role as mourner in ancient Greek culture, see Nicole Loraux, *Les mères en deuil* (Paris: Seuil, 1990). In his account of national burial customs and projects during World War I, Anderson notes as a curious detail the fact that the U.S. "Congress felt obliged to finance the

round-trip tickets and other expenses of all mothers (not wives) who wished to visit their Europe-interred sons" (*S*, 53).

23. As Friedrich Kittler has shown, the mother becomes closely associated with "language" and language acquisition in German contexts in the early nineteenth century. Indeed, "The mother as primary instructor is, quite literally, an invention of 1800." See Kittler, *Discourse Networks: 1800/1900*, trans. Michael Metteer, with Chris Cullens (Stanford: Stanford University Press, 1990), 26. Kittler's is a culturally specific analysis in many respects (see his chapter "The Mother's Mouth," 25–69). But quite apart from the considerable direct influence of Pestalozzi and other German pedagogical theorists of the era on European and American educational theory and practice, it seems safe to say that in a very broad sense, Anderson's maternal figure constitutes part of his text's romantic legacy. For an account of the romantic-era "revolution in the nursery" in Britain and the British colonies that complements Kittler's account of the rise of maternal child care and the association of the mother with language in Germany, see Katie Trumpener, *Bardic Nationalism: The Romantic Novel and the British Empire* (Princeton: Princeton University Press, 1997), 193–241.

It should be added, however, that Anderson is highly aware of the rhetorical and ideological power of the figure of the family. His fine gloss on Renan's famous comment that "l'essence d'une nation est que tous les individus aient beaucoup de choses en commun et aussi que tous aient oublié bien des choses" (872) ("the essence of a nation is that all individuals have many things in common and also that they have forgotten many things" [11]) identifies the trope of the family as the nation's exemplary device for forgetting what it remembers. Violent events become "reassuringly fratricidal" when both parties are retrospectively absorbed into the familiarity of a "France" or a "United States": a war thus becomes a "Civil" War; a bloody anti-Hugenot pogrom becomes "la Saint-Barthélemy" (*IC*, 200). Speaking of that second example (which is drawn from Renan), Anderson comments that "we become aware of a systematic historiographical campaign, deployed by the state mainly through the state's school system, to 'remind' every young Frenchwoman and Frenchman of a series of antique slaughters which are now inscribed as 'family history'" (*IC*, 201). The Nation as Motherland can then mourn and celebrate both her sons, thanks to the forgetful power of the memory that preserves the event only by presupposing the nation.

24. Norma Alarcón, Caren Kaplan, and Minoo Moallem, "Introduction: Between Woman and Nation," in Kaplan, Alarcón, and Moallem, eds., *Between Woman and Nation: Nationalisms, Transnational Feminisms, and the State* (Durham, N.C.: Duke University Press, 1999), 10. Anderson's ambivalent naturalization of imagination, nation, and language in these passages may be understood as the flip side of his *under*estimation of nationalism's drive to "naturalize" itself. His much-criticized effort to oppose nationalism to racism ("nationalism thinks in terms of

historical destinies, while racism dreams of eternal contaminations"; *IC*, 149) partly stems, I think, from his effort to resist his own denaturalizing critique. Etienne Balibar is surely right to stress that the "ideal nation" requires something besides language to define itself: language (as Anderson, for that matter, also points out) "assimilates everyone, but holds no one" to the extent that it can be learned or lost; hence the need for the "fiction of a racial identity" as a supplemental principle of closure. See Balibar, "The Nation Form: History and Ideology," in Balibar and Immanuel Wallerstein, *Race, Nation, Class: Ambiguous Identities*, trans. Chris Turner (London: Verso, 1991), 97, 99. (As Balibar remarks, "One's 'mother' tongue is not necessarily the language of one's 'real' mother" [99].) It must also be said that Anderson's account oversimplifies the relationship between racism and historicism: racism's stereotyping idiom is bound up both with the typographical technologies that made the dissemination of stereotypes effective and with the typology of aesthetic historicism, whereby the master race prefigures—and, through its dominion, works to achieve—the ever-deferred accomplishment of modernity as the communion of peoples.

25. Benedict Anderson, "Introduction," in Balakrishnan, ed., *Mapping the Nation*, 8.

26. Samuel Weber, *Mass Mediauras: Form, Technics, Media* (Stanford: Stanford University Press, 1996), 101 (Weber's italics).

27. On the ideological effectiveness of contemporary nationalist culture's endless stream of banal, quotidian imagery—anthems, flag motifs, and so on—see Michael Billig, *Banal Nationalism* (London: Sage Publications, 1995).

28. Johann Gottlieb Fichte, *Reden an die deutsche Nation* (Hamburg: Felix Meiner, 1955), 11; *Addresses to the German Nation*, trans. R. F. Jones and G. H. Turnbull (London: Open Court Company, 1922), 2. In what follows, double page numbers separated by a slash refer to the German- and English-language texts of *Addresses to the German Nation*, in that order. The Jones and Turnbull translation will be modified in the interest of accuracy or emphasis.

29. For a history of the reception of Fichte's lectures, see Xavier Léon, *Fichte et son temps, II: Fichte à Berlin (1799–1813), deuxième partie: La lutte pour l'affranchissement national (1806–1813)* (Paris: Armand Colin, 1959). Etienne Balibar points out that the phrase "war of national liberation" was first coined during Prussia's uprising against Napoleon in 1813 and adds the interesting detail that, a century later, Fichte's text was literally taken into the trenches. In 1915, the German general staff had hundreds of thousands of copies printed and placed in soldiers' backpacks. See Balibar, "Fichte and the Internal Border: On Addresses to the German Nation," in *Masses, Classes, Ideas: Studies on Politics and Philosophy Before and After Marx*, trans. James Swenson (New York: Routledge, 1994), 232 n. 2. Fichte himself, it is only fair to add, hesitated before giving his support to the 1813 war, worrying (rightly) that it was being waged on behalf of reactionary rather than progressively nationalist constituencies.

30. Because at the beginning of this chapter I suggested that in a very broad sense one can think of Benedict Anderson as writing within a romantic tradition, I should pay for that generalization by recalling that if we take romanticism as what a traditional literary history calls *die romantische Schule*, Fichte does not belong to it, though certainly his relation to Jena romanticism and its aftermath is hardly simple. "By a remarkable irony," Xavier Léon writes, "the ideas that the *Addresses* popularized, and that Fichte's genius animated and made enter history, were for the most part German romantic theses: theses that Fichte, in the end, had borrowed only in order to combat the romantics" (133). If Fichte stands opposed to Hegel as the nationalist to the statist, his nationalism intends to have little in common with what he saw as the Catholic and monarchical tendencies of A. W. Schlegel's lectures on literature and art of 1803–4 (from which Fichte borrows liberally, as Léon shows). For some lucid orienting remarks on Fichte's relation to romanticism, see Ernst Behler, *German Literary Theory* (Cambridge: Cambridge University Press, 1996).

31. Fichte's approach to the classic question of the origin of language is set forth in Jere Paul Surber, *Language and German Idealism: Fichte's Linguistic Philosophy* (Atlantic Highlands, N.J.: Humanities Press, 1996), which includes a translation of Fichte's 1795 monograph "On the Linguistic Capacity and the Origin of Language" ("Von der Sprachfähigkeit und dem Ursprung der Sprache"). Partly in order to protect his revision of Kant against Hamann's critique of critical philosophy (as inattentive to its own dependence on a historically developed language), Fichte seeks, in this short and intriguing early paper, to reformulate the question of language's origin in transcendental terms, so that language may be understood as a product of reason's free purposiveness. In this account, language manifests itself originally as the "hieroglyphic language" of an *Ursprache*, in which signs, although arbitrarily posited by the will, are still mimetically connected to nature. As the *Ursprache* becomes an actual historical *Sprache*, it disappears without a trace: "Even with a people that remains free of all external influences, never mingles with another people, never changes its dwelling place, etc., the primitive natural language will gradually perish and be replaced by another which carries in itself not even the slightest trace of the former. Thus, it would be a mistake to believe that the Greeks, Romans, and others never had an *Ursprache* because there are no remnants of it in them. Those original sounds [*Urtone*] have gradually disappeared from the *Ursprache* as they were replaced by signs which better corresponded to the civilized spirit of the people" ("On the Linguistic Capacity," 144; for the German text see *Johann Gottlieb Fichtes sämmtliche Werke*, ed. I. H. Fichte ([Berlin: Veit, 1845–46], 8:340). Further references to the *Sämmtliche Werke* will be indicated by *SW* and volume and page number.

32. Teutons, for Fichte, are inherent leaders, and their genes, as it were, win out, but there is no such thing as a pure Teutonic race any more, and Fichte has no interest in measuring degrees of purity: "Little importance would be attached

to the fact that the Teutonic stock [*die germanische Abstammung*] has intermingled with the former inhabitants of the countries it has conquered; for, after all, the victors and masters of the new people [*Volk*] that arose from this intermingling were none but Teutons. Moreover, in the mother-country [*im Mutterland*] there was an intermingling with Slavs similar to what took place abroad with Gauls, Cantabrians, etc., and perhaps of no less extent; so that it would not be easy at the present day to demonstrate a greater purity of descent [*Abstammung*] than the others" (60–61/54–55).

33. For a fine study of Fichte's concern for linguistic purity, see David Martyn, "Borrowed Fatherland: Nationalism and Language Purism in Fichte's *Addresses to the German Nation*," *Germanic Review* 72, no. 4 (1997): 303–15. Drawing on modern studies of linguistic borrowing, Martyn shows that "the 'domestic' language is diverse—foreign—from the start" (309) by showing that practically no sentence in the *Addresses*, despite Fichte's deliberately "Germanic," Lutheran style, fails to contain hidden borrowings. Even a word like *Bildung*, as Martyn notes, "owes its formation to a double foreign influence. Coined as a translation of *imaginatio* to mean 'idea' or 'conception,' it later acquired the pedagogical sense that it has in the word *Bildungsroman* under the influence of the English *formation*, for it was first used with that meaning" (306). A hint of the gravity—or, if one wishes, the absurdity—of Fichte's predicament may be had from the fact that his only word for Teutons is *Germanen*, and that his title and topic hang on the equally latinate *Nation* (*natio*, the birth of a child, people, nation).

34. Fichte's writings are consistent in their Protestant emphasis on choice: "What sort of philosophy one chooses depends . . . on what sort of person one is," as the famous line from the First Introduction to the *Wissenschaftslehre* (*Science of Knowledge*) has it. "For a philosophical system is not a dead piece of furniture that we can reject or accept as we wish; it is rather a thing animated by the soul of the person who holds it. A person indolent by nature or dulled and distorted by mental servitude, learned luxury, and vanity will never raise himself to the level of idealism." Fichte, *Science of Knowledge, with the First and Second Introductions*, ed. and trans. Peter Heath and John Lachs (Cambridge: Cambridge University Press, 1982), 16; *SW*, 1:434.

35. Readers of the *Wissenschaftslehre* will recall the fundamental role of the imagination (*Einbildungskraft*) in generating the possibility of phenomenal experience. See *Science of Knowledge*, 188 (*SW*, 1:208) and 194 (*SW*, 1:216–17), where Fichte proposes that the imagination's wavering (*Schweben*) between irreconcileables "extends the condition of the self therein to a moment of *time*." Fichte's reworking of Kant's schematizing imagination ultimately results in the claim that "all reality—for us being understood, as it cannot be otherwise understood in a system of transcendental philosophy—is brought forth solely by the imagination" (202; *SW*, 1:227).

36. A vivid picture (and parody) of this sort of educational scheme may be had

in Goethe's descriptions of the Pedagogical Province in *Wilhelm Meisters Wanderjahre* (book 2, chaps. 1, 2, and 8).

37. "Reading and writing can be of no use in the purely national education, so long as this education continues. But it can, indeed, be very harmful; because, as it has hitherto so often done, it may easily lead the pupil astray from direct perception to mere signs" (Fichte, 152/162).

38. Samuel Taylor Coleridge, *On the Constitution of Church and State*, ed. John Colmer, in *The Collected Works of Samuel Taylor Coleridge*, ed. Kathleen Coburn (Princeton: Princeton University Press, 1976), 10:48. Coleridge's editor John Colmer notes that "writers in many fields seized on [the phrase *nisus formativus*], which means 'formative urge, impulse, or force,' with its German equivalent, *Bildungstrieb*" (48, n. 1).

39. Hence Fichte's determination to publish each address as soon as it was delivered, despite the battles he consequently had to fight with the government censor.

40. "In this way," as Anderson comments, "we can observe how the national dead and the national unborn, in their uncountable billions, mirror each other, and provide the best sureties of the ineradicable Goodness of the nation" (*S*, 364).

41. Pushed to its extreme point as National Socialist spectacle, the aesthetic nation represses its bad faith by recoding the impossibility of its own imagining as the frisson of self-destruction. On the peculiar amalgamation of kitsch and death in Nazi rhetoric, see Saul Friedländer, *Reflections of Nazism: An Essay on Kitsch and Death* (Bloomington: Indiana University Press, 1993 [1982]).

CHAPTER 2

1. Carl Woodring, *Politics in English Romantic Poetry* (Cambridge, Mass.: Harvard University Press, 1970), 31. Fichte's early *Der geschlossene Handelsstadt* (1800) provides an interesting counterexample, in which the trope of the body politic retains all its medieval particularity.

2. Mary Poovey, *Making a Social Body: British Cultural Formation, 1830–1864* (Chicago: University of Chicago Press, 1995), 7–8.

3. For a full consideration of the trope of the "imagined community" of the nation, see the previous chapter; this phrase comes to us, of course, from Benedict Anderson, *Imagined Communities: Reflections on the Origin and Spread of Nationalism*, 1ev. ed. (London: Verso, 1991 [1983]). On the culture industry, see Max Horkheimer and Theodor W. Adorno, *Dialektik der Anfklärung* (1944) (*Dialectic of Enlightenment*; New York: Continuum, 1982), 120–67. For a recent consideration of the development of nationalism in Britain, see Linda Colley, *Britons: Forging the Nation 1707–1837* (New Haven: Yale University Press, 1992).

4. Matthew Arnold, *Culture and Anarchy*, in *"Culture and Anarchy" and Other Writings*, ed. Stefan Collini (Cambridge: Cambridge University Press, 1993), 98,

214 Notes to Pages 76–77

emphasis in original. Unless otherwise noted, all my quotations from Arnold's works are taken from this edition, which collects "Democracy" (1861) and "The Function of Criticism at the Present Time" (1864), in addition to *Culture and Anarchy* (1869). When necessary for clarity of reference, short titles will accompany page numbers.

5. As noted in the Introduction (see n. 28), one may consult David Lloyd and Paul Thomas, *Culture and the State* (New York: Routledge, 1998) for a strongly argued account of the gradually hegemonic force of the discourses and institutions of aesthetic culture in Victorian Britain.

6. Terry Eagleton, *The Ideology of the Aesthetic* (Oxford: Blackwell, 1990), 13.

7. Immanuel Kant, *Critique of Judgment*, trans. Werner S. Pluhar (Indianapolis: Hackett, 1987), 47 (sect. 3).

8. Northrop Frye, *The Anatomy of Criticism* (Princeton: Princeton University Press, 1957), 119. Harold Bloom offers images of the "astral body" in *Omens of Millennium: The Gnosis of Angels, Dreams, and Resurrection* (New York: Riverhead Books, 1996) that are not dissimilar from Frye's. But this figure circulates well beyond the orbit of Blakean romanticists: Fredric Jameson, for instance, cites and reinflects Frye in *The Political Unconscious: Narrative as a Socially Symbolic Act* (Ithaca: Cornell University Press, 1981): "A social hermeneutic will . . . restore a perspective in which the imagery of libidinal revolution and of bodily transfiguration once again becomes a figure for the perfected community. The unity of the body must once again prefigure the renewed organic identity of associative or collective life, rather than, as for Frye, the reverse" (74). One catches hints of this vision in much contemporary utopian writing, e.g., Norman O. Brown's rhapsodies on "a body freed from all sexual organizations" in *Life Against Death: The Psychoanalytical Meaning of History* (Middletown, Conn.: Wesleyan University Press, 1970), 291. Consider too the freely modified versions of Leonardo da Vinci's *homo ad circulum* that the U.S. space program chose as the emblem for the second manned Skylab mission in 1973. (The images sent out with the *Voyager* probes in 1977 included a female as well as a male figure modeled on the da Vinci drawing.) An aesthetic–humanistic dream of transcendence marks much of the fiction and real-life practice of space exploration, and would merit extensive analysis.

On Kant, a qualification is in order: Kant's "ideal of beauty" is not, strictly speaking, an image of a fulfilled historical telos; it is, however, an "archetype of taste" that we strive to "produce" within ourselves (*Critique of Judgment*, 80).

9. On the "pure cut" of aesthetic framing (that must also be, at certain crucial points, impure), see Jacques Derrida, "Parergon," in *The Truth in Painting*, trans. Geoffrey Bennington and Ian McLeod (Chicago: University of Chicago Press, 1987), my short discussion of Kant and the problem of form this book's Introduction, and my considerably more detailed discussion in the opening chapter of *Phantom Formations: Aesthetic Ideology and the Bildungsroman* (Ithaca: Cornell University Press, 1996).

10. David Farrell Krell, *Contagion: Sexuality, Disease, and Death in German Idealism and Romanticism* (Indianapolis: Indiana University Press, 1998).

11. Paul Youngquist, "De Quincey's Crazy Body," *PMLA* 114, no. 3 (1999): 351. Youngquist writes of the body as the text's "material ground," yet he seems to mean by that phrase a kind of aesthetic eudaemonia capable of swallowing up all anxieties of representation or being. The fantasy is not dissimilar to that at work in Terry Eagleton's text, as discussed below. One of the most influential recent literary–critical works on the body, Elaine Scarry's *The Body in Pain: The Making and Unmaking of the World* (New York: Oxford University Press, 1985), grounds itself in precisely this fantasy: for Scarry, the body is the prelinguistic "physical basis of reality," the "mother-lode" of technology and signification (137).

12. Judith Butler, *Bodies That Matter: On the Discursive Limits of "Sex"* (New York: Routledge, 1993), 66–67, Butler's italics.

13. Sigmund Freud, *Das Ich und das Es*, in *Gesammelte Werke*, ed. Anna Freud et al. (Frankfurt am Main: S. Fischer Verlag, 1967 [1940]), 13:253; *The Ego and the Id*, in *The Standard Edition of the Complete Psychological Works of Sigmund Freud*, ed. James Strachey (London: Hogarth Press, 1961), 19:26.

14. Butler discusses this paradox at some length in the pages that precede the passage I cited above; see 57–66. Freud's speculations on the "bodily ego" in *The Ego and the Id* are developed in a footnote: "I.e., the ego is ultimately derived from bodily sensations, chiefly from those springing from the surface of the body. It may thus be regarded as a mental projection of the surface of the body" (26). As Butler comments, "Although Freud's language engages a causal temporality that has the body part precede its 'idea,' he nevertheless confirms here the indissolubility of a body part and the phantasmatic partitioning that brings it into psychic existence," an insight that Lacan of course develops (59).

15. After this chapter had been written and sent off for publication, I belatedly came across Judith Butler's essay "How Can I Deny That These Hands and This Body Are Mine?", in *Material Events: Paul de Man and the Afterlife of Theory*, ed. Barbara Cohen et al. (Minneapolis: University of Minnesota Press, 2001), 254–73: an essay that takes up the materiality of the body in terms immediately relevant to a critique of aesthetics. Butler writes: "Although the body depends upon language to be known, the body also exceeds every possible linguistic effort of capture. It would be tempting to conclude that this means that the body exists outside of language, that it has an ontology separable from any linguistic one, and that we might be able to describe this separable ontology. But this is where I would hesitate, perhaps permanently, for as we begin that description of what is outside of language, the chiasm reappears: we have already contaminated, though not contained, the very body we seek to establish in its ontological purity" (257). Butler goes on to provide a reading of Descartes with reference to Paul de Man's reading of the figure of the body in Kant's *Critique of Judgment*, where, as Butler rightly observes (and as we shall confirm in Chapter 3), de Man proposes the dismembered body as

the figure for the uncanny "limits of figuration" (268)—the figure, that is, for a materiality prior to any figuration or phenomenalization. We may allow Butler's closing sentence to sum up the discussion: "If there is a materiality of the body that escapes from the figures it conditions and by which it is corroded and haunted, then this body is neither a surface nor a substance, but the linguistic occasion of the body's separation from itself, one that eludes its capture by the figure it compels" (271–72).

The difficulty posed by the figure of the body in the aesthetic tradition is legible in Jean-François Lyotard's remarkable meditations on the aesthetic body: "To be esthetically (in the sense of the first Kantian Critique) is to be there [*être-là*], here and now, exposed in space-time and to the space-time of something that touches before any concept and even any representation. This *before* is not known, obviously, because it is there before we are. It is something like birth and infancy (Latin *in-fans*)—there before we are. The *there* in question is called the body. It is not I who am born, who is given birth to. I will be born afterwards, with language, precisely in leaving infancy. My affairs will have been handled and decided before I can answer for them—and once and for all: this infancy, this body, this unconscious remaining there my entire life. When the law comes, with my self and language, it is too late. Things will already have taken a turn. And the law in its turn will not manage to efface the first turn, this first touch. Esthetics has to do with this first touch, which touched me when I was not there." Lyotard, "Prescription," *L'Esprit Créateur* 31, no. 1 (1991): 18. Lyotard's figure of the "touch" captures the imperative to think the body in terms of inscription—the inscription of meaning prior to meaning—at the same time that his Lacanian thematization of language as law, etc., tends toward a literalization of "language" that allows the body to be imagined as resolutely pre- and nonlinguistic—as the "real," the absolute referent. It is perhaps impossible to avoid this referential fantasy; but I would insist, with Butler as I interpret her, that the materiality of Lyotard's "first touch, which touched me when I was not there" is always a linguistic materiality insofar as it opens the possibility of form, meaning, and body (a body that, in Butler's phrase cited above, eludes "the figure it compels").

16. William K. Wimsatt, "Organic Form: Some Questions About a Metaphor," in *Romanticism: Vistas, Instances, Continuities*, ed. David Thorburn and Geoffrey Hartman (Ithaca: Cornell University Press, 1973), 21. The trope of the text as body goes back to the *Phaedrus*: "every discourse [*logos*] should be composed like a living body, so that it lacks neither hands nor feet." Plato, *Phaedrus*, in *Opera*, II, ed. John Burnet (Oxford: Oxford University Press, 1971 [1901]), 264c; compare Aristotle's *Poetics*, 7.

17. Wimsatt is paraphrasing G. N. G. Orsini, "The Organic Concept in Aesthetics," *Comparative Literature* 21 (1969): 27. M. H. Abrams's discussion of Coleridge's theory of organic form offers another intriguingly overcharged meditation

on the power of figurative language: "Indeed, it is astonishing how much of Coleridge's critical writing is couched in terms that are metaphorical for art and literal for a plant: if Plato's dialectic is a wilderness of mirrors, Coleridge's is a very jungle of vegetation. Only let the vehicles of his metaphors come alive, and you see all the objects of criticism writhe surrealistically into plants or parts of plants, growing in tropical profusion. Authors, characters, poetic genres, poetic passages, words, meter, logic become seeds, trees, flowers, blossoms, fruit, bark, and sap" (169). For a discussion of this passage in *The Mirror and the Lamp*, see Jonathan Culler, "The Mirror Stage," in *The Pursuit of Signs: Semiotics, Literature, Deconstruction* (Ithaca: Cornell University Press, 1981), 157–58.

18. Kathy Alexis Psomiades, *Beauty's Body: Femininity and Representation in British Aesthetics* (Stanford: Stanford University Press, 1997), 19.

19. I would add to Psomiades's discussion that the feminine body recurs elsewhere in Eagleton's work as a figure for "the truth," particularly in *The Rape of Clarissa: Writing, Sexuality, and Class Struggle in Samuel Richardson* (Minneapolis: University of Minnesota Press, 1982), where we find appeals to "the 'real' of the woman's body, that outer limit upon all language" (61). There is a considerable literature on the figure of woman as truth (a trope that unfolds rapidly into that of woman as figure—that is, surface, false appearance, etc.); see Jacques Derrida, *Spurs: Nietzsche's Styles*, trans. Barbara Harlow (Chicago: University of Chicago Press, 1981).

20. It is perhaps worth emphasizing that such a claim in no way denies the referential force of medical or biological descriptions of the body. Yet even scientific descriptions of the body obtain their referential force historically and remain linguistic practices that may be understood as constructing what they describe to the extent that they remain "sedimented with discourses on sex and sexuality," as Butler put it (29). An informed arguing of this point may be found in the work of the molecular biologist and cultural critic Anne Fausto-Sterling; see her *Sexing the Body: Gender Politics and the Construction of Sexuality* (New York: Basic Books, 2000). Fausto-Sterling's main claim is that "our bodies are too complex to provide clear-cut answers about sexual difference" (4)—chromosomal sex, for instance, as she shows in considerable detail, is not a "truth" external to interpretation, though in promising such referential stability, it has a range of political and social effects. In the present essay, my point is to emphasize, and tease out the consequences of, the body's role as a figure of linguistic referential force.

21. William Bennett, "To Reclaim a Legacy: Report on Humanities in Education," *Chronicle of Higher Education* (November 28, 1984), 17.

22. For instance: "Once the inspiration of humanistic study in England and America, Arnold has now become something of an embarrassment. He represents for many an abandoned path or a path to be abandoned." Eugene Goodheart, "Arnold at the Present Time," *Critical Inquiry* 9 (1983): 451. See also Morris

Dickstein, "Arnold Then and Now: The Use and Misuse of Criticism," *Critical Inquiry* 9 (1983): 469–507; and for an essay exemplary of the full-throated neoconservative appeal to Arnold, see Joseph Epstein, "Matthew Arnold and the Resistance," *Commentary* 73, no. 4 (1982): 53–60.

23. Gerald Graff, *Professing Literature: An Institutional History* (Chicago: University of Chicago Press, 1987).

24. The legacy of Arnoldianism is not always straightforward. Harold Bloom, for instance, positions himself within the aestheticist tradition of Pater and Wilde, rejecting the Arnoldian humanist conviction that art, or the study of art, has an effect on the world; Bloom thus propounds a theory of literary influence that, in a Wildean spirit, understands the task of criticism to be the seeing of the object as it really is *not*. But aestheticism represents in the end a version of aesthetic humanism, and despite Bloom's (loudly and frequently) pronounced aversion to Matthew Arnold, readers of Arnold or Schiller will recognize aesthetic (and ultimately theological) topoi in Bloom. There is the fall away from the original; there is the canon's historical and the poet's personal development from naive to ever more self-conscious, sentimental poetry, with a corresponding emphasis on the ever-increasing difficulty of modern art: "One of the functions of criticism, as I understand it, is to make a good poet's work even more difficult for him to perform, since only the overcoming of genuine difficulties can result in poems wholly adequate to an age consciously as late as our own." Bloom, *A Map of Misreading* (New York: Oxford University Press, 1975), 10.

25. In calling on the figure of Burke to such ends, Arnold is visiting a topos that dates at least to Hazlitt's "Character of Mr Burke" (1807): "It has always been with me a test of the sense and candor of any one belonging to the opposite party, whether he allowed Burke to be a great man." *The Complete Works of William Hazlitt*, ed. P. P. Howe (London and Toronto: J. M. Dent and Sons, 1932), 7:305. (Hazlitt, himself very much of "the opposite party," of course, did not always write charitably about Burke.) Arnold knew Hazlitt's work well and inherited the term *disinterestedness* from him.

26. George Eliot, *Middlemarch*, ed. Rosemary Ashton (Harmondsworth: Penguin, 1994 [1871–72]), 86. For a study of the pressures to which this text submits aesthetic discourse, see my *Phantom Formations*, chap. 5.

27. Friedrich Schlegel, *Kritische Friedrich-Schlegel-Ausgabe*, ed. Ernst Behler with Jean-Jacques Anstett and Hans Eichner (Paderborn: Schöningh, 1958), 18:82.

28. R. H. Super, the editor of the *Complete Prose Works*, adds the bracketed word "not" here, and Collini's edition preserves Super's emendation; cf. *The Complete Prose Works of Matthew Arnold*, vol. 3, *Lectures and Essays in Criticism* (Ann Arbor: University of Michigan Press, 1962).

29. It is not entirely a coincidence that the newspaper serves Benedict Anderson as the exemplary technological precondition of nationalism. See *Imagined Communities*, and, for discussion, my previous chapter.

30. Mary Poovey, *Uneven Developments: The Ideological Work of Gender in Mid-Victorian England* (Chicago: University of Chicago Press, 1988), 143. Arnold's fantasies about Wragg may also be understood in the broader context of the challenge encountered by Victorian domestic ideology in the 1860s, by which point, in the wake of middle-class feminist agitation for employment and property rights for women, "the threat posed to the equation of female nature and domesticity or maternity was perceived to be increasingly serious" (Poovey, 155). Also of interest in this context is the increasingly maternal representation of Britannia over the romantic and postromantic era that Anne Mellor tracks in a recent paper, "Materializing the English Nation: The Triumph of Britannia," given at the North American Society for the Study of Romanticism's meeting in Tempe, Arizona, on September 16, 2000; see also Mellor's arguments about ways in which "British national identity is reconfigured as feminine" in the opening decades of the nineteenth century, in *Mothers of the Nation* (Indianapolis: University of Indiana Press, 2000), 139 (see esp. 139–46). Peter Mellini and Roy T. Matthews's article "John Bull's Family Arises," *History Today* 37 (May 1987): 17–23, arrives at a similar conclusion via a survey of representations of Britannia. Britannia made her first appearance on first-century Roman coins; she was revived in the sixteenth century as an emblem of English glory. But according to Mellini and Matthews, only after the Napoleonic wars did she become "a matronly Graeco-Roman goddess" (17). By the mid-nineteenth century, "in a sense she exemplified the perfect Victorian woman as well as the nation's ideals, and, increasingly, she became associated (or confused?) with Queen Victoria" (23). I thank Susan Wolfson for originally drawing my attention to Mellor's discussion in her book and Leanne Maunu for alerting me to Mellini and Matthews's article.

31. Julia Kristeva, *Powers of Horror: An Essay on Abjection*, trans. Leon S. Roudiez (New York: Columbia University Press, 1982), 71. In Wilde's "The Critic as Artist," the naive Ernest, half-remembering Arnold, edits out the pun: "By the Ilyssus, says Arnold somewhere, there was no Higginbotham [sic]. By the Ilyssus, my dear Gilbert, there were no silly art congresses. . . . The Greeks had no art critics" (*Intentions* [London: Methuen, 1913 (1891)], 109). Arnold's choice of names to deplore has a self-consciously literary—and literarily self-parodic—side to it: "Nehemiah Higginbottom" is the alias Samuel Taylor Coleridge used to sign three self-parodic sonnets in 1797.

32. Cathy Caruth has pointed out to me the felicity of Arnold's having "stumbled" on the paragraph about Wragg; the verb conjures up a vulnerable, falling body—potentially, a damaged or fragmented body. For an extended study of the falling body as a figure for unreliable and excessive linguistic referentiality, see Caruth, "The Falling Body and the Impact of Reference (de Man, Kant, Kleist)," in her *Unclaimed Experience: Trauma, Narrative, and History* (Baltimore, Md.: Johns Hopkins University Press, 1996), 73–90.

CHAPTER 3

1. For fuller discussion see, in addition to this book's Introduction, the opening chapter of my *Phantom Formations: Aesthetic Ideology and the Bildungsroman* (Ithaca: Cornell University Press, 1996).

2. In his recent *The Wild Card of Reading: On Paul de Man* (Cambridge, Mass.: Harvard University Press, 1998), Rodolphe Gasché remarks the "general dreariness of the more recent de Man studies in North America" (269), but the evidence, I think, is against him. Gasché's book forms part of a slender but steady stream of intelligent, and at times brilliant, readings of de Man over the past twenty years. I shall be citing some of the work I most admire in the pages that follow, but in passing, we may note here two significant recent collections that testify to the vitality of "recent de Man studies in North America": *Critical Encounters: Reference and Responsibility in Deconstructive Writing*, ed. Cathy Caruth and Deborah Esch (New Brunswick: Rutgers University Press, 1995), and *Material Events: Paul de Man and the Afterlife of Theory*, ed. Tom Cohen, Barbara Cohen, J. Hillis Miller, and Andrzej Warminski (Minneapolis: University of Minnesota Press, 2000). The broader influence of de Man on literary and cultural study today is a subject worthy of a substantial essay. One would need to track a very wide range of phenomena, e.g., the interest of gender and queer theorists such as Judith Butler or Eve Sedgwick in modes of linguistic performativity, in addition to the more specific mobilization of a de Manian vocabulary of rhetorical reading in psychoanalytic or gender-identity contexts by Cynthia Chase, Lee Edelman, Neil Hertz, and others (see nn. 78 and 80, and attendant discussion, in this book's Introduction); or the work of Cathy Caruth and Shoshana Felman on trauma (see nn. 19 and 20 to the present chapter). For the various efforts, of which the present book is one, to discover in de Manian theory a resource for thinking about questions of technology, mediation, ethics, and ideology, see, e.g., Deborah Esch, *In the Event: Reading Journalism, Reading Theory* (Stanford: Stanford University Press, 1999); Thomas Keenan, *Fables of Responsibility: Aberrations and Predicaments in Ethics and Politics* (Stanford: Stanford University Press, 1997); and Samuel Weber, *Mass Mediauras: Form, Technics, Media* (Stanford: Stanford University Press, 1996).

3. Frank Lentricchia, *Criticism and Social Change* (Chicago: University of Chicago Press, 1983), 39.

4. We may recall the comment of John Guillory's cited in the Introduction: "It would not have been necessary for so many theorists and antitheorists, de Manians and anti–de Manians, to 'respond' to these revelations if theory itself were not perceived to be implicated in the figure of de Man." Guillory, *Cultural Capital: The Problem of Literary Canon Formation* (Chicago: Chicago University Press, 1993), 178. I have discussed Guillory's interesting, but in my opinion erroneous, account of de Manian theory briefly in the Introduction and in *Phantom Formations* (1–37,

211–13); because of the considerable success that Guillory's book has enjoyed, it is perhaps worth noting that the present chapter—an early version of which was published in 1990—may be taken in part as a refutation *avant la lettre* of Guillory's claim that "what de Man has no patience for at all, not even the patience to name, is the notion of transference" (193). As we shall see, de Man constantly names and reflects on transference; indeed, de Manian theory might plausibly be described as a theory of transference.

5. Paul de Man, *Allegories of Reading: Figural Language in Rousseau, Nietzsche, Rilke, and Proust* (New Haven: Yale University Press, 1979), 4. (The opening chapter, "Semiology and Rhetoric," was originally published as an essay in 1972.) Subsequent references to *Allegories of Reading* are indicated parenthetically in the text by acronym *AR* and the page number. Quotations from de Man's other books are indicated by page number and acronym, as follows: *Aesthetic Ideology*, ed. Andrzej Warminski (Minneapolis: University of Minnesota Press, 1996) = *AI*; *Blindness and Insight: Essays in the Rhetoric of Contemporary Criticism*, 2nd ed. (Minneapolis: University of Minnesota Press, 1983) = *BI*; *Critical Writings, 1953–1978*, ed. Lindsay Waters (Minneapolis: University of Minnesota Press, 1989) = *CW*; *The Resistance to Theory* (Minneapolis: University of Minnesota Press, 1986) = *RT*; *The Rhetoric of Romanticism* (New York: Columbia University Press, 1984) = *RR*; *Romanticism and Contemporary Criticism: The Gauss Seminar and Other Papers*, ed. E. S. Burt, Kevin Newmark, and Andrzej Warminski (Baltimore, Md.: Johns Hopkins University Press, 1993) = *RC*.

6. The closing cadence is slightly less portentous in the original French: "avant de pouvoir devenir une histoire." De Man, "La critique thématique devant le thème de Faust," *Critique* 120 (May 1957): 404.

7. The refusal of pathetic language, of course, hardly impedes, and if anything encourages, the recurrence of a pathetic tone. I am drawing attention here to one thematic regularity among several in a general rhetoric of mourning that one encounters throughout de Man's work. For a study of the rhetoric of sacrifice in de Man, see Minae Mizumura, "Renunciation," *Yale French Studies* 69 (1985): 81–97; see also the essays of Neil Hertz cited in nn. 33 and 34 below. For a sustained reflection on the role of affect in de Man, see Rei Terada, *Feeling in Theory: Emotion After the "Death of the Subject"* (Cambridge, Mass.: Harvard University Press, 2001). A particularly rich thematization of the temporal pathos of history occurs in the fourth of de Man's 1967 Gauss lectures, "Time and History in Wordsworth," *RC*, 74–94. The lecture holds special interest for critics interested in de Man's shift from existential to rhetorical terminologies, since he gave the lecture again in 1972, modified in ways that the editors record in footnotes.

8. René Wellek, *A History of Modern Criticism: 1750–1950* (London: Jonathan Cape, 1955), 1:255. For Hegel's famous claim that Schiller broke through "Kantian abstraction and subjectivity of thinking," see G. W. F. Hegel, *Aesthetics: Lectures*

on Fine Art, trans. T. M. Knox (Oxford: Clarendon Press, 1974), 61; *Vorlesungen über die Ästhetik*, in *Werke*, ed. Eva Moldenhauer and Karl Markus Michel (Frankfurt: Suhrkamp, 1970 [1835]), 13:89.

9. Schiller's name appears with some regularity in de Man's work, usually signifying a certain misreading of Rousseau (see *RR*, 20–26 and passim, and *AR*, 137, 176, 208). However, Schiller only becomes a figure of emblematic stature when de Man begins to write explicitly on the reception of Kant's *Critique of Judgment*.

10. Schiller, the vulgarizer of Kant, the overpragmatic dramatist or overidealistic poet incapable of genuine philosophical cogitation, is a stock character in German literary history from Schiller's own time onward. Schiller's patron, the Duke of Augustenburg, wrote apropos of an early version of the *Aesthetic Education*: "Our good Schiller is not cut out for a philosopher; he needs a translator to elaborate his fine phrases with philosophic precision, and to transpose him from the poetic into the philosophic mode." Hans Schulz, *Schiller und der Herzog von Augustenburg in Briefen* (Jena, 1905), 153, as quoted by Elizabeth M. Wilkinson and L. A. Willoughby in their introduction to their translation of Schiller, *On the Aesthetic Education of Man, in a Series of Letters* (Oxford: Clarendon Press, 1967), cxxxviii. For a summary of the main lines of Schiller's twentieth-century reception, and a glowing defense of the Education, see Wilkinson and Willoughby, xlii–lxvii.

Theodor W. Adorno's remarks on Schiller in *Ästhetische Theorie* (*Aesthetic Theory*) are reminiscent of de Man's: "The fetishization of the concept of genius that begins with Kant as the fetishization of dirempted, abstract subjectivity—to put it in Hegelian terms—already in Schiller's votive offerings took on a quality of crass elitism. [Schiller's] concept of genius becomes the potential enemy of artworks; with a sidelong glance at Goethe, the person back of the work is purported to be more essential than the artworks themselves. In the concept of genius, the idea of creation is transferred with idealistic hubris from the transcendental to the empirical subject, to the productive artist. This suits crude bourgeois consciousness as much because it implies a work ethic that glorifies pure human creativity regardless of its aim as because the viewer is relieved of taking any trouble with the object itself: The viewer is supposed to be satisfied with the personality—essentially a kitsch biography—of the artist." Adorno, *Aesthetic Theory*, trans. Robert Hullot-Kentor (Minneapolis: University of Minnesota Press, 1997), 171; *Ästhetische Theorie*, ed. Gretel Adorno and Rolf Tiedemann (Frankfurt am Main: Suhrkamp, 1970), 255–56.

11. Edmund Husserl, *Ideen zu einer reinen Phänomenologie und Phänomenologische Philosophie, I: Allgemeine Einführung in die reine Phänomenologie*, ed. Walter Biemel (Hague: Martinus Nijhof, 1950 [1913]), 64; *Ideas: General Introduction to Pure Phenomenology*, trans. W. R. Boyce Gibson (New York: Collier Books, 1962), 97.

12. Werner Hamacher, "Lectio: De Man's Imperative," in Lindsay Waters and

Wlad Godzich, ed., *Reading de Man Reading* (Minneapolis: University of Minnesota Press, 1989), 185.

13. See, for a careful treatment of this predicament, Cynthia Chase's chapter on de Man, "Giving a Face to a Name," in her *Decomposing Figures: Rhetorical Readings in the Romantic Tradition* (Baltimore, Md.: Johns Hopkins University Press, 1986), 82–112.

14. Immanuel Kant, *Kritik der Urteilskraft*, in *Werkausgabe*, ed. Wilhelm Weischedel (Frankfurt am Main: Suhrkamp, 1974); *Critique of Judgment*, trans. Werner S. Pluhar (Indianapolis: Hackett, 1987), sect. 29 ("General Comment on the Exposition of Aesthetic Reflective Judgments").

15. De Man's reading of Kant and his notion of formal materialism has attracted considerable informed commentary. See, among others, Rodolphe Gasché, "In-Difference to Philosophy" and "Apathetic Formalism," now collected in *Wild Card*, 48–90, 91–113. Most of the essays in the collection *Material Events* engage or at least touch on de Man's interpretation of Kant. See in particular Andrzej Warminski, "'As the Poets Do It': On the Material Sublime," 3–31.

16. Fredric Jameson, *The Political Unconscious: Narrative as a Socially Symbolic Act* (Ithaca: Cornell University Press, 1981), 100. The difficult thought being elaborated in de Man's work, however, turns precisely on the inadequacy of the phenomenal trope of the horizon or "limit" as a figure for historical force. A compact critique of the idealization of the nonrepresentational space of history may be found in Wlad Godzich's introduction to *RT*, xvii–xviii.

17. I have engaged the question of history from a rhetorical standpoint in my chapter on Flaubert in *Phantom Formations*, 171–200. A helpful discussion of de Man's notions of materiality and history may be found in Kevin Newmark, *Beyond Symbolism: Textual History and the Future of Reading* (Ithaca: Cornell University Press, 1990), 195–230.

18. De Man's tone is by no means always pathetic in these moments. In two late texts that are very much about history and have remained conditioned by oral delivery—"The Task of the Translator" and "Kant and Schiller"—the persona is frequently that of cheery provocateur. Near the beginning of "Kant and Schiller," for instance, de Man defines history thus: "History . . . is not thought of as a progression or a regression, but is thought of as an event, as an occurrence. There is history from the moment that words such as 'power' and 'battle' and so on emerge on the scene. At that moment things happen, there is occurrence, there is event. History is therefore not a temporal notion, it has nothing to do with temporality, but it is the emergence of a language of power out of a language of cognition" (*AI*, 133). These remarks—a little like the famous closing sentence about wars and revolutions—are at once oddly dramatic and thoroughly serious, provocatively staged ("there is history from the moment that words such as 'power' and 'battle' and so on emerge on the scene") and accounted for by previous argumentation

(the reference is to the previous lecture on Kant, where de Man, as we saw above, located a rupture in Kant's text in its passage from the cognitive model of the mathematical sublime to the dynamic sublime's vocabulary of "power").

19. Cathy Caruth, "Introduction," *American Imago*, special issue on Psychoanalysis, Culture and Trauma, 48, no. 1 (1991): 4. Caruth has extended these reflections in *Unclaimed Experience: Trauma, Narrative, and History* (Baltimore, Md.: Johns Hopkins University Press, 1996).

20. For an important practical elaboration of history as trauma, see, in addition to Caruth's work, Shoshana Felman and Dori Laub, *Testimony: Crises of Witnessing in Literature, Psychoanalysis, and History* (New York: Routledge, 1992). This collection includes Felman's reading of de Man's wartime journalism. For a searching reflection on the wartime journalism in this general context, see Cynthia Chase, "Trappings of an Education," in *Responses: On Paul de Man's Wartime Journalism*, ed. Werner Hamacher, Neil Hertz, and Thomas Keenan (Lincoln: University of Nebraska Press, 1989), 44–79.

21. Louis Althusser, "Ideology and Ideological State Apparatuses," in *Lenin and Philosophy and Other Essays*, trans. Ben Brewster (New York: Monthly Review Press, 1971), 159–62. There are a number of tempting points of congruence between Althusser's theoretical writing and de Man's: an insistence on the irreducibility of ideology; an attempt to think history as "a process without a telos or a subject" (*Réponse à John Lewis* [Paris: Maspéro, 1973]); a refusal to confuse history with "'empirical' temporality" (*Reading Capital*, trans. Ben Brewster [London: New Left Books, 1970], 105). For a closely argued mediation between Althusser and de Man, see Michael Sprinker, *Imaginary Relations: Aesthetics and Ideology in the Theory of Historical Materialism* (London: Verso, 1987). I have discussed the problematics of "aesthetic ideology" at length in *Phantom Formations*, 1–37.

22. The caginess of de Man's formulation becomes evident when one considers that the word "drive" here translates the notion of *Trieb* with which Schiller, as we'll see in a moment, domesticates Kant's critical system. Similarly subtle gestures of give and take abound in these late texts of de Man's. When he writes of a certain Schillerian tradition that it "condenses the complex ideology of the aesthetic in a suggestive concatenation of concepts" (*RR*, 264), for instance, he is actually describing the achievement of Wilkinson and Willoughby's edition of Schiller's *Aesthetic Education*. Schiller's text, in other words, is as much a construction of its "reception" as a force in its own right. Wilkinson and Willoughby's fine bilingual edition, with its two-hundred-page introduction and extensive commentary, constitutes one of the most monumental—and monumentalizing—gestures of canonization in recent scholarship. Quotes from the *Aesthetic Education* in what follows are from this edition and are indicated by letter and paragraph number.

23. Readers who are not Germanists, and who intend to work through de Man's essay in greater detail, may benefit from a sense of the dates and occasions

of the Schiller texts. Schiller began to read Kant's *Critique of Judgment* intensely in the spring of 1791, and wrote the relatively obscure essay "Vom Erhabenen" in the spring of 1793. Also in 1793, Schiller composed for the Duke of Augustenburg the letters that, massively transformed and elaborated, became the *Aesthetic Education* of 1795. In 1801 Schiller discarded the first half of "Vom Erhabenen" and republished its second half under the title "Über das Pathetische" in *Kleinere prosaische Schriften*. The usual scholarly guess is that, eight years after its composition, Schiller found the essay's first half too dependent on Kant. Schiller revised the *Aesthetic Education* for republication in *Kleinere prosaische Schriften* in 1801, but the changes were relatively minor: the significant transformations in Schiller's aesthetic theory had occurred between 1793 and 1795. De Man will speak of "Vom Erhabenen" as "early Schiller" for this reason. To avoid confusion, it should also be noted that in 1795 Schiller published another essay on the sublime, "Über das Erhabene," which de Man mentions but does not discuss.

24. As I hope to show later—and as de Man would doubtless be the first to acknowledge—Schiller's text is more strained and complex at this point than de Man's comments (which I am more or less reproducing here) immediately suggest. But it is certainly true that "the human" functions as a pragmatic, conceptually arbitrary principle of closure in the *Aesthetic Education*. When complications grow troublesome, Schiller is given to saying things like, "But enough! Self-consciousness is there" (19.11); and at a crucial point in the treatise, not far removed from the passages that concern us, we are told that Reason must posit humanity and beauty— i.e., the *Wechselwirkung* that defines the beautiful and the human—because Reason is Reason. "But how there can be beauty, and how humanity is possible, neither reason nor experience can tell us" (15.4).

25. Joseph Goebbels, *Michael: Ein deutsches Schicksal in Tagebuchblättern* (Munich: F. Eber, 1933 [1929]), 21; cited by Wilkinson and Willoughby, cxlii. For an instructive account of Schiller's importance for the Nazi culture industry, see Georg Ruppelt, *Schiller im nationalsozialistischen Deutschland: Der Versuch einer Gleichschaltung* (Stuttgart: J. B. Metzlersche Verlagsbuchhandlung, 1979).

26. Carl von Clausewitz, *On War*, ed. and trans. Michael Howard and Peter Paret (Princeton: Princeton University Press, 1976), 77 (I, 1.3).

27. From the perspective of aesthetic formalism, as we have seen, the material event takes as its privileged figure the mutilation of a (human) body, and Cathy Caruth rightly suggests that such moments open the possibility of rethinking humanism: "such mutilation also designates the reassertion of a referential moment [within a sheerly formal system], a referentiality that is not, however, to be understood within the phenomenal, formalizable opposition of empirical and conceptual knowledge. In terms of the example, we could say that while the force of the enumeration mutilates the body as a whole, it at the same time establishes, in this disarticulation of limbs, or naming of parts, the very specificity of a human, as opposed to puppet, body." Caruth, "The Claims of Reference," in *Critical Encounters*,

102–3. (Caruth refers here both to de Man's reading of Kant and to his reading of Kleist's "Über das Marionettentheater" in "Aesthetic Formalization in Kleist.") For another effort to rethink humanism in relation to de Man's work, see my "Humanizing de Man," *Diacritics* 19, no. 2 (1989): 35–53.

28. This chapter leaves aside, but wishes to recall and evoke, the Heideggerian subtext constantly legible in de Man's work, and especially prominent in this chapter of *Allegories of Reading*. Though de Man's terms are dictated by the task of interpreting Rousseau's text, it is not entirely coincidental that the operative, disputed term should be the inauthentic (that is, im-proper: *uneigentlich*) affect "fear" rather than the authentic *Angst* of a *Dasein* turning away from itself. De Man's intervention here would ultimately have to be thought in relation to the occurrence or *Ereignis*: to history as *Geschichte*, as that which occurs, as in the line of Hölderlin's that encapsulates de Man's invocation and displacement of Heidegger: "Es ereignet sich aber das Wahre." For Heidegger's classic discussion of *Angst*, see par. 40 of *Sein und Zeit* (Tübingen: Max Niemeyer Verlag, 1967 [1927]), 184–91; *Being and Time*, trans. John Macquarrie and Edward Robinson (New York: Harper and Row, 1962), 228–35.

29. Paul de Man, "A Letter from Paul de Man," *Critical Inquiry* 8, no. 3 (spring 1982): 509, 510. For a study of de Man's shift in position with regard to Rousseau's "giant" metaphor, see Hans-Jost Frey, "Undecidability," *Yale French Studies* 69 (1985): 124–133.

30. J. Hillis Miller, *The Ethics of Reading: Kant, de Man, Eliot, Trollope, James, and Benjamin* (New York: Columbia University Press, 1987), 59. For a fuller discussion of the general question of the ethical in de Man's writing, see my review of Miller's *Ethics of Reading* in "Humanizing de Man," *Diacritics* 19, no. 2 (1989): 35–53.

31. Here de Man's work has been seen to converge with various poststructuralist and post-Levinasian efforts to conceive of ethics as the risk of an uninsurable relationship to the other. For a recent study that works to make this connection, see Keenan, *Fables of Responsibility*.

32. Carol Jacobs, "On Looking at Shelley's Medusa," *Yale French Studies* 69 (1985): 166.

33. Neil Hertz, "Lurid Figures," in *Reading de Man Reading*, 82–104; here 90, 100.

34. In "More Lurid Figures," *Diacritics* 20, no. 3 (1990): 2–27, Hertz suggests that de Man's writing "bears the traces of a particular, thoroughly contingent event of his life"—his mother's suicide by hanging (8). Hertz tends to emphasize the defensive function of these lurid figures, but he also proposes that the mobilization of such marks of "the reader-critic's own fascination" is what allows de Man to "press his understanding of figuration . . . to the explicit and rewarding discussions of reading-as-prosopopeia that characterize his work after *Allegories of Reading*"

(13–14). The figure of the Medusa is treated in Hertz's chapter "Medusa's Head," in *The End of the Line: Essays on Psychoanalysis and the Sublime* (New York: Columbia University Press, 1985); for Freud on the Medusa, see "Das Medusenhaupt," in *Gesammelte Werke*, ed. Anna Freud et al. (Frankfurt am Main: S. Fischer Verlag, 1967 [1941]), 17:47; "Medusa's Head," in *Collected Papers*, ed. James Strachey (London: Hogarth Press, 1950), 5:105. For a historical and anthropological treatment of the Gorgo, see Jean-Pierre Vernant, *Mortals and Immortals: Collected Essays*, ed. Froma I. Zeitlin (Princeton: Princeton University Press, 1991), 95–150.

35. Jacques Derrida, *Glas*, trans. John P. Leavey Jr. and Richard Rand (Lincoln: University of Nebraska Press, 1986), 47. On erection and stoniness, see the discussion of Hegel and Freud in *Glas*: "But what is the stone, the stoniness of the stone? Stone is the phallus. Is that any answer? . . . And what if, occupying no center, having no natural place, following no path of its own, the phallus has no signification, eludes every sublimating relief (*Aufhebung*), extracts the very movement of signification, the signifier/signified relation, from all *Aufhebung*, in one direction or the other, both types coming down ultimately to the same?" (45–46).

36. Sigmund Freud, "Zur Einführung des Narzißmus" (1914), in *Gesammelte Werke*, 10:155; "On Narcissism: An Introduction," *Standard Edition of the Complete Psychological Works of Sigmund Freud*, ed. James Strachey (London: The Hogarth Press, 1953–74), 14:89. Freud, of course, was to rewrite the *Spieltrieb* as the repetition compulsion in *Jenseits des Lustprinzips* (*Beyond the Pleasure Principle*; 1920) — a text that, from our present perspective, might be described as the most extravagant refiguration and critique that Schiller's treatise ever received.

37. Sarah Kofman, *The Enigma of Woman: Woman in Freud's Writings*, trans. Catherine Porter (Ithaca: Cornell University Press, 1985), 72. Kofman traces connections between the Medusa and the narcissistic woman of the "On Narcissism" essay, suggesting ways in which mothers, in Freud, collect attributes of monstrosity, death, necessity, phantasmatic power. Her interpretation emphasizes Freud's half-acknowledged fear of the inaccessible woman as "enigma" or other; "On Narcissism," she suggests, opens up a possibility that Freud elsewhere forecloses: "that of conceptualizing the enigma of woman along the lines of the [narcissistic] great criminal rather than the hysteric" (65). Along these lines, one could say that Schiller's Juno aestheticizes (as "god-like woman" and "woman-god") the "otherness" of woman within a phallocentric order.

38. One may recall here Adorno's remarks in *Ästhetische Theorie*, cited earlier (n. 10), on how Schiller's concept of genius, "with a sidelong glance at Goethe," transfers "the idea of creation . . . with idealistic hubris from the transcendental to the empirical subject" (*Aesthetic Theory*, 171; *Ästhetische Theorie*, 255). Goethe's fascination with the Juno Ludovisi dates from his Roman sojourn; he installed a cast of the colossal bust ("my first sweetheart in Rome") in his rooms in 1787 and talked of taking it back with him to Weimar, but he was eventually forced to leave

it behind. In 1823, eighteen years after Schiller's death, Goethe obtained another replica, which dominates the "Juno-Zimmer" in what is now the Goethe Museum in Weimar. Schiller's invocation of the statue is tantamount to an explicit act of homage and would of course take its place in the narrative of idealization, insecurity, and envy that constituted the Schillerian half of one of Western literature's more ponderously canonized friendships.

39. Anyone who feels that the aestheticization of politics really belongs to a vanished era might begin by consulting Josef Chytry's neo-Schillerian *The Aesthetic State: A Quest in Modern German Thought* (Berkeley: University of California Press, 1989). Chytry's book is a valuable thematic survey, but it is even more impressive as an ideological symptom: sincerely humanist in its aspirations, disturbingly violent in its totalizing fantasies. Throughout his text, Chytry personifies the Aesthetic State as a woman, and this overdetermined gesture realizes its apotropaic potential in Chytry's rhapsodic concluding pages: "'Aphrodite' transcends all possibility of harm, disfigurement, or oppression, since it is self-contradictory to imagine her in any but a consuming relation to possible assailants. Should conditions cry out for rectification, she manifests as political revolution in the form of Dionysos: his fair locks sway the women of the corrupt polis to the forest, whence the vigor of their outraged ecstasy dismembers the stubborn opponent of *Vereinigung*" (497).

CHAPTER 4

1. Hans Eichner, "Lucinde," in Friedrich Schlegel, *Kritische Friedrich-Schlegel-Ausgabe*, ed. Ernst Behler with Jean-Jacques Anstett and Hans Eichner (Paderborn: F. Schöningh, 1958), V, lv. References to Schlegel's texts are drawn from this edition; citation is by volume and page number. It should be noted that the canonization of *Lucinde* in our era has occurred thanks in great part to the extraordinary philological and critical work of Ernst Behler and Hans Eichner.

Translations are mine unless otherwise noted, though I have tried to key my citations to published English translations whenever possible, with page references given as German (volume and page number)/English. Translations not my own have sometimes been silently modified. Unless otherwise noted, English pagination refers to Peter Firchow's *Friedrich Schlegel's "Lucinde" and the Fragments* (Minneapolis: University of Minnesota Press, 1971).

2. Søren Kierkegaard: *The Concept of Irony, with Continual Reference to Socrates*, ed. and trans. Howard V. Hong and Edna H. Hong (Princeton: Princeton University Press, 1989), 286.

3. Wilhelm Dilthey, *Leben Schleiermachers* (Berlin: G. Reimer, 1870), 492.

4. Rudolf Haym, *Die Romantische Schule: Ein Beitrag zur Geschichte des deutschen Geistes*, 2nd ed. (Berlin: Weidmannsche Buchhandlung, 1906), 501.

5. For a helpful overview of *Lucinde*'s reception, see Eichner, xlvi–lv.

6. At the cost of a further irony, since the genre of the *Bildungsroman* is itself an ironic mirage. For discussion, see my *Phantom Formations: Aesthetic Ideology and the Bildungsroman* (Ithaca: Cornell University Press, 1996). The "Lehrjahre" chapter is also arguably *Lucinde*'s flattest, most woodenly narrated episode; Schlegel has set a high price on comprehensibility.

7. I refer here of course to two of Schlegel's more famous epigrammatic definitions of irony: "Ironie ist klares Bewußtsein der ewigen Agilität, des unendlich vollen Chaos" (II, 263); "Ironie ist eine permanente Parekbase" (XVIII, 85). I shall return briefly to the vast and much-discussed topic of Schlegel's notion of irony later in this chapter, but for reasons of economy I am forced to refer readers interested in this topic to the copious secondary literature. For a recent, strongly argued account of Schlegelian irony as dialectical synthesis, see Eric Miller, "Masks of Negation: Greek eironeia and Schlegel's Ironie," *European Romantic Review* 8, no. 4 (1997): 360–85. Other important accounts of Schlegel's irony that move in a similar direction include the following: Beda Allemann, *Ironie und Dichtung* (Pfullingen: Neske, 1956); Rüdiger Bubner, "Zur dialektischen Bedeutung romantischer Ironie," in *Die Aktualität der Frühromantik*, ed. Ernst Behler (Paderborn: F. Schöningh, 1987), 85–95; and Ingrid Strohschneider-Kohrs, *Die romantische Ironie in Theorie und Gestaltung* (Tübingen: Niemeyer, 1960). This chapter discovers at work in Schlegel's text an irony better described by Paul de Man, "The Concept of Irony," in *Aesthetic Ideology* (Minneapolis: University of Minnesota Press, 1996), 163–84; see also Georgia Albert, "Understanding Irony: Three Essays on Friedrich Schlegel," *MLN* 108 (1993): 825–48; and Kevin Newmark, "*L'Absolu littéraire*: Friedrich Schlegel and the Myth of Irony," *MLN* 107 (1992): 905–30.

8. Judith Butler, *Bodies That Matter: On the Discursive Limits of "Sex"* (New York: Routledge, 1993), 9.

9. Philippe Lacoue-Labarthe, "The Unpresentable," trans. Claudette Sartiliot, in Philippe Lacoue-Labarthe, *The Subject of Philosophy*, ed. Thomas Trezise (Minneapolis: University of Minnesota Press, 1993), 116–57, here 117. Lacoue-Labarthe chose not to collect this essay in his *Le sujet de la philosophie* (Paris: Flammarion, 1979). The essay originally appeared as "L'Imprésentable," *Poétique* 21 (1975): 53–95. Subsequent references to this essay over the next few pages are to the English-language version and are given parenthetically in the text.

10. Lacoue-Labarthe characterizes his essay as the "first part" of a longer work—"the first part, which can be considered as an introduction to the (a) 'reading of *Lucinde*'" (183 n. 4). To my knowledge, a second part never appeared, though years later Lacoue-Labarthe published a short, relatively informal essay that discusses *Lucinde*, "L'avortement de la littérature," in *Du féminin*, ed. Mireille Calle (Sainte-Foy, Quebec: Le Griffon d'argile, 1993).

11. G. W. F. Hegel, *Vorlesungen über die Ästhetik*, in *Werke*, ed. Eva Moldenhauer and Karl Markus Michel (Frankfurt am Main: Suhrkamp, 1970), 14:116. Subsequent references to Hegel's texts are to this edition of the collected works and

are noted by volume and page number. For the English translation, see G. W. F. Hegel, *Aesthetics: Lectures on Fine Art*, trans. T. M. Knox (Oxford: Clarendon Press, 1975), 1:508.

12. The point, for Lacoue-Labarthe, is that Hegel's handwritten note "Lucinde" was inscribed next to lines in paragraph 164 in which the inability to grasp the ethical dimension of marriage is called "impertinence [*die Frechheit*]." Oddly, Lacoue-Labarthe does not refer to the "oral addition" to paragraph 164 that one finds in Eduard Gans's 1833 edition of the *Philosophy of Right*. Gans's "additions," drawn from student notes taken at Hegel's lectures, are controversial (for a succinct account of the editorial questions involved, see Moldenhauer and Michel's afterword to vol. 7 of the *Werke*, 7:524–31), but it seems a bit peculiar that Lacoue-Labarthe would ignore them, given that his main object of analysis, the *Aesthetics*, is itself made up entirely of lecture transcripts. The addition or *Zusatz* to paragraph 164, in any case, mentions *Lucinde* explicitly and supports Lacoue-Labarthe's argument quite dramatically: "Friedrich von Schlegel in his *Lucinde*, and a follower of his in the *Briefe eines Ungenannten* [i.e., Schleiermacher], have put forward the view that the wedding ceremony is superfluous and a formality which might be discarded, because love is the substance of marriage and the celebration therefore detracts from its worth. Surrender to sensuality is here represented as necessary to prove the freedom and inwardness of love—an argument not unknown to seducers." Hegel goes on to reinforce the principles of gender difference that he enunciates in this section of the *Philosophy of Right*: "It must be noticed in connection with the relationship of man and woman that a girl in surrendering her body loses her honor, which is not the case for the man, who has a field for ethical activity outside the family. A girl is destined in essence for the marriage tie." Hegel, *Grundlinien der Philosophie des Rechts oder Naturrecht und Staatswissenschaft im Grundrisse: Mit Hegels eigenhändigen Notizen und den mündlichen Zusätzen*, in *Werke*, 7:317–18. *Philosophy of Right*, trans. T. M. Knox (Oxford: Clarendon Press, 1967), 263.

13. We may note briefly that the paragraph that elicited Hegel's marginal note "Lucinde" is richly suggestive in ways that Lacoue-Labarthe does not pursue. In the *Philosophy of Right*, Hegel argues that the stipulation of a contract involves the genuine transfer of the property in question—that, in other words, a contract is a performative (or, in Hegelian language, a contract is "the being of my resolved will," "das Dasein meines Willensbeschlusses" [par. 79; III, 162]). Thus, in Paragraph 164, the marrying parties' declaration of consent to enter into marriage, and the recognition of this declaration by the community, constitutes the actuality [*Wirklichkeit*] of marriage: "The knot is tied and constituted as ethical only through the progress of this ceremony, whereby through the use of signs, of language, as the most spiritual being of spirit [*als das geistigste Dasein des Geistigen*], the substantial thing in the marriage is brought completely into being" (VII, 315/113). Language makes marriage an ethical reality because it is language's func-

tion to symbolize and thus grant determinate existence to ideas: "Once made, a covenant taken by itself in distinction from its performance is something held before the mind [*ein Vorgestelltes*], something therefore to which a particular determinate existence must be given in accordance with the appropriate mode of giving determinate existence to ideas by rendering them in signs [*Zeichen*]. This is done, therefore, by expressing the stipulation in formalities such as gestures and other symbolic actions, particularly by declaring it with precision in language, the most worthy medium for the expression of our mental ideas" (par. 78, VII, 161). At this point, Hegel cross-references his challenging discussion of the sign in paragraph 458 of the *Enzyklopädie der philosophischen Wissenschaften*, in which the sign is defined as "any immediate intuition [*unmittelbare Anschauung*] representing a quite different content than that which it has for itself [*für sich*];—the pyramid into which a foreign soul is transferred and preserved" (X, 270). It is at this point in the *Enzyklopädie* that Hegel distinguishes the sign from the symbol, characterizes the sign as the expression and product of the free power of intelligence and links the sign to memory (*Gedächtnis*). The passage has elicited strong interpretations from Jacques Derrida, "The Pit and the Pyramid: Introduction to Hegel's Semiology," in Derrida, *Margins of Philosophy*, trans. Alan Bass (Chicago: University of Chicago Press, 1982), 69–108; and Paul de Man, "Sign and Symbol in Hegel's *Aesthetics*," in de Man, *Aesthetic Ideology*, ed. Andrzej Warminski (Minneapolis: University of Minnesota Press, 1996), 91–104. In paragraph 164 of the *Philosophie des Rechts*, in other words, the complex question of the sign intersects with what Lacoue-Labarthe, in the passage quoted below, calls Hegel's "sexual symbolic." It is possible that Hegel's marginal note "Lucinde" was spurred by his disapproval not just of *Lucinde's* supposed ethical levity but of its specifically semiotic, which is to say *literary*, playfulness.

14. Drucilla Cornell, "The Future of Sexual Difference: An Interview with Judith Butler and Drucilla Cornell," conducted by Pheng Cheah and Elizabeth Grosz, *Diacritics* 28, no. 1 (1998): 24, 23. For an extended account of the ethical and cognitive necessity of the "feminine" in this poststructuralist sense, see Drucilla Cornell, *Beyond Accommodation: Ethical Feminism, Deconstruction, and the Law* (New York: Routledge, 1991).

15. G. W. F. Hegel, *Phänomenologie des Geistes*, par. 475, in *Werke*, 3:352; *Phenomenology of Spirit*, trans. A. V. Miller (Oxford: Clarendon Press, 1977), 288. It should be noted that complex and powerful acts of reading have resulted from (ironic) feminist appropriations of Hegel's phrase. "No red-blooded woman, after all, can fail to enjoy the irony of wearing Hegel's slur as something of a crown," Carol Jacobs writes ironically in her "Dusting Antigone," *MLN* 111 (1996): 889–90. See also Luce Irigaray, *Speculum of the Other Woman*, trans. Gillian C. Gill (Ithaca: Cornell University Press, 1985), esp. 214–26. Important readings of Hegel that suggest the complexity and ambiguity of his texts' deployment of sex and gender difference include Jacques Derrida, *Glas*, trans. John P. Leavey Jr. and Richard Rand

(Lincoln: University of Nebraska Press, 1986); and Werner Hamacher, "pleroma," in G. W. F. Hegel, *Der Geist des Christentums: Schriften 1796–1800*, ed. Werner Hamacher (Frankfurt am Main: Ullstein, 1978).

16. Catriona MacLeod, "The 'Third Sex' in an Age of Difference: Androgyny and Homosexuality in Winckelmann, Friedrich Schlegel, and Kleist," in *Outing Goethe and His Age*, ed. Alice A. Kuzniar (Stanford: Stanford University Press, 1996), 194–214, here 214. See also Sara Friedrichsmeyer, *The Androgyne in Early German Romanticism: Friedrich Schlegel, Novalis, and the Metaphysics of Love* (New York: Peter Lang, 1983); and Kari Weil, *Androgyny and the Denial of Difference* (Charlottesville: University Press of Virginia, 1992). Feminist readings that interpret the novel as a fundamentally male fantasy include the following: Barbara Becker-Canterino, "Schlegels Lucinde: Zur Frauenbild der Frühromantik," *Colloquia Germanica* 10 (1976–77): 128–39; Eva Domoradzki, *Und alle Fremdheit ist verschwunden. Status und Funktion des Weiblichen im Werk Friedrich Schlegels: Zur Geschlechtigkeit einer Denkform* (Innsbruck: Institut für Sprachwissenschaft der Universität Innsbruck, 1992); and Sigrid Weigel, "Wider die romantische Mode: Zur ästhetischen Funktion des Weiblichen in Friedrich Schlegels Lucinde," in *Die verborgene Frau: Sechs Beiträge zu einer feministischen Literaturwissenschaft*, ed. Inge Stephan and Sigrid Weigel (Berlin: Argument-Verlag, 1983), 67–82.

17. Martha Helfer, "'Confessions of an Improper Man': Friedrich Schlegel's *Lucinde*," in *Outing Goethe and His Age*, 177.

18. Of the many studies that have recently advanced our understanding of the play of the "homoerotic" in various European cultures, perhaps the most indispensable are those of Eve Sedgwick: see her *Between Men: English Literature and Male Homosocial Desire* (New York: Columbia University Press, 1985); and *Epistemology of the Closet* (Berkeley: University of California Press, 1990).

19. As Schlegel was in fact to write many years later, at the beginning of the third of his Dresden lectures of 1829: "True irony . . . is the irony of love" (X, 357).

20. Furthermore, because love and friendship slide easily into each other in *Lucinde*, the pain of friendship reappears, linked to the wounding powers of language, as that of a woman submitted to (presumably heterosexual) intercourse: "Let words or men try to bring a misunderstanding between us! That deep pain would quickly ebb and soon resolve itself into a more perfect harmony. I'd pay as little attention to it as a woman in love does to the slight hurt she suffers in the heat of pleasure" (V, 12/49).

21. Kierkegaard, 275: irony, in the wake of Schlegel and Tieck's misreading of Fichte, "functioned as that for which nothingness was an existent, as that which finished with everything, and also as that which had the absolute power to do everything."

22. Sigmund Freud, *Das Ich und das Es*, in *Gesammelte Werke*, ed. Anna Freud et al. (Frankfurt am Main: S. Fischer Verlag, 1967 [1940]), 13:255; *The Ego and the*

Id, in *The Standard Edition of the Complete Psychological Works of Sigmund Freud*, ed. James Strachey (London: Hogarth Press, 1953–74), 19:16.

23. Butler, *Bodies That Matter*, 10–11. See also Butler's earlier *Gender Trouble: Feminism and the Subversion of Identity* (New York: Routledge, 1990).

24. See esp. "Melancholy Gender / Refused Identification," in Butler, *The Psychic Life of Power: Theories in Subjection* (Stanford: Stanford University Press, 1997) 132–50; here 140.

25. As in the novel's bizarre closing section, "Tändelein der Fantasie" ("Dalliance of the Imagination"), for instance, where the first-person narrator fantasizes the premature death of his own (as yet presumably unborn) son, followed by an erotic approach to his brother's wife: "Full of thoughts I strew flowers on the grave of my too soon departed son, and then give them, filled with joy and hope, to the bride of my beloved brother" (81/129).

26. *Vorlesungen über die Ästhetik*, XIII, 93; *Aesthetics*, trans. Knox, 64. This because, in the abstract space of the Fichtean ego, "every particularity, every determination, every content is negated in it, since everything is destroyed in this abstract freedom and unity"; and the ego rejoices in an empty, yet corrosive potency: "Whatever is, is only through the ego, and what exists through me I can equally well annihilate again" (93/64; translation modified). "In no sphere of morals, law, things human and divine, profane and sacred, is there anything that would not first have to be posited by the ego, and that therefore could not equally well be destroyed by it. Consequently everything genuinely and independently real [*alles Anundfürsichseiende*] becomes mere appearance [*nur ein Schein*]" (94/64–65).

27. The phrase "diese sehr ernsten Scherze" is Goethe's description of *Faust* in a letter to Humboldt that was the last letter he wrote before his death (March 17, 1832); for commentary, see Ehrhard Bahr, *Die Ironie im Spätwerk Goethes* (Berlin: Schmidt, 1972), 13–39. From this perspective, one may understand Schlegel's irony as an irony *of* irony: an ironization of the aesthetic irony that Bahr discerns in Goethe, or of the philosophic–aesthetic irony that many critics have sought to discern in Schlegel (see n. 7 above). "Mit der Ironie ist durchaus nicht zu scherzen," Schlegel warns us (jokingly and seriously, of course) in "Über die Unverständlichkeit" (II, 369).

28. Apart from its generally Fichtean language of striving, self-determination, and so on, Schlegel's text may be parodying here one of Fichte's propositions in the *Grundlage des Naturrechts* (1797), which is that sexual difference refers back to the fundamental struggle of being and nonbeing (*Seyns und Nicht-Seyns*) and is thus ontologically prior to nature. Sexual difference, in fact, makes "Nature" possible by making form possible: without sexual difference, Nature's "shaping force [*bildende Kraft*]" would have nowhere to pause, and there would be a constant transformation of forms, a process of becoming in which no being could come to presence. "In that case no nature is possible," Fichte comments. "If nature was to be

possible, the species [*Gattung*] had to have an organic existence other than species, yet also exist as species in order to reproduce itself. This was only possible if the force shaping the species were distributed, and the species were split into two halves that absolutely belonged together and only made a self-reproductive whole in coming together." Fichte, *Grundlage des Naturrechts nach Principien der Wissenschaftslehre*, in *J. G. Fichte-Gesamtausgabe der Bayerischen Akademie der Wissenschaften*, ed. Reinhard Lauth, Hans Jacob, and Hans Gliwitsky (Stuttgart–Bad Cannstatt: Frommann, 1962), 1.4:96. Subsequent references to Fichte are to this edition. Fichte is extending Kant's definition of the organism as a "sich fortpflanzende bildende Kraft" and his discussion of the division of the sexes in paragraph 82 of the *Critique of Judgment*: "This pair is what first amounts to an organizing whole, even if not to an organized whole in a single body." Kant, *Critique of Judgment*, trans. Werner S. Pluhar (Indianapolis: Hackett, 1987), 313 (sect. 82); *Kritik der Urteilskraft*, in *Werkausgabe*, ed. Wilhelm Weischedel (Frankfurt am Main: Suhrkamp, 1974), 10:382.

29. Rodolphe Gasché, *The Tain of the Mirror: Derrida and the Philosophy of Reflection* (Cambridge, Mass.: Harvard University Press, 1986).

30. Fichte, *Grundlage der gesammten Wissenschaftslehre* (1794), in *Gesamtausgabe*, 1.2:261; *Science of Knowledge*, ed. and trans. Peter Heath and John Lachs (Cambridge: Cambridge University Press, 1982), 99. Werner Hamacher's analysis of the Fichtean proposition of the I discerns a tension that Hamacher describes as an incompatibility between constative and performative language: "The unconditioned proposition of the I, its fundamental principle, is pure positing and as such performance and event, action and process of the proposition; yet it is also a positivity [*das Gesetzte*], and as such already the product, the outcome, the fact of the proposition. As pure positing, it is open, irreferential, without context and significance; as positivity, it is closed, a fact, both the determined—and no longer determining—subject and the possible object of an assertion." Thus, "the double proposition inscribed in the Fichtean principle . . . tears this principle apart: the sheer performative, the positing called 'I,' is incapable of being stated; it is absolute excess beyond every possible objectification and every self-reflective subjectivity." Hamacher, *Premises: Essays on Philosophy and Literature from Kant to Celan*, trans. Peter Fenves (Cambridge, Mass.: Harvard University Press, 1996), 232, 235. See Hamacher's chapter, "Position Exposed: Friedrich Schlegel's Poetological Transposition of Fichte's Absolute Proposition," in *Premises*, 222–60.

CHAPTER 5

1. See esp. Maurice Blanchot, *La communauté inavouable* (Paris: Minuit, 1983), and Jean-Luc Nancy, *La communauté desoeuvrée* (Paris: Christian Bourgois, 1986), in addition to Jacques Derrida's efforts to think of a democracy "to come" in many

texts, but see esp. *Specters of Marx: The State of the Debt, the Work of Mourning, and the New International*, trans. Peggy Kamuf (New York: Routledge, 1994); also Ernesto Laclau and Chantal Mouffe, *Hegemony and Socialist Strategy: Towards a Radical Democratic Politics* (London: Verso, 1985).

2. Maurice Blanchot, "The Athenaeum," in *L'entretien infini* (Paris: Gallimard, 1969); *The Infinite Conversation*, trans. Susan Hanson (Minneapolis: University of Minnesota Press, 1993), 351, translation slightly modified.

3. German romanticism inspired sharply political commentary during and after World War II; see esp. A. O. Lovejoy, "The Meaning of Romanticism for the Historian of Ideas," *Journal of the History of Ideas* 2 (1941): 257–78; and Leo Spitzer's reply to Lovejoy, "'*Geistesgeschichte*' vs. History of Ideas as Applied to Hitlerism," *Journal of the History of Ideas* 5 (1944): 191–203. A fine summary and analysis of this debate may be found in Orrin N. C. Wang, *Fantastic Modernity: Dialectical Readings in Romanticism and Theory* (Baltimore, Md.: Johns Hopkins University Press, 1996), 26–36. As late as the 1960s, mainstream Anglo-American scholarship was blaming German romanticism, or more generally the "German mind," for having produced Hitlerism; see, e.g., Ronald Gray, *The German Tradition in Literature, 1871–1945* (Cambridge: Cambridge University Press, 1965).

4. Most recently, as ecocriticism or "green" criticism, as noted in the Introduction (see n. 64). The recent tendency to substitute "early modern" for "Renaissance" has generated discussions similar to, but also instructively different from, those about romanticism. Though marked by the usual exchanges between traditionalists and revisionists, the Renaissance / early modern debate has involved a competition between two terms rather than an obsessive circling around a single term: "romanticism" has proved harder to replace than "Renaissance," perhaps in part because the notion of romanticism, as we saw in this book's introduction and as McGann and many others recall, names the emergence of a historicism that made possible literary periodization (e.g., terms like *Renaissance*) in the first place. Denunciations of romanticism as "ideology" have become commonplace among British romanticists who nonetheless often have no term to offer in its stead, even on the occasions when they suggest getting rid of it; see, e.g., Anne K. Mellor and Richard E. Matlak, "General Introduction," *British Literature 1780–1830* (Fort Worth: Harcourt Brace, 1996), and my citations and comments in n. 66 of the Introduction. For a helpful summary of the Renaissance / early modern discussion, see Leah S. Marcus, "Renaissance / Early Modern Studies," in *Redrawing the Boundaries: The Transformation of English and American Literary Studies*, ed. Stephen Greenblatt and Giles Gunn (New York: Modern Language Association, 1992), 41–63.

5. McGann's title echoes, of course, the misleading but by now inevitable translation of Marx and Engels's *Die deutsche Ideologie*, but his use of the definite article is also motivated by his understanding of romantic ideology as aesthetic ideology in

the sense of elevating art and ideas—"imagination and poetry"—over material reality. Romanticism is thus ideology itself. See Jerome J. McGann, *The Romantic Ideology: A Critical Investigation* (Chicago: Chicago University Press, 1983).

6. For two exemplary positions, see Paul Foot, *Red Shelley* (London: Sidgwick and Jackson, 1980); and Donald H. Reiman, "Shelley as Agrarian Reactionary," in *Romantic Texts and Contexts* (Columbia: University of Missouri Press, 1987), 260–74.

7. Forest Pyle, "'Frail Spells': Shelley and the Ironies of Exile," in *Irony and Clerisy*, ed. Deborah White, *Romantic Circles Praxis Series* (http://www.rc.umd.edu/praxis/irony/pyle/frail.html), 7. Pyle suggestively links this political dimension of Shelley's writing to Walter Benjamin's notion, in the text cited in my epigraph, of a "*weak* Messianic power" capable of "blast[ing] open the continuum of history." Walter Benjamin, "Über den Begriff der Geschichte," *Gesammelte Schriften*, ed. Rolf Tiedemann and Hermann Schweppenhäuser (Frankfurt am Main: Suhrkamp, 1980), 1.2:694. "Theses on the Philosophy of History," in *Illuminations: Essays and Reflections*, ed. Hannah Arendt, trans. Harry Zohn (New York: Schocken Books, 1969 [1955]), 254. My argument will also have points of affinity with Jerrold Hogle's diagnosis of a "radical transference" at work in Shelley's texts in *Shelley's Process: Radical Transference and the Development of His Major Works* (New York: Oxford University Press, 1988), and with Hugh Roberts's emphasis on contingency and fragmentation in *Shelley and the Chaos of History: A New Politics of Poetry* (University Park: University of Pennsylvania Press, 1997).

8. *Letters of Percy Bysshe Shelley*, ed. Frederick L. Jones (Oxford: Clarendon Press, 1964), 2:191. The quotation about *The Mask*'s greatness is from Richard Holmes, *Shelley: The Pursuit* (New York: E. P. Dutton, 1975), 532, cited in Susan Wolfson, "Social Form: Shelley and the Determination of Reading," in *Formal Charges: The Shaping of Poetry in British Romanticism* (Stanford: Stanford University Press, 1997), 286 n. 6. As Wolfson notes, most commentary on *The Mask of Anarchy* has celebrated its power as a political poem.

9. Preface to *Prometheus Unbound*, in Donald H. Reiman and Sharon B. Powers, eds., *Shelley's Poetry and Prose* (New York: W. W. Norton, 1977), 135. Unless otherwise noted, all references to Shelley's poetry in what follows are to texts as given in Reiman and Powers and will be identified simply by book, stanza, or line numbers. Quotations from Shelley's prose that are taken from Reiman and Powers will be identified by acronym *SPP* and page number.

10. Wolfson, 203; see British Library f. 12V in Donald Reiman, ed., *"The Mask of Anarchy": A Facsimile Edition, with Scholarly Introductions, Bibliographical Descriptions, and Annotations*, vol. 2 of *Percy Bysshe Shelley* in *The Manuscripts of the Younger Romantics* (New York: Garland Press, 1985), 32.

11. For an extended examination of this aesthetic–nationalist fantasy, which Benedict Anderson calls the imagining of "unisonance," see Chapter 1.

12. See, e.g., Carlos Baker, who imagines the address to be spoken by "Liberty"

in *Shelley's Major Poetry: The Fabric of a Vision* (Princeton: Princeton University Press, 1948), 162, as does Jerrold Hogle forty years later in *Shelley's Process*, 137–38. Tempting though it is to extend the poem's allegorical cast of characters in this way, the text offers us no clear support for doing so—indeed, since this anonymous orator goes on to apostrophize Freedom and Liberty ("What art thou Freedom?" [209]; "It availed, Oh, Liberty!" [244]), poetic convention suggests that the speaker isn't the entity addressed. We do not even have a fully certified warrant for referring to the speaker as "the female orator," as Wolfson does (203). All we know is that the words arise "as if" a maternal Earth had cried aloud. (Wolfson also characterizes the "Shape" of 110 ff. as "a miraculous epiphanic feminine intervention," despite Shelley's use of neuter pronouns in those stanzas.) One of the few critics to emphasize that the Shape "elud[es] any identification" is Steven Goldsmith, in his *Unbuilding Jerusalem: Apocalypse and Romantic Representation* (Ithaca: Cornell University Press, 1993), 245 (though Goldsmith's reading of *The Mask* could hardly be more different from mine; for him, the Shape as an embodiment of "decentered" poetic language exists only in order to be negated, "so the rest of the poem can advocate a specific politial program" [245]). As many critics have shown, *The Mask* draws on contemporary political iconography and is certainly tempting its readers to personify the speaker as Britannia or a Britannic version of the French Revolution's Liberty, but as so often in this deceptively rough-hewn poem, what it gives with one hand it takes with the other. For a study of the poem in relation to the political iconography of the era, see Steven E. Jones, *Shelley's Satire: Violence, Exhortation, and Authority* (De Kalb: Northern Illinois University Press, 1994), 102 ff. (he personifies the orator as Britannia).

13. For reasons of economy, I haven't quoted these stanzas (though a little later I shall briefly discuss Anarchy's motto). Here is Goldsmith's helpful summary (the numbers in parentheses within this citation refer to line numbers in *The Mask*): "On his brow Anarchy bears the mark, 'I AM GOD, AND KING, AND LAW' (37). Every spoken line in the poem's first section merely rearranges this official declaration, as if its terms were the necessary and immutable givens of discourse and social relation. Anarchy's cohorts, for instance, sing, 'Thou art God, and Law, and King' (61), and lawyers and priests together whisper, 'Thou art Law and God' (69). As if to confirm the tautological unity of the official lexicon, the echoing voices join forces: 'Then all cried with one accord; / "Thou art King, and God, and Lord"' (70–71)" (Goldsmith, 243). I should perhaps note that my reading of *The Mask* is at odds with Goldsmith's claim that it represents a turn on Shelley's part away from the "bankrupt linguistic universals" of *Prometheus Unbound* and toward a pragmatic idea of "communication" (241). Goldsmith's is the sort of privileging of Shelley's "Popular Songs" that Wolfson is setting out to correct—though one should note that Wolfson and Goldsmith share many key assumptions, above all the notion that literary density is the narcissistic opposite of practical politics. Goldsmith's book is in part an extended chastisement of a deconstruction that he

imagines to be engaged in "freeing language and its human values from the weight of historical determination" (212).

14. Jones, *Shelley's Satire*, 102. Jones notes that Shelley also does this in *The Devil's Walk*.

15. Actually, the stanza is even more ambiguous than that: "Clothed with the Bible, as with light, / And the shadows of the night, / Like Sidmouth, next, Hypocrisy / On a crocodile rode by" (22–25). Depending on how one adjudicates the appositions, Hypocrisy is like Sidmouth in being clothed with the Bible, etc., or in riding a crocodile. The historical figure thus blurs into the allegorical figure.

16. Marcel Proust, *Du côté de chez Swann*, in *A la recherche du temps perdu* (Paris: Gallimard, Bibliotheque de la Pléiade, 1954), 1:81. Marcel is imagining a resemblance between the Giotto figure and a pregnant kitchen maid who is seemingly "unable to comprehend the meaning" of the "symbol" she bears in her womb. For a reading of this passage, see Paul de Man, *Allegories of Reading: Figural Language in Rousseau, Nietzsche, Rilke, and Proust* (New Haven: Yale University Press, 1979), 73–78.

17. Speculation on Shelley's use of the masque genre has generally not gotten much further than the claim that Shelley is drawing on and debunking an aristocratic genre. See Stuart Curran, *Shelley's Annus Mirabilis: The Maturing of an Epic Vision* (San Marino: Huntington Library, 1975), 181–92, for a classic discussion of this point.

18. For a political analysis of *The Mask*, see Michael Scrivener, *Radical Shelley: The Philosophical Anarchism and Utopian Thought of Percy Bysshe Shelley* (Princeton: Princeton University Press, 1982): "The idea of massive non-violent response, in the context of a general strike and an egalitarian assembly, is a way for Shelley to express his revolutionary vision while at the same time relieving some of the anxiety this vision produced in him" (210). Wolfson, as we have seen, sharpens that judgment into a perception of "contradictory elements" in Shelley's political stance (202). It has also proved possible to relate *The Mask*'s "ambivalence . . . toward popular violence" to "a profound ambivalence in the reform movement itself." See Jones, *Shelley's Satire*, 109.

19. Fredric Jameson, *The Political Unconscious: Narrative as a Socially Symbolic Act* (Ithaca: Cornell University Press, 1981), 20, 19. "The all-informing process of *narrative*" Jameson takes to be "(here using the shorthand of philosophical idealism) the central function or *instance* of the human mind" (13, Jameson's italics).

20. I would thus agree with James K. Chandler's characterization of *The Mask* as displacing "the everyday time of the periodicals into a quasi-apocalyptic framework, anticipating the displacement of 'empty homogenous time' by 'messianic time' in Benjamin's twentieth-century analysis." Chandler, *England in 1819: The Politics of Literary Culture and the Case of Romantic Historicism* (Chicago: University of Chicago Press, 1998), 529. See also Forest Pyle's comparable remarks on Shelley and Benjamin, as cited in n. 7.

21. To Ollier, September 6, 1819; *Letters*, ed. Jones, 2:117.

22. To Peacock, September 21, 1819; *Letters*, ed. Jones, 2:120. For Beatrice's line, see *Cenci*, III, i, 86–87.

23. "Aye, something must be done; / What, yet I know not . . . something which shall make / The thing that I have suffered but a shadow / In the dread lightning which avenges it; / Brief, rapid, irreversible, destroying / The consequence of what it cannot cure" (*Cenci*, III, i, 86–91; the ellipses are Beatrice's).

24. Sometimes the demonstration undergoes awkward, almost comical elaboration, as in "The Sensitive-Plant," where the Lady goes to great lengths to erase the damage she does in tending her garden: "Her step seemed to pity the grass it prest . . . And wherever her aery footstep trod / Her trailing hair from the grassy sod / Erased its light vestige" (II, 21, 25–27). She removes "all killing insects and gnawing worms / And things of obscene and unlovely forms"; but she removes them gently, exiling them to the "rough woods" in "a basket of grasses and wild flowers full, / The freshest her gentle hands could pull" (41–42, 44, 45–46). The irony, of course, is that she still has to pull up grass and flowers, and that there has to be a place called the "rough woods" for the killing insects to go on happily killing in. Shelley mercilessly rewrote these images in *The Triumph of Life* (see esp. lines 405–10).

25. The word's persistence within the sword may thus be taken as the mark of language's persistence within and beyond the apocalyptic dream of the "tremendous deed." From this perspective, "Shelley's poetry is the record of a perpetually renewed failure," as J. Hillis Miller writes: "It is the failure ever to get the right formula and so end the separate incomplete self, end lovemaking, end politics, and end poetry, all at once, in a performative apocalypse in which words will become the fire they have ignited and so vanish as words, in a universal light. The words, however, always remain, there on the page, as the unconsumed traces of each unsuccessful attempt to use words to end words." Miller, "The Critic as Host," in *Deconstruction and Criticism*, ed. Harold Bloom (New York: Continuum, 1979), 237.

26. For a rhetorical study of the complexities of language and speech in *Prometheus Unbound*, see Carol Jacobs, "Unbinding Words: *Prometheus Unbound*," in *Uncontainable Romanticism: Shelley, Brontë, Kleist* (Baltimore, Md.: Johns Hopkins University Press, 1989).

27. Edward Trelawny, *The Last Days of Shelley and Byron*, ed. J. E. Morpurgo (Garden City, N.Y.: Anchor Books, 1960), 61.

28. Earl R. Wasserman, *Shelley: A Critical Reading* (Baltimore, Md.: Johns Hopkins University Press, 1971), 87. Wasserman's observation is made in the context of his larger account of free will and causality in Shelley's work generally: "In Shelley's Manichean system, in which evil is an autonomous and pressing potentiality, the Count is the original and unmotivated point at which transcendent evil enters human reality and begins its causal sequence, simply because the Count *permits* it to enter by assuming man is necessarily evil" (87).

29. Shelley predicted the shape of his play's reception in his preface, writing of "the restless and anatomizing casuistry with which men seek the justification of Beatrice, yet feel that she has done what needs justification" (*SPP*, 240). Interpretation of *The Cenci* turns endlessly on whether and to what extent Beatrice is morally responsible for her crime, and has done so since the earliest reviews, as Stuart Curran shows in *Shelley's "Cenci": Scorpions Ringed with Fire* (Princeton: Princeton University Press, 1970), 24, passim. For a helpful survey of modern criticism on the issue, see Hogle, *Shelley's Process*, 365 n. 95. Hogle's own analysis of how Beatrice's choice "contorts her into the patterns of patriarchal language" (154) is particularly suggestive.

30. For a rhetorical reading of *The Cenci* that emphasizes the split between action and understanding, see Roger Blood, "Allegory and Dramatic Representation in *The Cenci*," *Studies in Romanticism* 33 (fall 1994): 355–89.

31. These observations perhaps gloss Jacques Lacan's suggestive remark that the sadist, projecting outward the death he cannot accept as his own, imagines that he can thereby cast "the pain of existence onto the Other, without realizing that in this manner he also changes into an 'eternal object.'" Jacques Lacan, *Ecrits* (Paris: Seuil, 1966), 778.

32. Walter Benjamin, "Das Kunstwerk im Zeitalter seiner technischen Reproduzierbarkeit," in *Gesammelte Schriften*, ed. Rolf Tiedemann and Hermann Schweppenhäuser (Frankfurt am Main: Suhrkamp, 1980), 1.2:508; "The Work of Art in the Age of Mechanical Reproduction," in *Illuminations*, 242.

33. Anne McWhir, "The Light and the Knife: Ab/Using Language in *The Cenci*," *Keats-Shelley Journal* 37 (1989): 150.

34. Shelley, *A Philosophical View of Reform*, in David Lee Clark, ed., *Shelley's Prose, or, The Trumpet of a Prophecy* (Albuquerque: University of New Mexico Press, 1954), 253.

35. Some months after an earlier version of this chapter had been published, I encountered in Deborah White's *Romantic Returns: Superstition, Imagination, History* (Stanford: Stanford University Press, 2000), a fine discussion of the echoing similarities between the description of the poet in the closing sentences of the *Defence* and that of the soldier in *A Philosophical View of Reform*. "The soldier," White observes, "stands as a negative reflection of the poet, a type of historical agency that exceeds responsible norms. As such he exposes the risk to which the poet subjects himself when he serves a power that comes from the future and athwart the will—the risk that poetry, too, may enslave humanity" (127). White emphasizes the irreducibility of such exposure to risk: "Poetry points ahead and away from itself, and yet the promise of its truth in each and every case leads one back . . . to the supplemental truth that one may, after all, have been *mis*led—that promises are, quite literally, made to be broken" (128).

CODA

1. "Shock absorber" is Elissa Marder's witty phrase to sum up the apotropaic function of women in Baudelaire's poetry; see her *Dead Time: Temporal Disorders in the Wake of Modernity* (Stanford: Stanford University Press, 2001).

2. Paul de Man, *Aesthetic Ideology*, ed. Andrzej Warminski (Minneapolis: University of Minnesota Press, 1996), 89.

3. De Man's reading of Rousseau's "giant" was discussed in Chapter 3, as was, somewhat more briefly, Neil Hertz's remarkable study of the role of "lurid figures" in de Man's writing. The phrase "a terror glimpsed" is plundered from de Man's commentary on Ferdinand de Saussure's notes on the possibly anagrammatic structuring of Latin poetry: "Saussure's caution supports the assumption of a terror glimpsed. As is well known, he claims to have interrupted his inquiries partly because he could find no historical evidence for the existence of the elaborate codes he had reconstructed, but principally because he could not prove whether the structures were random, the outcome of mere probability, or determined by the codification of a semiosis." De Man, "Hypogram and Inscription," in *The Resistance to Theory* (Minneapolis: University of Minnesota Press, 1986), 37.

4. "Technology in some way is always implicated in the feminine," Avital Ronell writes. "It is young; it is thingly. Thus every instrument of war can be given a feminine name." In such a picture—Ronell is glossing Heidegger's famous discussion of the Van Gogh shoes in "Der Ursprung des Kunstwerkes" ("The Origin of the Work of Art"; 1935–36)—the feminine never quite arrives: "she is what is missing," Ronell suggests, because she "has gotten in the way of things." Ronell, *Finitude's Score: Essays for the End of the Millennium* (Lincoln: University of Nebraska Press, 1994), 247. (Although Heidegger attributes the shoes to a peasant woman as part of his elucidation of the shoes as "equipment," no woman appears in the Van Gogh painting, an absence that Ronell reads as telling: "To what extent does the passage through the work leave the woman wasted, used up, or worn out, like the shoes that wear her spirit down? . . . The woman who fills the shoes does not exactly exist as an aesthetic object, prepared for sensuous apprehension. *She is absent from the shoes that hold her*" [247].)

5. Drucilla Cornell, "The Future of Sexual Difference: An Interview with Judith Butler and Drucilla Cornell," conducted by Pheng Cheah and Elizabeth Grosz, *Diacritics* 28, no. 1 (1998): 24, 23.

6. The importance of the role played by radio technology in early to midtwentieth-century mass politics is well known. For a canny fictional reimagining of (postcolonial, midcentury) nationalism, see Salman Rushdie, *Midnight's Children* (New York: Penguin Books, 1991 [1980]), in which the first-person narrator becomes "a sort of radio" capable of picking up the mental voices of the children born at the (homogenized, clock-time) moment of India's birth (midnight, August

15, 1947) (189). Benedict Anderson's figures of the "imagined community" and of a (technically produced) "unisonance" become here a fantasy of telepathy. Despite being associated with the mass circulation of newspapers ("Telepathy, then; the kind of thing you're always reading about in the sensational magazines" [192]), telepathy is a transcendent supertechnics with "no need of machines" (191)— which is to say that it is a dream of communicational transparency: "In the beginning, when I was content to be an audience—before I began to *act*—there was a language problem. The voices babbled in everything from Malayalam to Naga dialects, from the purity of Lucknow Urdu to the southern slurrings of Tamil. I understood only a fraction of the things being said within my skull. Only later, when I began to probe, did I learn that below the surface transmissions—the front-of-mind stuff which is what I'd originally been picking up—language faded away, and was replaced by universally intelligible thought-forms which far transcended words" (192).

7. Alan Liu, "Local Transcendence: Cultural Criticism, Postmodernism, and the Romanticism of Detail," *Representations* 32 (1990): 75–113, here 76.

8. Alan Liu, "The Power of Formalism: The New Historicism," *ELH* 56 (1989): 721–71, here 734. Liu develops in this article an extensive critique of the so-called New Historicism as a specular encounter with romanticism. On the postmodern sublime, see Fredric Jameson, *Postmodernism, or the Cultural Logic of Late Capitalism* (Durham, N.C.: Duke University Press, 1990); and J. F. Lyotard, "Answering the Question: What Is Postmodernism?" in *The Postmodern Condition: A Report on Knowledge*, trans. Geoff Bennington and Brian Massumi (Minneapolis: University of Minnesota Press, 1984). See also my "Pynchon's Postmodern Sublime," *PMLA* 104 (1989): 152–62. As noted in this book's introduction, one may consult, on the interplay between notions of romanticism and postmodernity, Orrin Wang, *Fantastic Modernity: Dialectical Readings in Romanticism and Theory* (Baltimore, Md.: Johns Hopkins University Press, 1996).

9. Tilottama Rajan, "The University in Crisis: Cultural Studies, Civil Society, and the Place of Theory," *Literary Research / Recherche littéraire* 18, no. 35 (2001): 8–25, here 12, 14. I offer a more extensive consideration and critique of Rajan's essay in my response to it: "Crisis and Culture: Theory, Cultural Studies, and the University," in the same issue of *Literary Research / Recherche littéraire*, 31–35. Much has been written about cultural studies in recent years. For an essay particularly attentive to the symbiosis between globalism and localism, see Timothy Bahti, "Anacoluthon: On Cultural Studies," *MLN* 112, no. 3 (1997): 366–84.

10. Bill Readings, *The University in Ruins* (Cambridge, Mass.: Harvard University Press, 1996), 99, 27.

11. Wlad Godzich, *The Culture of Literacy* (Cambridge, Mass.: Harvard University Press, 1994), 12.

12. On the delusiveness of the myth of the "end of history," see, among others, Jacques Derrida, *Specters of Marx: The State of the Debt, the Work of Mourning, and*

the New International, trans. Peggy Kamuf (New York: Routledge, 1994), 59–64, passim.

13. Readers deeply skeptical of my insistence on the ambivalent symbiosis between aesthetics and technics will probably have put this book down some time ago, but if not, they may wish to consult some of the texts of the late nineteenth-century aestheticist movement, of which J. K. Huysmans' *A rebours* is one of the most interesting. Keen to escape the vulgarity of the modern world of mass politics and mechanical reproduction, des Esseintes retreats to a bower of decadence where he makes elaborate technical arrangements for the reliable—that is, mechanical—production of aesthetic pleasure, e.g., his *orgue à bouche,* or "mouth organ," an apparatus by which drops of various liquors can be placed on his tongue, in an elaborate parody of symbolist synesthesia: "Des Esseintes would drink a drop here and there, enjoying internal symphonies, to the point of obtaining on his palate sensations analogous to those which music provides for the ear." And so on. *A rebours* (Paris: G. Crès, 1922 [1884]), 60.

14. One of the many ironies of the "political" assault on romanticism is that its efforts to open the canon frequently wind up reinforcing national traditions and borders. Romanticism has traditionally been a rich field for comparatists precisely because the texts, authors, and movements that national literary histories wind up calling "romantic" appear under different circumstances and at different times in each national tradition. We have noted in passing the tendency among a few prominent scholars and anthologists of British romanticism to jettison, or at least pretend to jettison, the troublesome word *romanticism* as part of an attempt to reduce the definition of their "period" to a slab of homogenous empty time, framed by variously arrived-at dates. These are inevitably dates indexed to a national literary history—e.g., the anthology I discussed briefly in this context in the Introduction, Anne K. Mellor and Richard E. Matlak, *British Literature 1780–1830* (New York: Harcourt Brace, 1996). (This particular anthology—which is a very well planned and useful one, I should add—announces itself forthrightly as a collection of *British* literature, and then restricts itself to a block of time conventionally associated with British romanticism. The dates chosen would make little sense in any other national context.) There is of course nothing inherently wrong with using the nation as one's cookie cutter; one simply should not pretend that, in doing so, one has escaped the force field of the aesthetic. We should note, finally, that it is hardly surprising that American scholars should be turning more and more to the nation (as linguistic community) for a limiting device in an era when American scholarship grows ever more monolingual in a world presumed to speak English, and as the existence of foreign national literatures within the American academy grows ever more tenuous.

15. I explore the interplay of addiction and culture at some length in my introduction, cowritten with Janet Brodie, to *High Anxieties: Cultural Studies in Addiction,* ed. Brodie and Redfield (Berkeley: University of California Press, 2002). The

most sustained reading of addiction in relation to the question of technology is to be found in the work of Avital Ronell; see esp. *Crack Wars: Literature, Addiction, Mania* (Lincoln: University of Nebraska Press, 1992); see also David Clark, "Heidegger's Craving: Being-on-Schelling," *Diacritics* 27 (1997): 8–33. The literature on romanticism and addiction or intoxication is extensive. For a recent study that moves in directions congruent with those being pursued here, see Orrin N. C. Wang, "Romantic Sobriety," *Modern Language Quarterly* 60, no. 4 (1999): 469–93.

16. Theodor W. Adorno, *Ästhetische Theorie*, ed. Gretel Adorno and Rolf Tiedemann (Frankfurt: Suhrkamp, 1970), 293; *Aesthetic Theory*, trans. Robert Hullot-Kentor (Minneapolis: University of Minnesota Press, 1997), 197.

Index

Abrams, M. H., 216–17n17
Adorno, Theodor, 182, 184n5, 213n3, 222n10, 227n38
aesthetics: and body, 11, 76–81, 89–92, 137, 174–76, 214n8, 216n15; and education, 2, 12–14, 28, 46–47, 56, 65–69, 75–76, 174, 187–88n14, 188–89n19, 189–90n25; and gender, 34–40, 80–81, 89–92, 104–5, 112, 121–24, 127, 130–34, 174–77, 200n72, 200–201n73, 201n74, 201n75; history of, 9–14, 75, 189n24, 190n28, 190n29; and ideology, 3, 12, 18, 24–27, 30, 32, 110, 124, 184n6, 194n45, 198n62; and judgment, 2–3, 11–12, 16–18, 89–90, 105–7, 194n46; and nationalism, 14–16, 21–23, 40, 46–50, 55–61 *passim*, 71, 75–76, 157, 174–75, 177, 181–82, 187n11, 206n12, 208n19, 213n41; and politics, 1–8 *passim*, 12–16, 21–22, 40–42, 46–47, 55, 68–69, 75–76, 86, 90, 92, 99, 111–12, 124, 148, 150–71, 177–82, 183n3, 190n28, 192n36, 200n69, 204n6, 222n10, 228n39; and romanticism, 9, 29–34, 41–42, 149, 174, 178–79; and technics, 15–29 *passim*, 60, 180–82, 192n36, 193n42, 243n13; and theory, 5–9, 18, 22–28 *passim*, 114, 118, 174, 194–95n47

Alarcón, Norma, 59
Albert, Georgia, 229n7
Allemann, Beda, 229n7
Althusser, Louis, 109, 224n21
Anderson, Benedict, 14, 40, 60, 174–78 *passim*, 182, 205n7, 236n11, 242n6; and aesthetic education, 55–56, 59, 174; and aestheticization of shock experience, 48, 52–58 *passim*, 71, 174; and gender, 58–59, 174–75, 209n23; and imagination, 47, 49–50, 54–55, 59–60; and mourning, 56–59, 174; and print capitalism, 50–52, 207n15. Works: *Imagined Communities*, 45, 47–59, 71–73, 75, 209n23, 209–210n24, 213n3, 218n29; "Introduction" to *Mapping the Nation*, 60; *The Spectre of Comparisons*, 60, 207n15, 208n20, 213n40

Ankersmit, F. R., 204–5n6
Aristotle, 19, 216n16
Armstrong, Nancy, 201n74
Arnold, Matthew: and gender, 40, 88–92, 174–76; and literature, 82–85; and politics of culture, 2, 13–14, 75–76, 86. Works: *Culture and Anarchy*, 13–15, 46, 75–77; "Democracy," 76; "The Function of Criticism," 2, 40, 76, 81–92, 107, 127, 174–76

106–7, 175, 215–16n15, 225n27; and formal materialism, 18, 41, 104–7, 191–
92n34, 215–16n15, 223n15; and gender,
41, 100, 116–18, 124; and history, 97–
98, 107–9; and language, 7–8, 22–25,
28, 100–114, 117–18, 173; as personification of "theory," 6–7, 95–96, 187n11;
and reception, 5–9, 41, 95–100 *passim*,
114–16, 124, 185n9, 185–86n10, 186–
87n11, 188n15, 220n2, 220–21n4; and
rhetorical reading, 5, 7, 18, 28, 100–115
passim, 124; and romanticism, 32–33,
41, 95, 199n68; and Schiller, 99, 109–
12, 222n9; and wartime journalism,
96, 99, 185–86n10. Works: "Aesthetic
Formalization in Kleist," 109, 193n42,
224n22, 226n27; *Allegories of Reading*,
28, 97, 99–102, 113–15; "The Concept
of Irony," 229n7; "The Contemporary
Criticism of Romanticism," 32–33;
"The Dead End of Formalist Criticism," 97; "Foreword to Carol Jacobs'
The Dissimulating Harmony," 107;
"Hypogram and Inscription," 112,
241n3; "Kant and Schiller," 103, 109–
12, 118–19, 223–24n18; "A Letter from
Paul de Man," 113; "Literary History
and Literary Modernity," 108; "Phenomenality and Materiality in Kant,"
104–7, 175, 215–16n15; "The Resistance to Theory," 7–9, 22–26, 28–29,
114; "The Rhetoric of Blindness," 113;
"Shelley Disfigured," 103, 114; "Sign
and Symbol in Hegel's *Aesthetics*," 50;
"Thematic Criticism and the Theme
of Faust," 97, 221n6
de Quincey, Thomas, 78
Derrida, Jacques, 17, 54, 57, 185–86n10,
186n11, 192n37, 193n39, 195n48, 207–
8n18, 217n19, 231n13, 234–35n1; *Glas*,

39, 117, 231n15; "Parergon," 16–17,
20, 214n9; *Specters of Marx*, 52, 234n1,
242–43n12
Dickstein, Morris, 217–18n22
Dilthey, Wilhelm, 125–26
Domoradzki, Eva, 232n16

Eagleton, Terry, 11, 76, 80–81, 189n24,
217n19
Edelman, Lee, 37–38
education. *See under* aesthetics
Eichner, Hans, 125, 197n58, 228n5
Eliot, George, 87
Ender, Evelyne, 202n79
Engell, James, 205n8
Epstein, Joseph, 218n22
Esch, Deborah, 220n2

Fausto-Sterling, Anne, 217n20
Felman, Shoshana, 203n79, 224n20
Felski, Rita, 201n73
feminine, 35–36, 58–59, 72, 91, 128, 130–
33, 142–47, 176, 200n72, 201n73,
201n74, 201n75, 217n19, 219n30,
227n37. *See also* gender; phallocentrism
Ferguson, Frances, 197n57
Fichte, Johann Gottlieb: and aesthetic
education, 66–68; and gender, 72–73,
174, 233n28; and Germanness, 49, 62–
73 *passim*; and imagination, 49, 65–73
passim, 212n35; and language, 61–64,
69, 211n31, 212n33; and romanticism,
61, 211n30. Works: *Addresses to the
German Nation* (*Reden an die deutsche
Nation*), 40, 48–49, 61–73, 127, 174,
176–77, 211–12n32, 213n37, 213n39;
Foundations of Natural Law (*Grundlage des Naturrechts*), 233–34n28; "On
the Linguistic Capacity" ("Von der
Sprachfähigkeit"), 211n31; *Science of*

Cultural Memory | *in the Present*

Marc Redfield, *The Politics of Aesthetics: Nationalism, Gender, Romanticism*

Emmanuel Levinas, *On Escape*

Dan Zahavi, *Husserl's Phenomenology*

Rodolphe Gasché, *The Idea of Form: Rethinking Kant's Aesthetics*

Michael Naas, *Taking on the Tradition: Jacques Derrida and the Legacies of Deconstruction*

Herlinde Pauer-Studer, ed., *Constructions of Practical Reason: Interviews on Moral and Political Philosophy*

Jean-Luc Marion, *Being Given That: Toward a Phenomenology of Givenness*

Theodor W. Adorno and Max Horkheimer, *Dialectic of Enlightenment*

Ian Balfour, *The Rhetoric of Romantic Prophecy*

Martin Stokhof, *World and Life as One: Ethics and Ontology in Wittgenstein's Early Thought*

Gianni Vattimo, *Nietzsche: An Introduction*

Jacques Derrida, *Negotiations: Interventions and Interviews, 1971-1998*, ed. Elizabeth Rottenberg

Brett Levinson, *The Ends of Literature: The Latin American "Boom" in the Neoliberal Marketplace*

DATE DUE
